Food and Philosophy

Food and Philosophy
SELECTED ESSAYS

SPENCER K. WERTZ

TCU Press
Fort Worth, Texas

Library of Congress Cataloging-in-Publication Data

Names: Wertz, Spencer K., author.
Title: Food and philosophy : selected essays / by Spencer K. Wertz.
Description: Fort Worth, Texas : TCU Press, [2016] | Includes index.
Identifiers: LCCN 2016016741 | ISBN 9780875656380 (alk. paper)
Subjects: LCSH: Food--Philosophy. | Taste--Philosophy. | Food
   consumption--Philosophy. | Cooking--Philosophy.
Classification: LCC B105.F66 W47 2016 | DDC 641.3001--dc23
LC record available at https://lccn.loc.gov/2016016741

TCU Press
TCU Box 298300
Fort Worth, Texas 76129
817.257.7822
www.prs.tcu.edu
To order books: 1.800.826.8911

Designed by Bill Brammer
www.fusion29.com

For Linda,
with whom I shared life
and passion for food

Contents

Acknowledgments

Several of these essays appeared in journals over the past two decades. I wish to thank the editors for permission to reprint these articles. Chapter 1 appeared in *Philosophy Today*, vol. 50, no. 2 (Summer 2006); chapter 2 appeared in *Asian Philosophy: An International Journal of the Philosophical Traditions of the East*, vol. 17, no. 3 (November 2007); chapter 3 was printed in the *Journal of Aesthetic Education*, vol. 47, no. 1 (Spring 2013); chapter 4 appeared in the Journal of Aesthetic Education, vo. 49, no. 3 (Fall 2015); chapter 5 was in GAE, vol. 47, no. 3 (Fall 2013); chapter 6 was published in *History Research*, vol. 3, no. 2 (February 2013); chapter 7 appeared in the *International Journal of Applied Philosophy*, vol. 14, no. 1 (2000); chapter 8 was printed in the *Journal of Comparative Literature and Aesthetics*, vol. 22, nos. 1-2 (1999); chapter 9 was published in the *Journal of Agricultural and Environmental Ethics*, vol. 18, no. 2 (2005); chapter 10 was published in the *International Journal of Applied Philosophy*, vol. 19, no. 1 (Spring 2005); chapter 13 was recently published in *Collingwood and British Idealism Studies*, vol. 22, no. 2 (2016). These articles have been rewritten with each other in mind as representing a fairly new area of philosophy that I call "Food and Philosophy." I want to thank the students in my Master of Liberal Arts (MLA) course, "Food and Philosophy," who read most of these essays in one form or another over the years. Their input improved them considerably.

The acquaintances and scholars of Convivium: The Philosophy and Food Roundtable have been very helpful with their advice and suggestions on several of the chapters. I have learned a lot from them individually (especially through email exchanges) and collectively in conferences or meetings. Also the members of the Agriculture, Food & Human Values Society, in their joint meetings with the Association for the Study of Food and Society, have provided stimulating conferences on food and initiated much of the intellectual atmosphere and motivation for several of these essays. Chapter 1 was read at the Culinary Institute of America in Hyde Park, New York, in June 2004, at a panel titled "Temporality and Food," part of a conference titled "From Agriculture to Culture: The Social Transformation of Food," which was a series of joint meetings of the Agriculture, Food & Human Values Society and the Association for the Study of Food and Society; chapter 2 was presented in Portland, Oregon, in June 2005, at a Food and Philosophy session in the conference called "Visualizing Food and Farm," the series of joint meetings of the Agriculture, Food & Human Values Society and the Association for the Study of Food and Society; and chapter 5 was read at Boston University's Programs in Gastronomy, Boston, Massachusetts, in June 2006, at a food conference entitled "Place,

Taste, and Sustenance: The Social Spaces of Food and Agriculture," the joint meetings of the Agriculture, Food & Human Values Society and the Association for the Study of Food and Society. Chapters 3, 4, 7, 8, 9, 11, and 13 were read at the annual meetings of the Rocky Mountain Division of the American Society for Aesthetics in Santa Fe, New Mexico, in July 2009, 2015, 2000, 1996, 2001, and 2014 respectively. Chapter 9 was also an invited paper given at a symposium entitled "Know Thyself: Food and the Human Condition," Mississippi State University, Starkville, Mississippi, in April 2002, and the other participants' comments were helpful in the final draft.

My greatest debt is to my wife, Linda Loflin Wertz, whose masterful eye has made these essays more readable. This book is dedicated to her. Also, I wish to thank Dan Williams and his editorial staff, especially Kathy Walton, of the TCU Press for editing the manuscript and seeing it through the final stages of printing.

Introduction

Food and Philosophy is a relatively new area of philosophy that lies in the intersection of the two activities. Obviously, there is much to do about food that has nothing to do with philosophy, and conversely, a lot of philosophy is not concerned—even remotely—with food, but there is an interesting middle ground. This middle ground is the preoccupation of the following chapters. By "food," I mean agriculture, preparation, and cooking, in addition to the food products and their consumption. These activities have cultural and social significance besides philosophical concerns. Those concerns can be conceptual, ethical, aesthetic, historical, or scientific and are usually manifested in issues and arguments over controversial points. The chapters that make up this book are conceptual investigations that cover a broad range of these issues. Let us look briefly at each of these thirteen chapters.

Chapter 1, entitled "Philosophy of Food History," addresses three fundamental problems: (1) the duplication of sensations and taste, (2) the understanding of other recipes, and (3) the sorts of judgments that are included or excluded in a historical narrative. First the duplication problem: how can we duplicate or reproduce flavors and tastes when tastes and sensations are private, unique, subjective, and nonrecurring? Under a Cartesian view of sensation, it is impossible—they cannot be duplicated or reproduced. One of the principals holding this view is R. G. Collingwood. But the literature and history of food abounds with instances where many insist that tastes and sensations *can* be duplicated. Novelists, chefs, and gourmands think that dishes and whole cuisines can be reproduced. This takes us to the second problem: how can someone understand a recipe from another period or culture? (The problem of other recipes is analogous to Arthur Danto's problem of other periods in his book, *Narration and Knowledge*.) In ancient times, Roman recipes are notoriously silent about certain things—for instance, the quantities of ingredients. Or a recipe just mentions adding wine in a preparation. Is it red or white and is it sweet or dry? Quality is an issue, too. How does modern-day pork compare to ancient Roman pork? To anticipate an answer, the Italians over the centuries have preserved the ancient breeds of pigs, so we can taste the Roman pork of old. Personally I see no comparison between today's American mass-produced pork and the Italian pork. The American pork we find in the supermarket is generally tasteless and can be tough if care is not given to it in cooking. Italian pork, in contrast, has more flavor and takes on the herbs and spices more readily than its American counterpart. I have found it more tender and tasty. I remember a few years ago eating a fabulous lunch in Tuscany during a wine tour; the cut of meat was what we refer to as pork loin, but it tasted nothing like what we normally have in the states. Alas.

The issues above have led to serious disagreement among historians of food (these include the likes of Revel, Tannahill, Civitello, Coe, Fernández-Armesto, Toussaint-Samat, Willan, Wright, Bober, Super, Giacosa, Bottéro, Albala, Flandrin, and Montanari). Some—Ken Albala, for example—argue that five-hundred-year-old recipes are to be viewed for their own sake by the reader. They should not be interpreted by some historian, and even worse, adapted to the contemporary kitchen by some chef or cook. Others disagree and argue that we miss out on a great deal of a culture or society if we do not try to reproduce its cuisine. So recipes are to be interpreted and, in fact, most recipes are replete with history. Their context or "atmosphere" provides cultural clues that would be overlooked if the foods of the past and other periods were not appreciated or tasted. Histories with a vision bias can be corrected by utilizing the other senses, such as taste. Historians who employ this methodology in their narratives are known as "sensory historians." Historians of food were among the first in this group, and they thought that recipes were to be experimented with. Food can also be seen as a unifier, in that what is eaten takes both body and mind to appreciate it, so dualism seemingly vanishes in attempting to understand the complex behavior that surrounds the phenomenon of food. "The history of dining is not a history of eating," Collingwood rightfully declares; "it is in virtue of his rationality that he not only eats but dines." If we have use of rationality here, then we have pros and cons of what we are eating, and there must be arguments and reasons for these opinions; hence reason provides us with an avenue for philosophy to enter the culinary picture.

The history of food as an academic discipline (a fairly new one at that—starting in 1973) opens up new vistas for the philosophy of history, which takes us to the third problem. What sorts of judgments, like culinary and comparative judgments, are included in a narrative of food history? Again, historians disagree about their inclusion. A discussion of the historians' reasoning on these three problems occupies a substantial part of this opening chapter. Because this study represents the embryonic stage of the philosophy of food history, it is crucial that the historians speak for themselves. Consequently, there are more quotations from their narratives than usual, but this is enlightening. And I weave their arguments and central points around the three basic philosophical issues that I think are pivotal to an analytic philosophy of food history.

Chapter 2, "The Five Flavors and Taoism: Lao Tzu's Verse Twelve," moves to a curious claim about the five flavors; namely that they cause people to have no taste or that the five flavors jade the palate. The five flavors are: sweet, sour, salty, bitter (these four are the traditional elements of taste in the West, recognized by the science of taste), and spicy or hot as in "heat" (*picante*, not *caliente*). As a side note before the introduction of chili peppers, black pepper and ginger provided the heat. Several plausible interpretations of the verse will be discussed along with visualizing the five flavors through the five colors (yellow, green, black, red, and white) and elements (earth, wood, water, fire, and metal). To the Western mind, the claim "The five flavors cause them [persons] to not taste" is counterintuitive; on the contrary, the presence of the five flavors in a dish or in a meal would expand or enhance the senses and the palate, i.e., taste would be augmented by the five flavors. So what is the plausible meaning of the Taoistic claim? To answer this question, I look very briefly at the history of the doctrine of the five flavors and the history of Chinese cuisine. Lao Tzu probably has Confucian feasts in mind in making such a claim, but other interpretations are discussed.

Chapter 3, "The Elements of Taste: How Many Are There?" attempts to answer the question, what is the number of tastes or flavors we have? Is it five as most Chinese believe? None as the ancient Taoists asserted? Four as Western science traditionally claims? Recently, *umami* has been added to the traditional four: sweet, sour, salty, and bitter (the Chinese added another: spicy or pungent). Aristotle and Raghavan Iyer (of India) thought there were seven components of taste: sweet, sour, salty, bitter, astringent, pungent, and harsh. In 2001, Gray Kunz and Peter Kaminsky argued for fourteen in their book, *The Elements of Taste*. Not to be outdone, Brillat-Savarin thought there is an infinite number of tastes because each one is unique. Some recent studies by Richard D. Mattes on rats show that fats do have taste and can be chemically detected in their blood, so we may be adding a sixth component to the scientific perspective: fat. And even more recently, carbs (carbohydrates) have been added to the list. The number of elements continues to expand with experimentation and the development of analysis of the gustatory experience. Many of these elements are shared by the world cuisines, which tells us something about human nature or constitution.

In chapter 4, "Leibniz and Culinary Cognitions: A Speculative Journey," I argue that the origin of our ideas about food as we know it today began to be seriously entertained during the modern period of Western philosophy—mainly by examples of concepts. Locke, Hume, and Leibniz all thought that food was a complex idea, but their accounts were vastly different. Locke and Hume gave similar accounts: the complex idea of an apple (Hume's illustration) consists of its simple ideas—color, smell, taste, size, ripeness (to the touch), and so on. These simple ideas or impressions are thought of as clear and distinct. "Simple" for Leibniz is an abstraction, and perceptions cannot be separated from ideas, so complexity is more easily achieved in his scheme of things. What would happen to these simple qualities if apples were made into a sauce? We don't know, because none of the three philosophers addressed this issue, although Leibniz's answers come the closest. Surprisingly, Leibniz—our rationalist—has a better account of the perceptual process in regard to food than our two empiricists. I mainly draw on the passages on perception and ideas in their writings and compare Locke and Hume with Leibniz in the process.

Chapter 5, "Taste and Food in Rousseau's *Julie, or the New Heloise*," discusses these newly emerging topics surrounding food practices as they were developed in Jean-Jacques Rousseau's epistolary novel (1761). It is in the midst of his tale of Julie and those who were close to her that Rousseau develops a philosophical position that he labels "the epicureanism of reason," as opposed to an epicureanism of the senses, whose advocates he calls "vulgar epicureans." The hallmarks of his epicureanism are abstinence, moderation, and simplicity. These three features are examined, and abstinence is found to be the most controversial in regard to taste. Rousseau attacks the food practices of the vulgar epicureans—those who practiced the urban, Parisian cuisine, and he applauds the country life and its cuisine. The argument is as follows: One is to cultivate "a taste for the innocent pleasures that moderation, order, and simplicity enhance." In other words, taste appears in simple things rather than in those that are smothered in riches. "All dishes [at the table] are common, but each excellent in its kind, their preparation is simple and yet exquisite." Widely read at the time, the novel made European culture self-conscious and forced it to pay attention to aspects of living that had gone unnoticed or underappreciated, including taste and food. The voices of Julie and her tutor turned lover, Saint-Preux, provide a lively critique of French (and Swiss) society and its values.

Chapter 6, "Hume's Culinary Interests and the Historiography of Food," is a discussion of David Hume's culinary interests and how they are reflected in his correspondence, essays, and historical narrative. It is in the latter that we find his culinary interests exhibited in a fair amount of detail—outlining a historiography of food. In fact, we discover a "subtext" of the history of food in Hume's general history of England. Discussed are foodstuffs as raw (economic) commodities, food as it is prepared and brought to the table, and food as part of a social ritual of manners. All these facets of food practices interested Hume throughout his life (1711-1776) and in his history of the British Isles (ca. 55 BCE to 1688).

In chapter 7, "Revel's Conception of Cuisine: Platonic or Hegelian?," I claim that Jean-François Revel (1924-2006) is the first contemporary philosopher to take food seriously and to offer a topology for food practices. He draws a distinction between different kinds of cuisine—popular (regional) cuisine and erudite (professional) cuisine. With this distinction, he traces the evolution of food practices from the ancient Greeks and Romans down through the Middle Ages and into the Renaissance and the Modern Period. His contribution has been acknowledged by Deane Curtin, who offers an interpretation of Revel's conceptual scheme along

Platonic lines. In this chapter, I review Curtin's interpretation, find it wanting in certain respects, and develop an alternative reading of Revel along Hegelian lines. This latter interpretation, I believe, does greater justice to Revel's topology for food practices.

In chapter 8, "The Analogy between Food and Art: Tolstoy and Eaton," I reexamine Leo Tolstoy's analogical argument between food and art, look at Professor Marcia Eaton's analysis and criticism, and suggest (with her assistance) an alternative interpretation which centers around her definition of *art*. My study of the food question extends beyond *What Is Art?* to *Anna Karenina* and other sources. The core of the food analogy lies in the nutrition/pleasure confusion in which food is enjoyed by the commoners for its nutritional value (its real value), whereas the upper class engages in eating for pleasure's sake (rather than for nourishment). The same thing, Tolstoy believes, has happened with art: the upper class has identified art with pleasure (beauty), whereas they have missed art's real value—the communication of sincere feeling—which has been preserved only in peasant art or non-counterfeit art. Contrary to Eaton, I think the analogy is appropriate for the purpose for which Tolstoy employs it, i.e., to point out the weakness of inherent theories of aesthetic value and the strength of consequential theories of aesthetic value. Nonetheless both theories are needed to do justice to our aesthetic situations, like those that surround food and art.

Chapter 9, titled "Maize: The Native North American's Legacy of Cultural Diversity and Biodiversity," summarizes recent research that has focused on establishing the values of preserving biodiversity both in agriculture and in less managed ecosystems, and shows the importance of the role of cultural diversity in preserving biodiversity in food production systems. A study of the philosophy embedded in cultural systems can reveal the importance of the technological information for preserving genetic biodiversity contained in such systems and can be used to support arguments for the protection/preservation of cultural diversity. For example, corn or maize can serve as a paradigm of Native American thinking and can provide one of the few areas from which common philosophical conceptions can emerge. An examination of the cultivation of corn or maize as an agricultural activity and as a cultural activity in Native American literature reveals a philosophy that recognizes the importance of biodiversity and provides techniques for its preservation. Corn, and the food and the materials derived from it, is something thought out not by specialists but by the entire tribe and its ancestors, even if this thinking is done within what we might consider a framework of highly mythical notions. Importantly, this framework yields an understanding of both the genetics and nutrition of corn. A survey of these mythical notions (myths and stories) and agricultural practices makes this understanding apparent and exemplifies the value of cultural diversity and biodiversity.

Chapter 10, "Are Genetically Modified Foods Good for You? A Pragmatic Answer," reviews the arguments that make up the current controversy on genetically modified foods (commonly referred to as GMOs, for Genetically Modified Organisms), as well as an assessment of their cogency. The two main arguments for genetically modified foods are utilitarian (we can feed a greater number of people with them than without) and environmental (we can increase the food supply without diminishing the wilderness areas by displacing them with farm land). The arguments against evolve around the idea of unforeseen consequences that could have irreversible effects on the food supply and consumers. A major philosophical issue centers on advocates' claims that genetic engineering is equivalent to conventional breeding. Opponents deny the equivalence. Because of the uncertainties involved in GMOs, it is suggested that their labeling, in addition to non-GMOs' labeling, should be enforced so that the public can make their own decision as to what they should eat. The conclusion drawn from this debate is that we should proceed on a case-by-case basis because of the rapidly changing biotechnologies. Most recently, the GMOs debate has been renewed around the merits of the Golden Rice Project in developing countries.

Chapter 11, "Is There a Pornography of Food?," was prompted by an article on food porn by Andrew Chan that appeared in *Gastronomica* in 2003. He claims that TV cooking shows, *all* cooking shows, are pornography. Such a claim is counterintuitive—most cooking shows are either educational (e.g., Rachael Ray's *30 Minute Meals* or Ina Garten's *Barefoot Contessa*) or competitive (e.g., *Cupcake Wars* or *Iron Chef America*). However, a few cooking shows could be labeled food porn, but under a much weaker conception or definition than what Chan is operating with. In 1961 Roland Barthes observed that certain food images connote "a sublimated sexuality," especially in visual advertising, but also in today's cooking shows. Chan thinks that "food preparation is a form of foreplay," and food presentations on cooking shows are comparable to "human sex-toy actors in porno films." Such remarks are beyond belief and stretch the analogy between pornography and cooking shows towards the fallacy of false analogy, where dissimilarities are greater than similarities. The analogy may be useful in characterizing certain cooking shows, but the definition needs to be weakened. Pornography is thought of as objectionable because it treats women disrespectfully, as mere objects. Food porn, analogously, is objectionable because it disrespects food. How that disrespect is carried out is by exaggerating gastronomic features. In other words, disrespect is present when these features are manipulated or mistreated in food practices that have sexual suggestions running through them. Several examples of cooking shows or specific actions in the cooking process are discussed.

Chapter 12, "Chocolate and Its World," is encyclopedic in nature, i.e., all branches of knowledge are addressed here: botany, chemistry, history, production, consumption, and ethical issues that lie in their paths. The discussion of chocolate and its world is divided into four sections: I. The Substance (the nature of chocolate), II. Tools and Processing (the making of chocolate), III. Health Issues (the effects of chocolate), and IV. Cooking and Baking (chocolate as a food/dish).

Chemical compounds in chocolate are briefly described; they are caffeine, theobromine, serotonin, and phenylethylamine. The first two are alkaloids, which are also present in coffee and tea; they were chocolate mark the beginning of alkaloid consumption in Europe in the seventeenth century. Because of these chemicals, chocolate has been traced to the pre-Olmec period in Mesoamerica. Tools for making chocolate were special cylindrical vases the Mayans and later the Aztecs used for the drink. The cocoa beans were ground on a *metate*. Next they were fermented, roasted, dried, and made into wafers; the Mesoamericans added water or some liquid to them to make a chocolate drink. This was poured back and forth to create a foam that was thought to be the best part of the drink. Later a *molinillo,* or swizzle-stick, was used to create this effect. The drink was later served in a gourd or clay cup (*jicara*). The method for making chocolate that the Mayans and Aztecs developed remained the same in Europe until the nineteenth century, when the process was mechanized. The beans come from a pod that grows on the cacao tree, which usually grows near the equator. Under good conditions, the tree can be harvested twice a year. The process of making chocolate was refined by the Europeans, and they were able to make a solid bar out of the powdery substance. Soon, with increased production, it was enjoyed by more than the elite, but a moral shadow was cast over chocolate because of forced, slave, or child labor practices in plantations. Health issues addressed are whether chocolate is good for you and whether it is as addictive as a drug. Some flavonoids in chocolate are found to be beneficial. Some people claim that chocolate makes them "high," and there is some truth to this. Opioids found in chocolate increase a feeling of well-being. However, the effects of these are minimal. In addition to drinking and eating chocolate, we can ingest it by cooking and baking with it. Various chocolates were developed to accommodate these needs by varying the percentages of cocoa butter and solids along with other ingredients like sugar and vanilla. The resulting dishes are more often sweet rather than savory, although *moles* from Mexico are considered the national dish and are quite savory. Chocolate became the king of the sweet kitchen, reigning over cakes, pies, puddings, ice creams, and cookies, but new uses for chocolate have surfaced recently in both savory and sweet dishes.

Chapter 13, "Eating and Dining: Collingwood's Anthropology," focuses on Collingwood's conception of philosophical anthropology. Eating and dining are metaphors for the distinction between physical actions and culturally, socially laden actions, respectively. In a surprising move, he virtually dismisses physical anthropology and concentrates almost exclusively on cultural or social anthropology. A reason for this was the primitive state that physical anthropology was in at the time (1920s and 30s), so he virtually ignored it. And just as surprising is his modification of his slogan, "history is the history of thought," to include emotions in both history and anthropology. This is a significant move in his methodology of the human sciences, and it is in line with anthropology after Collingwood. I cite several recent anthropologists: Claude Levi-Strauss, Howard Morphy, and Ellen Dissanayake. All see emotions and feelings (plus much more) as the basis of magical practices in all social and cultural groups. Let us look at one of Collingwood's examples taken from *The Philosophy of Enchantment*. He announces: "Clothes are magic" (PE, 212); and his elaboration of this follows: "The wearing of clothes gives one a feeling of security or self-confidence. To take off one's clothes in public is to 'give oneself away,' to 'make an exhibition of oneself,' that is, to forfeit one's dignity. It makes one ridiculous or contemptible. This is a universal human feeling to be traced, I think, in every civilization. How far and in what ways it is allowed to develop into a principle governing social life depends on the extent and manner and kind of occasion on which people feel it necessary to stand on their dignity" (PE, 213). An example he uses is "People who generally go naked wear clothes on state occasions when they wish to feel and look impressive" (PE, 213). What are these inferences based on? Collingwood suggests that "since we can understand what goes on in the savage's mind only in so far as we can experience the same thing in our own, we must find our clue in emotions to whose reality we can testify in our own persons" (PE, 196). The implications of this methodological statement are spelled out in this chapter.

The chapters can be read independently of one another, but most are interrelated. Chapters 1 and 7 are about the twentieth-century French philosopher of food Jean-François Revel (1924-2006). Chapters 9 and 10 address issues in food ethics ranging from the culinary and agricultural traditions of the native North Americans to today's genetically modified foods (GMFs). The relation of art and food is addressed explicitly in chapter 8 on the analogical argument made by Tolstoy and criticized by Marcia Eaton; the relation is implicitly addressed by Revel in chapter 7. Three chapters deal with food and philosophers of the modern era: Leibniz (chapter 4), Rousseau (chapter 5), and Hume (chapter 6), although Locke and Hume are discussed in the chapter on Leibniz. The first three chapters in one way or another discuss the idea of corruption of taste and the transition of a peasant cuisine to a more sophisticated one. There are obviously more interconnections among the chapters than these, and I am sure you will discover them as you read through the book. Enjoy this new area of philosophy.

1

Philosophy of Food History

[The French] . . . talk about talking about food.

GERTRUDE STEIN

* * *

Preamble

There is *a topology of time* in regard to food activities that I shall briefly develop here as a context for a philosophical discussion of the history of food. This should help clarify the levels of meaning that are implicit in the phenomena of food. The broadest distinction that can be drawn is between *immediate* and *mediate* time. Immediate time, on one hand, is the present and recent past, and within this temporal category we can distinguish between the *consumption* and *preparation* of food. Preparation can be further divided into regional (popular) cuisine and erudite (professional) cuisine, as Jean-Francois Revel has done in his book, *Culture and Cuisine*.[1] These different types of cuisine can be further developed along the lines of slow food and fast food, where Revel's interplay between the regional and the erudite disappears and becomes an opposition; see Carlo Petrini's *Slow Food: The Case for Taste*.[2]

Mediate time, on the other hand, is the connection of food with the remote past. (I shall mainly be preoccupied with this idea.) Several examples come to mind. First is Roland Barthes's "Sugar and Other Systems," in which he suggests that food has a commemorative function; i.e., "food permits a person (and I am here speaking of French themes) to partake each day of the national past."[3] In detail, he says,

> In this case, the historical quality is obviously linked to food techniques (preparation and cooking). These have long roots, reaching back to the depth of the French past. They are, we are told, the repository of a whole experience, of the accumulated wisdom of our ancestors. . . . No doubt the myth of French cooking abroad (or as expressed to foreigners) strengthens this "nostalgic" value of food

considerably; but since the French themselves actively participate in this myth (especially when traveling), it is fair to say that through his food the Frenchman experiences a certain national continuity. By way of a thousand detours, food permits him to insert himself daily into his own past and to believe in a certain culinary "being" of France. (87)

One perfect example of inserting oneself into the past through food is the way in which Marcel Proust reinhabits the landscape of his childhood when he tastes a crumb of madeleine in a spoonful of tea. Another good fictional illustration of this point is in Willa Cather's novel, *Death Comes for the Archbishop*,[4] in which a conversation about a dark onion soup ensues:

> "Think of it, *Blanchet*; in all this vast country between the Mississippi and the Pacific Ocean, there is probably not another human being who could make a soup like this."
>
> "Not unless he is a Frenchman," said Father Joseph. He had tucked a napkin over the front of his cassock and was losing no time in reflection.
>
> "I am not depreciating your individual talent, Joseph," the Bishop [Latour] continued, "but, when one thinks of it, a soup like this is not the work of one man. It is the result of a constantly refined tradition. There are nearly a thousand years of history in this soup."

Furthermore, this continuity of culinary "being" is a widely shared belief among native North American tribes and communities; for instance, Jim Enote of the Zuni Pueblo remarks, "In essence partaking of food is more than a matter of physical sustenance, it is also a personal ritual to honor the long history of our people, which is a story intimate and dense with meaning."[5] Food ritualizing a national or tribal history and providing a culinary continuity with the past is a premise shared by several cultures. This particular function of food distinguishes the history of food in terms of how it accesses the past, which makes the discipline very interesting and at the same time problematic. So the history of food raises some intriguing philosophical questions. For instance, philosophers of history are interested in what sorts of judgments are included in a historical narrative and why. I shall look at two of these here: culinary judgments and comparative judgments.

Duplication Problem

The major historiographical problem of the history of food, as Revel sees it, is this: "The difficulty when one explores the past (and even the present) lies in appreciating the difference between silent cuisine and cuisine that talks too much, between the cuisine that exists on the plate and the one that exists only in gastronomical chronicles. Or else, to state the matter in a different way, the difficulty lies in discovering, behind the verbal facade of fancy cuisines, the popular, anonymous, peasant or 'bourgeois' cuisine, made up of tricks and little secrets that only evolve very slowly, in silence, and *that no individual in particular has invented*" (10; emphasis added). So Revel echoes Bishop Latour's remark. This intimate relationship between food and the past is also echoed in the Slow Food movement. Carlo Petrini states, "If fast food means uniformity, Slow Food sets out to save and resuscitate individual gastronomic *legacies* everywhere; . . . Slow Food urges people to recover the *memory* of regional gastronomic practices" (17; emphases added).

What makes this recovery possible is explained by food writer Michael Frank:

> Food can be counted on to produce a sensation in time present that will duplicate a sensation from time past. With its myriad connections to the nurturing and sustenance of mothers and grandmothers, nannies and governesses, food is an uncanny defogger of early memory. But not only of early memory: its habits and associations, the ritual of its acquisition and preparation, the quarrels it can provide and the solace it can provide have a way, I think, of recovering and linking a good deal of lost history.[6]

Frank eloquently expresses the recovery of historical reality by the duplication of sensations of the past in the present. Proust describes such a duplication in his passage about the madeleine. A somewhat similar appeal is made to a culinary situation in the novel *Like Water for Chocolate*, where Laura Esquivel ends with this poignant passage:

> Throughout my childhood I had the good fortune to savor the delicious fruits and vegetables that grew on that land. Eventually my mother had a little apartment building built there. My father Alex still lives in one of the apartments. Today he is going to come to my house to celebrate my birthday. That is why I am preparing Christmas Rolls, my favorite dish. My mama prepared them for me every year. My mama! . . . How wonderful the flavor, the aroma of her kitchen, her stories as she prepared the meal, her Christmas Rolls! I don't know why mine never turn out like hers, or why my tears flow so freely when I prepare them—perhaps I am as sensitive to onions as Tita, my great-aunt, who will go on living as long as there is someone who cooks her recipes.[7]

For Esquivel's narrator, duplication of the Christmas Rolls seems impossible, but as Frank concedes, their associations and the ritualistic habits that surround making them are enough for the memories to come back. (The novel begins with the preparation of Christmas Rolls in the January installment, where the above passage comes from the December installment and the narrator reflecting on that early episode.) It is these emotional memories that drive regional (popular) cuisines and that define the family, especially in Hispanic/Mexican culture. Fast Food dwells in immediate time and destroys both the idea and the actuality of Slow Food and its mediate time.

Now, let us examine the nature of food history. What is the unique task of the history of food as an academic discipline? Revel attempts to answer this question in his conclusion:

> Now that we have arrived at the middle of the nineteenth century, there is no further reason to continue this attempt to resurrect the lost gastronomical *atmosphére* of times past, for from this date onward we are at home with texts, tastes, customs. . . . What I wanted to know was what was hidden behind the words; when I read the account of a repast at the court of the dukes of Burgundy or in a thatched cottage described by Rousseau, I wanted to know *Wie es eigentlich gewesen ist*: how was it really? As it draws closer to us, the curtain of time past becomes more and more transparent until eventually it disappears and the spectacle is understood without any need for keys or translations. (267)

It goes almost without saying that Revel is talking about the European history of food. When we look at different cultures, we generally are not at home with their different texts, tastes, and customs. In writing about maize in the civilization of the New World, Sophie Coe notes that "modern ignorance of this concept of the basic carbohydrate staple has led to numerous misinterpretations of the sources which would have been impossible had the reader been brought up in a society which depended on a single staff of life."[8] That ignorance is fostered by our "post-industrial diet, which is unique in lacking a basic carbohydrate staple" (9). We interpreted the maize products of the Aztecs, the Maya, and the Inca, and the rice products of the Chinese and the Japanese as *bread*, which led us to misinterpret the cultural associations which were made with those products. Coe, John Super,[9] and others have assisted in correcting these misconceptions.

What about Frank's claim that food can be counted on to produce a sensation in time present that will *duplicate* a sensation from time past? Duplicate? In *The Idea of History*,[10] Collingwood conceived of "sensation as distinct from thought," and consequently as not a part of the historical process. "They [sensations and feelings] are the basis of our rational life," he concedes, "though no part of it" (231). His argument for this claim is centered on his famous remark: "All history is the history of thought" (215). And then he adds, "At bottom, he [the critical historian] is concerned with thoughts alone; with their outward expression in events he is concerned only by the way, in so far as these reveal to him the thoughts of which he is in search" (217). The crucial premise in Collingwood's argument is this: "The peculiarity which makes it historical is not the fact of its happening in time, but the fact of its becoming known to us by our re-thinking *the same thought* which created the situation we are investigating, and thus coming to understand that situation" (218; emphasis added).[11] Collingwood probably thought that you couldn't have the same sensation, because sensations are particular, private, unique, and nonrecurring.[12] We can call this the duplication problem.

But is this really the case? Can't you have the same sensation? It seems to me that you can if you take your example from food—something Collingwood didn't consider. I think Frank is right about this—that one can have the same sensation in the present that one had in the past. In fact, this notion appears to be a presupposition of cuisines. "The art of cooking," says Alma Lach, "lies in the ability to taste, to *reproduce* taste, and to create taste" (xx; emphasis added). When I was a child my grandmother, Tressie, used to make custards of which I was very fond. Following her handwritten recipe, I can duplicate or reproduce the dish and experience the same sensations or taste that I remember having. Trained or educated palates can identify the same sensations that yield a particular flavor in, for example, a bearnaise sauce. In this way, food can bridge the gap between the past and present—something Collingwood considered to be impossible— so he replaced historical realism with historical constructionism. Food provides us with a case for historical realism in that we can truly discover the past by recovering its past sensations and tastes by duplicating them through following original recipes. (I shall return to this distinction between realism and constructionism at the end of the chapter.)

Phyllis Pray Bober, in her *Art, Culture, and Cuisine: Ancient and Medieval Gastronomy*,[13] suggests this culinary realism in her appendix on menus and recipes in which she entitles one of the menus as "A Prehistoric Repast." These are admittedly her inventions, but they do give us an experienced glimpse into the remote past that is more than just thought. "Repast" is an interesting word in this context, since it means the time or occasion of eating a meal, especially one of a specified quality. That quality couldn't be recognized unless it is one that someone has had before, so it is a "re-past." "Reconstructing the exact taste of these things [that make up a meal] in their [contemporaries'] minds presented no problem," Revel claims, because "gastronomical imagination, in fact, precedes experience itself, accompanies it, and in part substitutes for it" (5). She gives an example: "Apicius gives us a number of recipes that allow us to imagine what sweets were like in his day" (69). However, "the use of spices in some of

[Apicius's] recipes is eerily modern," Linda Civitello observes; "a recipe for pears could have come out of California two thousand years later. 'Stew the pears, clean out the center, crush them with pepper, cumin, honey, raisin wine, broth and a little oil; mix with eggs, make a pie [custard] of this, sprinkle with pepper and serve.'"[14] Nevertheless, "a written recipe," Revel warns us, "is far removed from the finished product" (112). In detail:

> Between the two there lies the indefinable domain of tricks and knacks and basic tastes that are always implicit, never explained in so many words, because the books are addressed to people who speak the same language. Any recipe read in a house-wife's handbook on sale today in bookstores calls to the reader's mind a register of very precise tastes. When we are told to add this or that rare condiment to *moules marinieres*, we see immediately what the result will be because the expression *moules marinieres* immediately summons to mind a very particular flavor. When, on the contrary, carp tongues and livers of anglerfish braised in Spanish wine are mentioned, we cannot be sure of the gastronomical reality implied by this expression, for, in the first place, we do not know if this wine was sweet or dry, and we have no idea how long the cooking time was. (112)

Nor is Revel alone in this skeptical stance towards the duplication problem. "The problem is more complex than that of texture," Reay Tannahill explains, "partly because Roman recipes are uncommunicative about quantities, and partly because they include ingredients which are not only unfamiliar today but impossible to reconstruct with any guarantee of accuracy."[15] She asks, "What did Roman food really taste like?" (102). We simply don't know, because there were fundamental differences in the quality of the raw materials, such as the differences between Roman pork and modern-day pork. However, we *do* have an idea of what Roman pork was like because we still have the original Italian breeds of pigs, such as the black pig of the Apennine, the red pig, the Casertana, the Calabrese, and the Cavallina Lucana. "There [are] organizations devoted to conserving native breeds [who] have even gone so far as to propose that increasingly rare Italian pigs should be declared part of the national heritage, in order to preserve the genes and chromosomes of the animals, and the native Italian plants on which they feed," writes Daniela Garavini.[16] So if one wants to go to the trouble and expense, one *can* taste what Roman pork was like. (These Italian pigs taste more like wild boar; much better than American domestic pigs, which tend to be bland or tasteless.) However, Tannahill concedes that it is "possible to make certain deductions from what might be described as the *atmosphére* of Roman recipes, and to integrate them with what is known about Roman life and attitudes of mind" (103; emphasis added). It is interesting indeed to observe that both Revel and Tannahill talk about the *atmosphére* of times past or of Roman recipes. So if the contact with the past is not direct, it can be indirect or a byproduct, as the word *atmosphére* suggests. There is *some* contact, but it is somewhat removed. The earlier the historical period, the more problematic the recipes are for the historian of food. Contemporaries of a recipe understood the unspoken conventions and the product, so the recipe for them was "complete." Hence, we can refer to this situation as the problem of other recipes (which is analogous to the problem of other minds or other periods). Arthur C. Danto describes the problem of other periods as the "degree to which we might succeed in achieving an *internal* understanding of what it would have been like to live in periods other than our own."[17] The same may be said of foods of other periods which are substantially different from our own. These recipes, like Apicius's,[18] are guides or probes into the past which we as food historians have to reconstruct.

Sensory History

What makes this possible—the successful gastronomical imagination—is the social or cultural background (*atmosphére)* that makes the experience public. In *Making Sense of Taste*,[19] Carolyn Korsmeyer argues against the Cartesian view of sensation (which we find in Collingwood's account) and foresees that cultural factors, or what she calls "C factors," "militate *against* the privacy and idiosyncrasy of taste, demonstrating the extent to which it is a social and hence in some respects a public phenomenon." The consideration of taste in the context of food is what prompted Korsmeyer to challenge the Cartesian dogma concerning sensation as something inherently subjective and private. And once the challenge is met, a new conception of the past and history begins to unfold.

Historians have begun recently to pay attention to the senses as ways of understanding or "adding texture" to a historical narrative. As Emily Eakin pointed out in a *New York Times* article, "By focusing on senses other than sight, sensory historians provide necessary correctives to a vision-biased history."[20] Historians of food were the first to make this corrective measure. The first sensory historians were food historians. Revel has a good illustration of this idea:

> But as you leaf through the books of the time, and when you enter a kitchen, the smells are, nonetheless, not the same as in the fifteenth and sixteenth centuries: when you raise the potlids of the Middle Ages, there rises to your nostrils a harsh meaty steam with the odor of cloves, saffron, pepper, ginger, and cinnamon mingled with the acidity of verjuice; as you lean over the cooking vessels of the Renaissance you breathe in a sweet, fruity cloud that smells of cooked sugar and pear or currant juice, all silently boiling together. The Middle Ages was the era of seasoned stews, the Renaissance the age of tasty sweetmeats. (145)

In another example, Coe reflects on her narrative:

> This book started with the promise that it was going to recount and
> celebrate the contribution of the New World, its lands and its peo-
> ples, to the cuisines of the world. It is to be hoped that it is not an
> overly Europe-centered account of the food of the Aztecs, the Maya,
> and the Inca and what happened to it during the first few decades of
> their coexistence with a fourth tribe, the Europeans. It should show
> us that not everybody eats the way we do, and that other culinary
> cultures can provide us not only with actual things to eat, but with
> food for thought as well. As well as enriching our diet, this encoun-
> ter could also enrich our minds, and let us hope that this enrich-
> ment is but a beginning! (252)

But maybe everybody eats the same way when it comes to certain things.
In *Near a Thousand Tables: A History of Food*, Felipe Fernández-Armesto
opens his narrative with a discussion of the oyster: "Still, it [the oyster] is
the food that unites us with all our ancestors—the dish you consume in
what is recognizably the way people have encountered their nourishment
since the first emergence of our species."[21] We duplicate their sensual experience of eating: "Scrape the creature from its lair with your teeth, taste
its briny juice and squelch it slightly against the palate before swallowing it alive" (2), and enjoy "the slightly fetid, tangy smell of the inside of
the shell" (2). The oyster is a taste of the sea: saltiness, moistness, miner-
al-grain-like feeling on the palate, yet a freshness to all these elements. He
describes this act of eating as "a historic experience" (2). All this sounds
remarkably similar to Leo Tolstoy's statement: "So, thanks to man's capacity to be infected with the feelings of others by means of art, all that
is being lived through by his contemporaries is accessible to him, as well
as the feelings experienced by men thousands of years ago, and he has
also the possibility of transmitting his own feelings to others."[22] Sensory
historians of food are making this claim about food. Food has this capacity or tendency for Fernández-Armesto, or as Barthes puts it: "Food
has a constant tendency to transform itself into situation" (90). And like
Tolstoy, this transformation results in communication.[23] This recapturing
or reexperiencing of a culinary past some food historians think is a central
portion of their narratives.

"In the contemporary world, it has still been possible," says Fernández-Armesto, "to recapture or reexperience a primitive sense of the power of this combination" [fire and socialized eating] (11). He gives a good
example of this "reenactment:" "When we [the Dutch] eat it [Indonesian
rijsttafel] we reenter the world of Colonel Verbrugge" [the 1860s when
the Dutch colonialists shared feasts of *rajahs*] (145). Another good example comes from Maguelonne Toussaint-Samat: "Modern *nouvelle cui-*

sine, with its emphasis on fish which is barely cooked, has rediscovered his [Archestratus's (as reported by Athenaeus)] precepts. The recipe Athenaeus gives for bonito [a small tuna] wrapped in fig leaves and cooked in the embers is simple and good."[24] She must have tried this dish for her to make this claim. Whether culinary judgments are an integral part of a historical narrative on food or not is one of the philosophical issues in the history of food discipline. Fernández-Armesto, Toussaint-Samat, Coe, and Civitello think they are; Tannahill probably thinks not; and Revel stands in the middle—sometimes culinary judgments are warranted, other times they are not. One of the reasons Tannahill stands against the inclusion of culinary judgments is found in her advice in the preface to the second edition: "I should perhaps remind readers that this is a history book, not a cookery book, and urge them not to experiment with the foods described herein. Anyone who chooses to eat unusual and unfamiliar foods may suffer harmful effects" (xii).

This advice is well and good, but the experimentation with ancient or foreign recipes can provide insight into a culture that would otherwise be missed. (Perhaps "taste" or "sample" rather than "eat" would be the best choice of words here.) As Eakin suggests, history can be enhanced if our other senses are empowered in addition to vision and the thinking associated with it. This is precisely what Bober has done in her book: on the basis of her findings in art history from prehistory to the late Gothic international style, she has reconstructed menus and recipes from what she has observed from artworks. Her repasts are there for the curious to try and for the food historian to experiment with. Bober's work implies an analogy between the history of art and the history of food. As a historian of art, Bober is immensely advantaged because she is an artist or at least very familiar with the creative artistic process. Likewise the historian of food has a better grip on her subject she herself is a chef—someone who understands the cooking process and its products. Examples abound: James Peterson and his definitive work on sauces[25] and Anne Willan and her *Great Cooks and Their Recipes*.[26] Perhaps the best example is Clifford Wright, who based his book on a diachronic rather than synchronic model of food history.[27] "This book is a history with recipes," Wright informs us, that "are not historical—that is, recipes from the medieval era—but rather they are contemporary recipes that exist the way they do because of history, a somewhat different history-telling than you learned in school; they may be considered heirloom recipes pregnant with history itself" (xvi). History colors the foods we prepare and eat, for him, and it can endow them with spirit and meaning, as we have seen with Enote of the Zuni Pueblo. The experimentation is in cooking with our imagination elaborating upon what we do know about the context (i.e., *atmosphére*) of a recipe, which may be incomplete. Quantities are omitted in Roman recipes, for instance, but these can be approximated by what we know of other Roman habits and tastes—not reproduced exactly, but then the Romans may not have been exact in their cooking.[28] Precision in quantities is something that came along centuries later. "The ability of the cook, however, is at least as important as the quality of the raw materials, and in some ways rather more important than the recipes," Tannahill concedes. "A good and experienced cook can overcome the limitations of poor materials and inadequate recipes; a bad cook can ruin the finest and the best" (365). A food historian who knows nothing of his subject can ruin a culinary narrative, too.

The Three "Ts"

At this point, let us draw out some of the implications of the argument developed here so far. We have examined the philosophical issues surrounding the history of food from the standpoint of the philosophy of history. Collingwood tells us that the remote past is either an imaginative construction or something discovered. However, there appears to be a third alternative which he didn't contemplate: the past is both something discovered (in sensations and experiences in tasting and eating) and imagined (in recipes reproducing a dish or a meal); as Revel puts it, "the exact taste of these things [that make up a meal] in their minds [contemporaries] presented no problem," because "gastronomical imagination, in fact, precedes experience itself, accompanies it, and in part substitutes for it." For those of another era or culture, there is a problem that has to be dealt with carefully and experientially by the historian of food. The problem manifests itself in three areas of concern, and these are centered on the three *T*s: texture, taste, and technique.

- *Texture*: Surviving recipes remain cryptic about the texture of food during the Roman period (see Tannahill, 96), although the Romans ate with their hands (so there is the initial feel of the food before tasting it) in a semi-reclining position, so the foods served would have to be finger-food or served in bowls, like porridge.

- *Taste*: Despite David Hume's claim (29), taste is not universal. Foods that are described as "balanced" or "acceptable" are culturally dependent. Tannahill rhetorically asks, "Who is to say what a modern cook's taste has in common with that of a chef in a Roman villa?" (102-3). And she notes: "As the decades passed, Athenian tastes became more exotic" (83). In other words, taste is something that evolves not only in an individual but also in a society—something Hume acknowledges in the second half of his essay.

- *Technique:* Several methods yield results that affect the two items above: roasting, boiling, pit cooking, and frying. During the medieval period, meats were brine-cured and dry-salted, and fruits, vegetables, and meats were dried. Some of the questions raised about these foods and processes are: How is the food prepared? How is it cooked? What temperature? Doneness? and so on. Utensils, like cauldrons and spits, obviously affected the food products.

These areas shed light on each other. The consistency of food is seen in all three categories. For instance, a roast was boiled and then roasted in Roman times. One would think that either technique would be sufficient, but we need to remember that meat was sometimes spoiled and that to ensure that the contaminants were rendered inactive, it would need to be twice cooked. So it was literally cooked to death! Once cooked, it was then ground up and shaped into patties or balls and perhaps fried or sauced. These would be eaten with one's hands, so the texture of these meatballs or patties would be quite different than if they were eaten with a utensil like a fork. (Forks weren't commonly used until early in the nineteenth century.) As I mentioned earlier, the sensory historian of food would want to *taste* rather than *eat* them.

Another possibility for the sensory historian of food is to make comparative judgments. Civitello comments, for example, that "they [the Romans] also had a kind of bread soup with vinegar and mashed cucumber, the forerunner of gazpacho" (46). So analogies can be drawn from present cuisines to past ones to give the reader and the scholar an idea of what these dishes tasted like. Here is another example from her narrative: "Underlying much of Roman cooking was a pungent fermented fish sauce called *garum*, a unique combination of salt, sea, and sun. It originated in Greece and was perhaps the ancestor, in a roundabout way, of Worcestershire sauce" (40-41). Not all historians of food include comparative judgments, but those who write general histories, like Civitello, are the ones who employ this kind of judgment in their narratives, because of the kind of audience they appeal to. Some historians, Tannahill for instance, believe that comparative judgments impose upon the past by interjecting the present. Others believe that such analogies are helpful in understanding the past by noting similarities with the present. This view is known as presentism, and it holds that the past can only be understood in terms of the present, because that is where the historian presides; in other words, he or she cannot escape the present and it must be reflected in the narrative. Others think this perspective costs the historian his or her objectivity. "Good historians do not seek the past with our own vision and experience, distorted by our own perspective, our 'specific mentality,'" Jean Bottéro argues, "but as *those for whom it was the present* contemplated and dreamed it."[30] Another food historian who has an antipresentism stance is Ken Albala; in his *Food in Early Modern Europe*,[31] he declares: "It seems far more interesting and valuable to read an actual 500-year-old recipe than try to sift through a historian's interpretation of it, or, even worse, an adaptation of it for a modern kitchen."[32] So with this last comment, we find serious disagreement among food historians in regard to the culinary status of recipes. Contrary to Albala and Tannahill, Jean Bottéro, in his *The Oldest Cuisine in the World: Cooking in Mesopotamia*, includes the greatest number of details from the texts so that "would enable us to discover some of their [the ancient Mesopotamians'] unexpected secrets concerning eating and drinking as they understood and practiced them, *so that we might appreciate and taste things as they appreciated and tasted them*" (5; emphasis added). He echoes the same sentiment in the conclusion of his study:

> To recover, even in fragments, something of the authentic gastronomy created by the ancient Mesopotamians, perhaps the first people to engage in the art—might be a way to inspire in us consumers, indeed as impenitent gourmets, through a kind of complicity, the "sympathy" (in the etymological sense of the word) indispensable for whoever wishes to truly know their fellow humans, those from the most distant past as well as those of today. (125-6)

The difficulty with the solution to the duplication problem is encountered in the three *T*s, especially when we move back in time to the ancient or medieval periods or examine other cultures. This, as we have seen, has been noted by Revel. The closer we come to the contemporary period, the easier duplication is, again, for the reasons that Revel gives. This is what we expect from the history of food and how recipes evolved over time. To this characterization of food history, Albala, in his *Eating Right in the Renaissance*,[33] adds another methodological prescription: "The history of food should involve not only tracing culinary trends but uncovering the logic of how and why cucumbers and melons truly affect Renaissance men and women differently than they do us." (There was a fear of fruit and cucumbers corrupting the body.) The difficulty in uncovering this "logic" is knowing exactly what people in the past felt about certain foods, i.e., whether they produced balanced nourishment or inbalanced indigestion. Again Albala says:

> Food preferences [and taboos], being so central to identity, are perhaps even more revealing than taste in other media. If a picture speaks a thousand words, then what of the dish that savors of the homeland, or displays wealth and elegance, or smacks of simple frugality? Each of these tells a complete story about the person who

eats it. (4)

When we eat foods that we think are good or bad for us, our bodies react physically and emotionally. "In this sense, the nutritional precepts of the past," Albala adds, "are 'true' despite what we may think of them" (10). Because the precepts are true, we have the main condition for a logic. He then ends the section on methodology with these remarks:

> As with all the medical opinions discussed in this book, the condemnation of melons typifies the vast differences between the nutritional logic of the past and our own. It also highlights the fact that the fears and preferences of the past, though strange, were no less real to those who experienced them. They also reveal the workings of the Renaissance mind on a level unattainable by any other means. That ultimately is the goal of this book: to understand the period through its idea about food. (13)

So for the most part, the history of food, for Albala, coincides with the history of medicine. This is because diet has been brought into the food scene along with recipes, dishes, menus, cooking, and eating.

Conclusion

In closing, let us look at the nature of history again and the place of food history within the mainstream of history. Professor Super has an interesting personal account worth examining. He says in his Preface:

> After finishing that work [a history of Mexico], I began to realize that my attempts to explain social and economic change would have been more successful if placed within the context of the natural world. My working definition of social and economic history had been too narrowly conceived. I then began to look for ways to bridge the gap between the social and biological worlds, for a way to interpret the relationship between people and environment which might give insight into the processes of conquest and colonization. Food was the answer to me. (vii)

Super's broadened historical perspective is especially useful in studying the sixteenth-century Americas because of the Columbian Exchange, which is the exchange of old world food plants and livestock and new world fruits and vegetables. But causal interaction between social-political history and the natural environment occurred in other periods of history; Tannahill, Fernández-Armesto, and Civitello use such an "exchange" to discuss some of their accounts of "revolutions" in world history. Many conventional historians, however, deal with change in human institutions as if they are independent of the natural environment. Maybe other histo-rians will follow the lead of historians of food like Super.[34]

The ability of food to unify apparent opposites is also appreciated by Jean-Louis Flandrin and Massimo Montanari, who have observed that "the history of food [as an academic discipline] has demonstrated its ability to unify many different approaches. The old distinction between mind and body, intellect and substance, seemingly vanished in the face of the need to understand the complexity of human behavior with respect to food."[35] And to this dualistic list we can add Collingwood's separation of sensation from thought. The history of food provides us with a third alternative to historical understanding by unifying realism and constructionism. What people eat engages both body and mind, sensation and thought. Seeing this novel third alternative provided by the phenomenon of food gives the philosophy of history another new direction to explore.

Notes

1. Jean-François Revel, *Culture and Cuisine: A Journey through the History of Food,* translated from the French by Helen R. Lane (Garden City, New York: Doubleday, 1982). For a dialectical discussion of regional and erudite cuisines, consult chapter 7 below.

2. Carlo Petrini, *Slow Food: The Case for Taste*, translated from the Italian by William McCuaig (New York: Columbia University Press, 2001).

3. Roland Barthes, "Sugar and Other Systems: Towards a Psychosociology of Contemporary Food Consumption," *The Journal of Gastronomy* I (Fall 1984), 87. Translated from the French by Elborg Forster in 1979 from the 1961 publication in *Annales.*

4. Willa Cather, *Death Comes for the Archbishop* (New York: Alfred A. Knopf, 1926), 38. The same point is made by Alma Lach in her Preface to the *Hows and Whys of French Cooking* (Chicago: The University of Chicago Press, 1974), xix: "*Haute cuisine* is a logical system of cooking that has developed in France, especially Paris, over the past several centuries. Once the 'Hows and Whys' of this *system* are learned, the cook becomes an independent and creative worker who makes up recipes by imaginative adaptions of and refinements upon what generations of cooks and chefs have evolved and codified into standard French procedures." Revel makes a similar point; see chapter 7.

5. Jim Enote, "Forward," in Rita Edaakie, *Idonapshe/Let's Eat: Traditional Zuni Foods* (Albuquerque: University of New Mexico Press, 1999), vii.

6. Michael Frank, "The Underside of Bread: A Memoir with Food," in *Not for Bread Alone: Writers on Food, Wine, and the Art of Eating*, edited by Daniel Halpern (Hopewell, New Jersey: The Ecco Press, 1993), 56.

7. Laura Esquivel, *Like Water for Chocolate*, translated from the Spanish by Carol and Thomas Christensen (Anchor Books; New York: Doubleday, 1992), 241.

8. Sophie D. Coe, *America's First Cuisines* (Austin: University of Texas Press, 1994), 9.

9. John C. Super, *Food, Conquest, and Colonization in Sixteenth-Century Spanish America* (Albuquerque: University of New Mexico Press, 1988); and John C. Super and Thomas C. Wright (eds.), *Food, Politics, and Society in Latin America* (Latin American Studies Series; Lincoln: University of Nebraska Press, 1985).

10. R. G. Collingwood, *The Idea of History* (London: Oxford University Press, 1946), 216.

11. For a discussion of the phrase "the same thought," see S. K. Wertz, "Mediation and Context in Collingwood's Epilegomena," *Collingwood and British Idealism Studies* XVIII, no. 1 (2012): 96-99.

12. R. G. Collingwood, *The Principles of Art* (London: Oxford University Press, 1938); see his discussion of sensation in Book II: The Theory of Imagination, esp. pp. 157-174.

13. Phyllis Pray Bober, *Art, Culture, and Cuisine: Ancient and Medieval Gastronomy* (Chicago: University of Chicago Press, 1999), 269ff.

14. Linda Civitello, *Cuisine and Culture: A History of Food and People* (Hoboken, New Jersey:

John Wiley & Sons, Inc., 2004), 44.

15. Reay Tannahill, *Food in History* (New York: Stein and Day Publishers, 1973), 96. A second, revised edition published in 1988. This book is considered by some to be the first history of food and Revel's followed in 1979; the eighties and nineties saw an explosion of publications in the field.

16. Daniela Garavini, *Pigs and Pork: History, Folklore, Ancient Recipes* (Cologne: Konemann, 1996/1999), 33-35.

17. Arthur C. Danto, *Narration and Knowledge* (New York: Columbia University Press, 1985), 285.

18. Apicius, *Cookery and Dining in Imperial Rome*, edited and translated by Joseph Dommers Vehling (New York: Dover Publications, Inc., 1977). Original edition published in 1936.

19. Carolyn Korsmeyer, *Making Sense of Taste: Food and Philosophy* (Ithaca: Cornell University Press, 1999), 100; her emphasis.

20. Emily Eakin, "History You Can See, Hear, Smell, Touch and Taste," *The New York Times.* Saturday, December 20, 2003, A21.

21. Felipe Fernández-Armesto, *Near a Thousand Tables: A History of Food* (New York: The Free Press, 2002), 2.

22. Leo N. Tolstoy, *What Is Art?*, translated from the Russian original by Almyer Maude (Indianapolis: Bobbs-Merrill Educational Publishing Company, 1960), 52. First published in 1896.

23. For a discussion of the relation between food and art, see chapter 8.

24. Maguelonne Toussaint-Samat, *History of Food*, translated from the French by Anthea Bell (Oxford: Basil Blackwell, 1992), 300.

25. James Peterson, *Sauces: Classical and Contemporary Sauce Making* (Second Edition; New York: John Wiley & Sons, 1998).

26. Anne Willan, *Great Cooks and Their Recipes: From Taillevent to Escoffier* (London: Pavilion Books Limited, 2000).

27. Clifford A. Wright, *A Mediterranean Feast: The Story of the Birth of the Celebrated Cuisines of the Mediterranean, from the Merchants of Venice to the Barbary Corsairs* (New York: William Morrow and Company, Inc., 1999), xvi.

28. A good book that does this is Ilaria Gozzini Giacosa, *A Taste of Ancient Rome*, translated from the Italian by Anna Herklotz (Chicago: University of Chicago Press, 1992); and Mary Taylor Simeti in the Forward writes: "her book gives context [*atmosphére*] to the ancient recipes by explaining to us how and where the Romans bought, cooked, and ate their food, and makes the recipes themselves accessible to modern cooks, suggesting substitutes for unavailable ingredients and supplying the procedures and the quantities omitted in the originals" (vii).

29. David Hume, "Of the Standard of Taste" (1757), in *Essays Moral, Political and Literary* (Oxford: Oxford University Press, 1963), essay 23.

30. Jean Bottéro, *The Oldest Cuisine in the World: Cooking in Mesopotamia.* Translated by Teresa Lavender Fagan (Chicago: University of Chicago Press, 2004), 5; his emphasis.

31. Ken Albala, *Food in Early Modern Europe* (Westport, Connecticut: Greenwood Press, 2003), xvi.

32. For further discussion of presentism, see David L. Hall, "In Defense of Presentism," *History and Theory* 17 # 1 (1979): 1-15; and S. K. Wertz, *Between Hume's Philosophy and History: Historical Theory and Practice* (Landam, Maryland: University Press of America, 2000), 94,135.

33. Ken Albala, *Eating Well in the Renaissance* (Berkeley: University of California Press, 2002), 9.

34. On the concept of environmental history, see the theme issue (no. 42) in *History and Theory*, entitled "Environment and History," December, 2003; it is interesting to note that none of the contributors in this issue saw the connection between the natural and social worlds with food that Super did.

35. Jean-Louis Flandrin and Massimo Montanari (eds.), *Food: A Culinary History from Antiquity to the Present*, translated by Clarissa Botsford, Arthur Goldhammer, Charles Lambert, Frances M. Lopez-Morillas, and Sylvia Stevens (English edition by Albert Sonnenfeld; New York: Penguin Books, 2000), 6.

2

The Five Flavors and Taoism: Lao Tzu's Verse Twelve

* * *

In verse twelve of the *Tao Te Ching*, Lao Tzu makes a curious claim about the five flavors: namely, that they cause people not to taste or that they jade the palate. The five flavors are: sweet, sour, salty, bitter (these four are the traditional elements of taste in the West, recognized by the science of taste[1]) and spicy or hot as in "heat" (*picante*, not *caliente*). (Before the introduction of chili peppers, black pepper and ginger provided the heat.[2]) The whole verse is as follows:

1 The five colors cause men to not see;
2 The five tones cause them to not hear;
3 The five flavors cause them to not taste.
4 The race and the chase drive men mad,
5 And rare goods lead them astray.
6 When wise men govern this is why
7 They favor the belly, not the eye,
8 The one accept, the other deny.[3]

To the Western mind, the claim in line three (The five flavors cause them to not taste) is counterintuitive; on the contrary, the presence of the five flavors in a dish or in a meal would expand or enhance the senses and the palate; i.e., taste would be augmented by the five flavors and not diminished. So what is the reasoning behind this mysterious stanza?

What is the origin of the five flavors? Scholars engaged in collecting ancient traditions, Reay Tannahill notes, "heard tell of a sage, who was said to have lived in the time of the (probably legendary) Hsia dynasty [twenty-first to eighteenth centuries BCE], whose name was reputedly I Yin, and who was believed to have spoken of the importance of the Five Flavors."[4] By the fourth century BCE, comparatively early in Chinese cuisine,[5] the concept of the five flavors appears to have been established.

Indeed, the five flavors were so well entrenched that they appear as an element in philosophical debate. Lao Tzu argues that the five flavors actually ruin the sense of taste—because using any sense to the fullest would finally dull it.[6] This reasoning suggests that the five flavors must have been *intense* in the dishes that were served during Lao Tzu's era. In other words, these dishes were very sweet, too spicy, lots of salt, quite bitter, and really sour. But surely this is a faulty deduction. "The *keng* soup," K. C. Chang reports, "formed the basis of a metaphoric discourse by a Chou philosopher-politician, supposed to have taken place in 521 BC[E], as recorded in *Tso chuan*: 'Harmony may be illustrated by soup. You have the water and fire, vinegar, pickle, salt, and plums, with which to cook fish and meat. It is made to boil by the firewood, and then the cook mixes the ingredients, harmoniously equalizing the several flavours, so as to supply whatever is deficient and carry off whatever is in excess. Then the master eats it, and his mind is made equable.'"[7] In other words, the five flavors were combined in such a way in a dish or a meal to achieve balance and harmony.

In the ode *Shih*, it is said that "the ancient kings established the doctrine of the five flavours ... to make their minds equable and to perfect their government."[8] So the lessons in individual and political harmony came from culinary harmony. But it doesn't end there, because the five flavors were linked to cosmological theories based on the five elements—earth (sweet, grains and fruits), wood (sour), fire (bitter), metal (pungent or "hot"), and water (salt).[9] Food affirmed order, both cosmological and ritual/political order.[10] And speaking of order and "fives," Chinese cuisine can be characterized by the "five plus five" method or approach—the five general condiment types (extracts, pastes, marinades, dipping sauces, and garnishes) aid in balancing the five flavors.[11] For the moment, let us return to verse twelve before exploring the concept of the five flavors any further.

What does "taste" denote in line three? Is it Chinese cuisine in general? Or is it one of the regional cuisines that Lao Tzu has in mind? Or is it the elite's dishes of the lords and kings of the Warring States period? Probably the latter, because the first two options are ruled out by simple chronology. Chinese cuisine as haute cuisine and the regional cuisines all developed after Lao Tzu's time. It was during the Sung dynasty (between 960 and 1279) that the regional cuisines developed. Line five mentions "rare goods," and more than likely some of the condiments and spices that would be used to bring out one or more of the five flavors would be scarce and costly. Also lines four and five suggest a criticism of the common practice of elite banquets or feasts that were staged at the time, and Lao Tzu probably held such elite practices in disgust. Moss Roberts's comment is: "Judging by the pursuits named in lines 1-5, this stanza is addressed to an elite, probably a ruling elite, warning them (as in stanza 3) that indulgence can ruin popular morals. Laozi [Lao Tzu] is calling for discipline of the ruler's character through self-denial with regard to the prerogatives of ritual luxury" (53).

Roberts is probably right about this, but frugality with food and eating was one of the things central to the Chinese way of life and a part of the Chinese ethos. Frugality is mentioned as one of the "three treasures" that allows generosity.[12] Sumptuous feasts and wastefulness of food were frowned upon generally: overindulgence was something only the upper class could afford. The nobles, Lao Tzu proclaims, "are glutted with food and drink" (Tzu 53, Addiss/Lombardo translation). "Exotic foods and elegantly balanced flavors were for the rich," Tannahill observes, "but it is possible that the style of cooking nowadays regarded in the West as being 'typically Chinese' may be evolved in the peasant kitchen" (145). The Chinese are among the peoples of the world most preoccupied with food and eating, so it is not surprising to find several other food references in the *Tao Te Ching*. Let us look at some of these.

The next to the last stanza (eighty), lines eight through ten, speaks of keeping the kingdom small and its people few (line one), and to

8 Guide them back to early times,

9 When knotted cords served for signs,

10 And they took relish in their food. (Roberts translation, 186)

What was the food like? As Tannahill conjectures, it was probably of peasant origin, but not what we associate with Chinese cuisine today. What the peasants ate was not anything like what the scholarly Confucians or elites ate. As a dietary rule, the Confucians or elites must not eat anything that is overcooked nor undercooked, nor anything out of season, nor any dish that lacks its *proper* seasoning.[13] The Taoist would agree with most of this maxim, except that it would be guided by simplicity, the common, and naturalness, rather than the doctrine of the five flavors. What determines the appropriateness of a dish in terms of cooking is not a matter of convention but of nature. However, what the Confucian or elites and Taoist diets would have in common would be the process of preparing food based upon the division between *fan* (grains and other starches) and *ts'ai* (vegetables and meats).[14] This is the Chinese *fan-ts'ai* principle, which is seen as the basis of balance or harmony sought among their dishes or in a menu.

For the Taoist, the five flavors of food serve as acts of sensory acquisition based on desire rather than need. They serve to charm the senses of sight and smell as well as taste. If one cooks with the five flavors, then one will *want* more, so in addition to desire being ignited, there would be a violation of the maxim of moderate consumption (see note 14). Archie Bahm has an interesting reading of verse twelve that is in line with this idea of desire rather than need: "Desire for enjoyment of the various flavors misdirects the appetite from seeking foods which are truly nourishing."[15] In other words, what *motivates* the use of flavors is more objectionable than the flavors themselves, because these flavors are natural and commonplace. What are the natural, flavorful foods that are truly nourishing? Besides verse twelve speaking out *against* certain uses, i.e., Confucian or elites uses of the five flavors, the stanza speaks *for* certain foods and their cooking.

The next interpretation is suggested by verse thirty-five: "Music and sweets [fine food] Make passing guests pause, But the Tao emerges Flavorless and bland" (Addiss/Lombardo translation); or in another translation by Stephen Mitchell: "Music or the smell of good cooking may make people stop and enjoy. But words that point to the Tao seem monotonous and without flavor." These words, in other words, do not stop people to sense things or to direct their attention in ways that music and the smell of fine food do. Tao words are so bland that they are without flavor (see note 25), or they do not *distract*. Consequently, instead of verse twelve referring to rich, decadent use of the five flavors, it suggests that the flavors are perhaps not to be used at all. The natural way to cook food items is just by themselves, so that they flavor themselves with water, steam, smoke, or heat—adding some complexity. A good example of this is rice. "If anyone ever doubts the real flavour of things," the Lins announce, "let him eat plain rice."[16] Their explanation is as follows:

> Rice has its *hsien* (sweet natural taste). The *hsien* is concealed in the grains, and meted out bit by bit in the aftertaste. The dual nature of the taste (immediate and aftertaste) is what makes it impossible to duplicate. It is also difficult to describe; one can only call attention to it. Yuan Mei spoke of the "juices" of rice. These can be tasted if one chews plain, well-cooked rice. Water dilutes the "juices," soaking removes them, thus, in the cooking of rice no excess water can be tolerated.[17]

Plain flavors, like boiled rice and chicken congee or other congees, are perhaps what Lao Tzu had in mind in verse twelve in that the five flavors would mask these plain flavors. A variation of this thought comes from verse sixty: "Govern big countries like you cook little fish" (Addiss/Lombardo translation). The less you interfere with them, the better—whether it's small fish or large countries. Little governance whether in ruling or in cooking is the best advice. This gives a whole new meaning to "whole foods" or "natural foods." An extreme view of the bland interpretation would be that there is *no* human intervention in the cooking process—no spices, no additives of any kind. If the Tao is bland, then we expect to find this true of the food of the devout Taoist. As Lao Tzu paradoxically says,

"Taste without tasting" (verse sixty-three, Addiss/Lombardo translation).

And also in this, it seems that everything in the Chinese landscape comes in groups of five.[18] We have Chinese Five-Spice (cinnamon, star anise, fennel, clove, ginger, licorice, Sichuan peppercorn, and white pepper, so it's really eight spices), which has been associated with the five flavors. Indeed, five-spice powder encompasses the five flavors, but the two are not synonymous, for the five flavors are much broader in taste range. Equating the two would be too restrictive, since such an equation would limit the flavors to substances. In fact, the "five-spice powder" in Chinese is closer to five fragrances than to five flavors.

Chinese cuisine as it is known today derives from classical combinations of the five flavors, but the full range of Chinese cuisine goes well beyond the scope of the five-flavor formula. Consequently, if one examines Chinese cookbooks,[19] one finds few references to the five flavors.

What remains of the doctrine of the five flavors in Chinese cuisine today is little compared to its use in elegant Confucian feasts or banquets (of which we know little in detail).[20] A few contemporary recipes I have found include Martin Yan's "Five-Flavor Honey Wings" (appetizer), which consists of oyster sauce, cornstarch, cooking oil, sliced green onion, garlic, dried red pepper flakes, chicken stock, dark soy sauce, Chinese rice wine or dry sherry, Chinese five-spice powder, honey, and chicken wings.[21] Another is *Ng Heong Gai,* "Five Flavors Chicken" (Cantonese), which includes peanut oil, salt, ground pepper, ground star anise, chopped scallion, chopped ginger, light soy sauce, sherry, hoisin sauce, and a fryer or squabs.[22] These chicken dishes display a balance of ingredients: Yan's wings having a sweet finish, while *Ng Heong Gai* has a unique anise-ginger taste, but is still a typical Cantonese dish known for its mildness. The Taoist wouldn't object to these flavors *per se* unless they were inspired by desire of eliteness, with its emphasis upon scarcity and expense.

The first recipe I want to look at in some detail allegedly comes from the Tang dynasty, around 800 CE:

Five Flavors Pork Roast

1 tablespoon sugar
1 medium garlic clove, minced
½ cup soy sauce
1 teaspoon ginger, grated
1 cup red wine
½ teaspoon Five-Spice powder
1 teaspoon Sichuan peppercorns, ground
3 pounds boneless pork loin

Combine the first 7 ingredients for the marinade.
Add the pork loin and marinade over night, covered.
Preheat oven to 300 degrees F.
Roast the pork in the marinade for 1½ hours. Baste often.
After roasting, you can add a thickening agent (cornstarch or arrowroot)
to the marinade to make a sauce.[23]

Notice that this recipe has no salt, so a regular soy sauce with high sodium content would be better than a light soy sauce. Other than that, the five flavors are represented in the ingredients. This recipe is unusual because one doesn't find many recipes for large pieces of meat in Chinese cuisine. Meat was primarily used as a flavor enhancer rather than a main dish, but this is an exception (along with Peking Duck). Here is a second recipe with a different cooking technique:

Five Flavors Chicken

3¾ to 4 pounds chicken pieces
1 (1¼-inch) piece fresh ginger root, peeled and finely chopped,
  or 1½ teaspoons ground ginger
2 cloves garlic, minced
½ cup soy sauce
½ cup honey
3 tablespoons mirin (sweet sake wine), dry sherry, or gin
2 tablespoons cornstarch
1 cup steamed rice

Trim tips off wings and pull skin off other chicken pieces.
Mix ginger, garlic, soy sauce, honey, and spirits.
Dip each piece of chicken into sauce.
Place chicken in crockpot and pour remaining sauce over it.
Cover and cook on LOW. Wings will be ready in 5 to 5 ½ hours,
  other pieces in 6 hours.
(On HIGH, wings will take about 2 ½ hours, other pieces in 3 hours.)
Remove chicken to warmed serving dish.
Pour juices into skillet; blend cornstarch with a little of the cooled juices,
  then whisk into skillet.
Cook over low heat until thickened. Adjust seasonings, adding salt and
  pepper to taste.
Pour a little sauce over chicken and rice, pour remaining sauce into a
  pitcher, and serve.[24]

These four recipes for specific dishes using the five flavors are about all we can find in Chinese gastronomy, which strongly suggests that the five flavors did not have to be present in each dish, but rather were found in combination with a few accompanying dishes or in the composition of the entire dinner menu. So the *fan-ts'ai* principle which governed a meal would be seen as each division contributing to the five flavors: some flavors in *fan* (grains and other starches) and others in *ts'ai* (vegetables and meats). If this is the case, then the five flavors could be easily achieved and in an almost endless variety of ways. See the appendix below for how various fruits, vegetables, spices, and food products (like sauces) exemplify a given flavor. One may infer from all this that the five flavors are not as objectionable as Lao Tzu makes them out to be. They serve to balance or harmonize dishes or a meal so that their harmony is carried over to the individual or gourmand. Surely such a balance was something Lao Tzu himself was trying to achieve with nature, so why not in a meal? In spite of such argument, the verse remains unclear, especially in terms of what it is referring to. We don't have enough historical information about Chinese cuisine at the time of Lao Tzu to know the specific references or even the nature of the references he is making in his culinary comments. I have offered some conjectures here, and when we fill in the details of what we do know about the five flavors, the objections that Lao Tzu makes seem to be rather weak.

In some quarters, the five flavors *cannot* balance themselves—they need something else to harmonize them, like tea. The use of the five colors with five-flavor dishes testify to this point, too. So an issue raised here would be sufficiency versus insufficiency. Most of the discussion of the five flavors seems to take them as sufficient in themselves for harmonizing or balancing a dish or a meal. To assist the five flavors are the five colors, and they parallel each other: spicy—white, sweet—yellow, sour—green, bitter—red, and salty—black. So if a particular flavor is subtle, then its corresponding color can be used in presentation to help suggest that flavor to the diner. Of course, Lao Tzu objects to the five colors, too (see lines one and seven of verse twelve), so such parallels are irrelevant to the Taoist.

Or, as Lao Tzu has done, the five flavors can be viewed as irrelevant or unnecessary to cooking and eating. Wang's commentary (third century CE) is instructive here: the mouth or the palate should comply [*shun*] with its own character [*xing*]. When one doesn't use it in compliance with its character and individual capacity [*ming*], he or she thus perversely harms what it is by nature [*ziran*], and this is why the text characterizes it as the five flavors making one's mouth fail.[25] In other words, the five flavors harm the mouth's (or palate's) nature, because, to repeat, we are following convention rather than nature. Is this a good argument? I don't think so. As I said above, these five flavors *are* natural, since they are found in nature and are commonplace, so they should be compatible with the mouth's character [*xing*]. It is what is *done* with the five flavors that determines whether they are natural or conventional.

It is worth mentioning here the metaphoric connection with the usage of *five*. That is, the adjective *five* in verse twelve may refer to not only *the* five flavors, but also to *many* flavors, or an excessive number (or confusion) of flavors. The repeated use of five, or another number (like three or seven), is often a literary device as well in Chinese prose-making. For Lao Tzu, there is a confusion that results from an excessive number of flavors—or really, an excess of anything. The Tao has no flavor, because it contains all flavors; thus differentiation is inferior. The source of Tao is *wu*, nothingness or void; thus even any individuation or manifestation is inferior. The cooking of rice with no flavoring is a good example of this principle. Close to this perspective is Chuang Tzu in *The Inner Chapters* (Part Four: The essays of the Primitivist and episodes related to them), where he speaks of the Five Tastes as a way to lose one's nature because they "dirty the mouth and make it sickly"; in other words, they are harmful to life.[26]

Lao Tzu is the antithesis of gastronomy. "For the gastronome," Jean-Robert Pitte describes, "the more he practices, the more difficult it becomes for him to achieve complete satisfaction—[to] reach a higher degree of refinement" (8). But he keeps trying, for this is his goal. This is precisely what Lao Tzu is objecting to in the *Tao Te Ching*. But this objection is not something unique to Lao Tzu. In eighteenth-century Europe, France in particular, we find a parallel argument in Rousseau to the newly emerging *haute cuisine* and its enthusiastic reception by the French upper class. Indeed, Rousseau even wants to do away with taste! "With regard to Julie, he [Rousseau] writes, 'Her sense of taste has hardly been used; she never needs to revive it with excesses, and I often see her savoring with delight a child's treat that would be tasteless to all others.'"[27] This sounds very much like the Sage or the Master in the *Tao Te Ching* with the child as one who is closest to the Tao and finding taste in the tasteless. This is an intriguing idea—finding taste in the tasteless. In some respects this would take a refined palate to detect this circumstance, or is it as Rousseau describes it—one who hasn't tasted at all, for the first time, or very little? Another reading of the phrase could be "without the five flavors" for "tasteless." In any event, it is interesting to find philosophical critics of the newly emerging haute cuisine in both China and France with their arguments hinging on the conception of corruption of taste.[28]

Appendix

Spicy	Sweet	Sour	Bitter	Salty
ginger	sugar	bitter melon (fresh)	bitter melon (ripe)	salt
black pepper	honey	rice vinegar	Seville orange	soy sauce (reg.)
chili peppers	coconut	lemon	soy sauce (lite)	
Sichuan peppers	bell peppers	lime	garlic (raw)	
cinnamon	apples	dry wine	star anise	
mace	grapes	cranberry	dry mustard	
nutmeg	raisins	wild cherries	radicchio	
radish	hoisin sauce		radish	
cardamom	sherry		mustard greens	
	garlic (cooked)		endive	
	dates		arugula	
	onions (cooked)			
	rice (well-cooked)			
	Bing cherries			

Note: There is some overlap among these flavors or tastes.

Notes

1. See Carolyn Korsmeyer, *Making Sense of Taste: Food and Philosophy* (Ithaca: Cornell University Press, 1999), ch.3.

2. Bruce Cost, *Asian Ingredients: A Guide to the Foodstuffs of China, Japan, Korea, Thailand, and Vietnam* (New York: HarperCollins Publishers, Inc., 2000), 7.

3. Translation and commentary by Moss Roberts, *Laozi, Dao De Jing: The Book of the Way* (Berkeley: University of California Press, 2001), 53. Line in Romanized Chinese, with literal English translation in parentheses, is: *wu* (five) *wei* (flavor) *ling* (cause) *ren* (man) *kou* (mouth) *shuang* (: to miss the mark, or to make a mistake, or to harm the quickness) in *The Power of Tao: A New Translation of the Tao Te Ching*, R. L. Wing, trans. (Wellingborough, Northamptonshire, England: The Aquarian Press, 1986), no page numbers given, who translates line 3 as "The five flavors will jade one's taste." Wing's commentary is labeled "Controlling the Senses" and is, in part: "Those who follow the Tao carefully control input to the senses in order to refine their insights and maintain an accurate perspective of the world. A cacophony of sounds, sights, and tastes, along with an accelerated, materially oriented life, will stand in the way of character

development and inner clarity. Evolved Individuals [Masters or Sages] know that intellectual independence and social freedom come through control of the senses." Interestingly, there are no culinary references in these commentaries.

4. Reay Tannahill, *Food in History* (New York: Stein and Day, Publishers, 1973), 140n.

5. Tannahill, 145. This occurred during the Chou dynasty (twelfth century BCE-221 BCE).

6. Tannahill, 145. In the West, the culinary maxim is: if you don't use it [the palate], you lose it. "Gastronomy," writes Jean-Robert Pitte, "is a form of aestheticism acquired by constant, intensive cultivation of the senses, the most important, in this case, being taste." *French Gastronomy: The History and Geography of a Passion*, translated by Jody Gladding (New York: Columbia University Press, 2002), 5.

7. K. C. Chang, "Ancient China," in *Food in Chinese Culture: Anthropological and Historical Perspectives*, edited by K. C. Chang (New Haven: Yale University Press, 1977), 51n2.

8. Chang, 51n2, and translated by James Legge, *The Ch'un Ts'ew with the Tso Chuen*, in *The Chinese Classics* (Oxford: Clarendon Press, 1872), V, 684.

9. Frederick W. Mote, "Yuan and Ming," in Chang, *Food in Chinese Culture*, 228; and Michael Freeman, "Sung," in Chang, 176n7.

10. Freeman, 163; and he continues: "Attitudes about food were marked by a similar concern: to integrate this facet of human experience into a comprehensible whole" (170). Such integration is one of the basic philosophical impulses of the Chinese mind.

11. Corinne Trang, *Essentials of Asian Cuisine: Fundamentals and Favorite Recipes* (New York: Simon & Schuster, 2003), 64ff. "This 'five plus five' approach has spread outward from China, progressing throughout Asia in regional influences and localized ingredients, evolving into something closer to a class of specialized dishes than the salt and pepper, ketchup, and mustard we commonly use in the West."

12. Lao Tzu, *Tao Te Ching*, translated by Stephen Addiss and Stanley Lombardo (Indianapolis: Hackett Publishing Company, 1993), 67. Stephen Mitchell also has a translation with notes (New York: Harper & Row, Publishers, 1988). Unless otherwise noted, the verse numbers are the same as the page numbers in the various editions and translations that I cite.

13. Tannahill, 142. "Proper" seasoning would be in accordance with the doctrine of the five flavors.

14. Chang, "Introduction," 7-8. In *Essentials of Asian Cuisine*, Corinne Trang records: "Of the two food groups, *fan* is fundamental and indispensable, and is considered primary. *Ts'ai* is secondary. Without *fan* one cannot be nourished; without *t'sai* the meal is simply less tasty. Overindulgence in food and drink is discouraged as unbalanced and unhealthful. Waste is anathema. The proper amount of consumption is, as Chinese parents have said to their children for millennia, *chi fen pao* or '70 percent.' Chinese folklore is full of stories told to children about the negative consequences of waste." (46)

15. Archie J. Bahm, *Tao Teh King by Lao Tzu Interpreted as Nature and Intelligence* (Second Edition; Albuquerque, New Mexico: World Books, 1986), 19.

16. Hsiang Ju Lin and Tsuifeng Lin, *Chinese Gastronomy* (New York: Pyramid Publications, 1969/1972), 48.

17. Lins, 48. They add Li Liweng's remarks: "The essences of rice are in the cooking water. If the rice is lacking in flavour, it is because the water has not been measured out correctly. Add so much rice to so much water, as the doctor brews medicine. Measure out the water to the exact spoonful. You would not think it would make so much difference."

18. "The five phases were then [the Chou, Ch'in, and Han dynasties] associated with everything else imaginable: five colors, five tastes, five smells [rancid, scorched, fragrant, rotten, and putrid], five larger bodily organs, five smaller bodily organs, five limbs of the body, and everything else that could be forced into a set of about this size." E. N. Anderson, *The Food of China* (New Haven: Yale University Press, 1988), 43, 231.

19. Besides the sources cited in these notes, consult Jacqueline M. Newman, *Chinese Cookbooks: An Annotated English Language Compendium/Bibliography* (New York and London: Garland Publishing, Inc., 1987), and her recent book, *Food Culture in China* (Westport, Connecticut: Greenwood Press, 2004).

20. The last great, enlightened emperor, Qianlong, of the eighteenth century, gives us some insight into royal eating habits: "Qianlong was very fond of duck but he also liked chicken and pork. He did not like fish or any other seafood. He received a great deal of dried and fresh seafood in the form of tribute goods, often when on tours to the Northeast and elsewhere, but promptly gave almost all of it away. Like all good Manchus, he did not eat beef; surviving

menus of the court show no beef dishes at all. He loved birds'-nest soup and was an enthusiast for the traditional Manchu snacks and pastries called *bobo*. Otherwise, his tastes ran to the sophisticated Han Chinese cuisine of Suzhou in central China; he consistently ordered Suzhou food for himself even at formal banquets where one would think that Manchu food would have been a more appropriate choice." Chuimei Ho and Bennet Bronson, *Splendors of China's Forbidden City: The Glorious Reign of Emperor Qianlong* (The Field Museum; London and New York: Merrill Publishing Limited, 2004), 195.

21. Martin Yan, *Martin Yan's Invitation to Chinese Cooking* (San Francisco, California: Bay Books, 1999), 22. Martin Yan's "Mandarin Five-Flavored Boneless Pork Chops" recipe (which consists of soy sauce, dry sherry, cornstarch, five-spice powder, vegetable oil, ginger, garlic, celery, onions, a fresh Tai chili, and the pork chops) is included in Grace Young and Alan Richardson, *The Breath of a Wok: Unlocking the Spirit of Chinese Wok Cooking Through Recipes and Lore* (New York: Simon & Schuster, 2004), 188.

22. Wonoma W. and Irving B. Chang, and Helene W. and Austin H. Kutscher, *An Encyclopedia of Chinese Food and Cooking* (New York: Crown Publishers, Inc., 1970), 231.

23. The recipe was retrieved October 1, 2004, on the Web: http://www.geocities.com/NapaValley/4317/5pork.html.

24. This recipe was also retrieved October 1, 2004, on the Web: http://www.recipegoldmine.com/crockpotpoul/crockpot694.html.

25. *The Classic of the Way and Virtue: A New Translation of the Tao-te ching of Laozi as Interpreted by Wang Bi*, translated by Richard John Lynn (New York: Columbia University Press, 1999), 70.

26. A. C. Graham, *Chuang Tzu: The Inner Chapters* (Indianapolis: Hackett Publishing Company 2001), 202-3: "whoever keeps his nature subordinate to the Five Tastes . . . is not what I would call a fine man . . . nor when I call someone a fine man is it the Five Tastes that I am talking about, but simply a trust in the essentials of our nature and destiny." Chuang Tzu's interpretation is very similar to Wang's (see note 25).

27. Pitte, 53. Rousseau's statement can be found in *Julie, or the New Heloise: Letters of Two Lovers Who Live in a Small Town at the Foot of the Alps* (1761), in Rousseau, Jean-Jacques, *The Collected Writings*, vol. 6, translated by Philip Stewart and Jean Vaché (Dartmouth College; Hanover, New Hampshire: University Press of New England, 1997), 443: "her taste does not go flat; she never needs to revive it through excess, and I often see her savor with delight a child's pleasure that would be insipid to anyone else." Part Five, Letter II To Milord Edward. For further discussion of taste and food in Rousseau's *Julie, or the New Heloise*, see chapter 5.

28. Some of this discussion continues in the next chapter (3).

3

The Elements of Taste: How Many Are There?

> The perception created by the combination
> of olfaction and taste is called flavor.
> BRUCE GOLDSTEIN
> *Sensation and Perception*

* * *

How many tastes or flavors are there? Are there five as most Chinese believe? None as the ancient Taoists asserted? Four as Western science traditionally claims? Or are there six or seven or even fourteen? World cuisines are at odds on this issue, and I briefly explore here their reasons for their numbers. They have a consensus with some of the elements, which tells us something about the human makeup or constitution. The other elements reveal social and cultural differences and varying environmental conditions.

1. Chinese Five Flavors

The doctrine of the five flavors dates to the Xia Dynasty (circa twenty-first to sixteenth centuries BCE) where tradition has it that the sage I Yin spoke of the importance of the five flavors: sweet, sour, salty, bitter, and spicy or pungent. By the fourth century BCE, this five-flavor concept appeared to be firmly entrenched in Chinese cuisine. These five flavors were associated with a few dishes (actually five that I was able to find), which strongly suggests that the five flavors are not the focus of one dish, but rather are spread over several dishes or an entire meal. The *fan-cai (ts'ai)* principle that governs meals can be seen as each division contributing to the five flavors; some flavors are in the *fan* or grains and other starches, and others are in the *cai (ts'ai)* or vegetable and meat category.[1] Assuming this is the case, the five flavors can easily be achieved in an endless variety of ways.

The chart that follows shows how various fruits, vegetables, spices, and food products such as sauces exemplify a given flavor.

Spicy	Sweet	Sour	Bitter	Salty
ginger	sugar	bitter melon (fresh)	bitter melon (ripe)	salt
black pepper	honey	rice vinegar	Seville orange	soy sauce (reg.)
chili peppers	coconut	lemon	soy sauce (lite)	
Sichuan peppers	bell peppers	lime	garlic (raw)	
cinnamon	apples	dry wine	star anise	
mace	grapes	cranberry	dry mustard	
nutmeg	raisins	wild cherries	radicchio	
radish	hoisin sauce		radish	
cardamom	sherry		mustard greens	
	garlic (cooked)		endive	
	dates		arugula	
	onions (cooked)			
	rice (well-cooked)			
	Bing cherries			

The above listing is obviously incomplete, so feel free to extend it. Peaches, for instance, would go under "sweet." Tomatoes can be sweet and also go there; however, because of their acidity they should also be placed under "sour." So when using this chart note that there is some overlap among the flavors or tastes. Included in the chart are certain "classic" combinations, including ginger, sherry, lemon or rice vinegar, star anise, and regular soy sauce. Many of these are combined intuitively. Some combinations, including those that involve hoisin sauce, regular soy sauce, Sichuan pepper, rice vinegar, and star anise, are uniquely associated with Chinese cuisine. One gets a sense that the doctrine of "five flavors" is a cornerstone of Chinese gastronomy. The flavors or tastes are among many things in the Chinese landscape that come in groups of five. As discussed in chapter 2, there is the five-spice powder made up of cinnamon, star anise, fennel, clove, ginger, licorice, Sichuan pepper, and white pepper. As this example illustrates, there are often eight spices in the "five-spice powder," and such seasonings may include a combination of other spices not listed here. While five-spice powder does encompass the five flavors, the spices and the flavors are not one and the same. The five flavors are much broader in taste range, and to equate the five flavors with specific substances is too restrictive. In actuality, Chinese five-spice powder is closer to the five fragrances than to the five flavors. (For further discussion of the Chinese five flavors, see chapter 2.)

2. Western Science Four

The science of taste is principally interested in the receptors—the observable bumps called "papillae"—for all tastes that are distributed over the tongue. Sensitivities for the four basic tastes (sweet, sour, salty, and bitter) are for the most part located in different areas on the tongue. Sweetness is detected on the tip of the tongue; the sides of the tongue are most sensitive to sourness; the back of the tongue registers bitterness; and saltiness is identified along the sides and the front of the tongue.[2] So the selection of the four tastes is based on physiology.[3] Sensation and its location on the palate is the focus; consequently, isolation of the elements of taste is important.

In reviewing the research, Western science tends to be atomistic and reductionist, whereas the Chinese perspective is holistic and emphasizes temporal order (rather than spatial order). In Chinese gastronomy, food products are discussed in terms of initial (immediate) taste and aftertaste, along with the balance of flavors.[4] One of the best examples that embodies scientific methodology is Professor Ann C. Noble and her work on the wine aroma wheel at the University of California at Davis. It is a useful tool for learning to describe the complexity of wine flavors. The wheel consists of three tiers: in the center are general terms such as "vegetal," "fruity," and "chemical"; terms become more specific as one works toward the outer tier, which includes the most specific terms—for examples "bell pepper," "currant," and "sulfur."[5] Her wheel is also useful in finding more specific descriptors for food products. Accurate analysis is a goal of the scientific perspective.

It is puzzling that spicy or pungent is not listed as an element of taste. It is thought to be a combination of sour and bitter. But that doesn't seem to do justice to spicy food products.[6] Take, for instance, the habanero pepper. It is well known for being very aromatic as well as flavorful and very hot, but its aftertaste is what sets it aside from other peppers. The golden or yellow habanero has a citrus, orangey finish. The red habanero displays cherries at the end. And the chocolate or brown one is somewhere in between the taste profile of the other two. Here are Diana Kennedy's descriptions of the habanero: it is "fiercely *picante*, probably the strongest of the lot,"[7] and has "unequaled fragrance";[8] "not only are its looks exceptional but also its distinctive flavor, which is lingering and perfumed—so much so that it is often put into sauces to give flavor and not piquancy."[9] All this is missed if one just follows the scientific analysis of the habanero pepper. More is going on here than the stimulation of taste buds (which is the narrower sense of the word *taste*) and synapses firing off. "The term *flavor*," Bruce Goldstein prescribes, "is reserved for *perceptions* resulting when stimulation of the receptors for smell, touch, and sometimes pain [as happens sometimes with eating habanero peppers], are added to stimulation of the taste buds."[10] The two terms *taste* and *flavor*, however, are usually interchangeable in most of the other literature. In fairness to Western science, the practitioners are interested in the reception of taste rather than the taste itself—the perception—which is probably too subjective and complex for them to analyze. Nevertheless, the additional category of spicy (and its phenomenological analysis) contributes to a better description of the habanero. And the next few sections contribute an even better understanding of it.

3. Japanese Six Components

The Japanese contribute two important notions to the discussion of the elements of taste: *umami* and *washoku*. Building on the five flavors, *umami* is the mouth-watering feel on the palate. Free glutamate, an essential amino acid, produces the coating effect on the tongue. Any food that contains free glutamate can create this sensation of succulence. These foods include cheeses, dairy products, mushrooms, legumes, tomatoes, meats, fish, shellfish, and sometimes chocolate.

Washoku distinguishes Japanese cuisine from other, Western-inspired food products. The term literally means "harmony of food," and the harmony or balance comes from the five principles: the five flavors or tastes; the five colors; the five ways (*go ho*), which include steaming, broiling, simmering, and combinations of them; the five senses (i.e., the need of food to appeal to all of them—not just taste and smell); and the five outlooks (*go kan mon*), which are Buddhistic in nature.[11] Balancing culinary ingredients is a feature that Japanese cuisine shares with Chinese cuisine. The principles unfold in the course of a meal—just as the Chinese principle of five flavors does when the flavors come together with the different dishes that make up a meal rather than being embodied in a single dish. But simple single dishes can benefit from the washoku manner or five principles, e.g., miso soup with enoki mushrooms (5, 117). This is cooking from the heart (*kokoro*).

4. Indian Seven Traits

In addition to umami, the Indians add astringency to the elements of taste. As Raghavan Iyer describes it:

> This particular group of ingredients is in your face, hard-hitting, and pushy. They are not a *primary* taste element, but their presence in a curry is definitely noticeable. They are always used in minute amounts, since a little goes a long way. When you look at words like "harsh," "severe," "caustic," and "acerbic," used to describe the taste of astringency, ingredients like asafetida, turmeric, teflam seeds, and baking powder come to mind. Don't shy away from sprinkling these ingredients into sauces and spice blends, as they are essential flavor-building elements.[12]

"Astringency" is also a wine term that is associated with alcohol and tannin, and how dominant these are in taste. It is largely a tactile sensation, and words typically used to describe it are "puckery" (a neutral term), "hard," "harsh," "sharp," "rough," "bitter" (all negative terms), and "soft," "smooth," "velvety," "silky," "gentle," "tender," and "mellow" (positive terms).[13] Some of these terms would obviously apply to food ingredients, e.g., vinegar, and food products.

5. Donna Hay's Nine Flavors

In her book *Flavors*,[14] Donna Hay gives no general account of flavors or reasons why she selected the ones she did. Nevertheless, her flavors exemplify the five flavors: vanilla, lemon + lime (including kaffir lime leaves and lemongrass), ginger, chili (chile), garlic + onion (including leek); chocolate, salt + pepper; basil + mint; and cinnamon (sticks) + spice (i.e., coriander and cumin seeds, star anise, juniper berries, and Chinese five-spice). Hay starts each chapter with what she calls "basics," i.e., history and culinary facts about a given flavor or pair of flavors, then moves to "good ideas" of what to do with the flavor, like vanilla tea or grating lemon or lime peel, and lastly she moves to recipes for sweet and savory dishes using a flavor component. Hay's list seems to be more *flavorings* than *flavors*.[15]

6. Kunz and Kaminsky's Fourteen

The most ambitious project to date is Gray Kunz and Peter Kaminsky's phenomenological study of the elements of taste. They divide the elements into four categories: tastes that push (salty, *picante*, sweet), tastes that pull (tangy, vinted, bulby, spiced aromatic, floral herbal, and funky), tastes that punctuate (sharp/bitter), and taste platforms (garden, meaty, oceanic, and starchy). As Bryan Miller says in the foreword of *The Elements of Taste*, the book is food writer Kaminsky's deconstruction of chef Kunz's signature dishes.[16] The result is a language that can be used to describe the way good chefs think.[17]

"Tastes that push" are fundamental ones that heighten all the others in a recipe, what they call "the trinity" (5). They take ordinary foodstuffs and make them into a memorable dish or meal. "Tastes that pull" are ones that highlight underlying ones; for example, lemon or lime peel or juice and cooked onions bring other flavors forward on the palate. Sour tastes (what they call "tangy"), which are experienced sometimes in "vinted" or reduced wine in a sauce or vinegar, make the tongue feel like it is contracting (7). Onions sautéing in a pan yield a nose-filling aroma, and this smell is what Kunz and Kaminsky refer to as "bulby," since they are grown from bulbs (i.e., they are in the *Allium* family). "Sweet" is a good descriptor for this aroma, but raw, these bulby ingredients are sharply odoriferous on the palate. In wine circles, the terms "floral" and "herbal" are distinguished and denote different flavor profiles, but here they are combined to represent both ingredients: "Olive oil has a floral aspect that works well with herbs and makes it superior to other oils or butter when you want to bring out the garden vegetable side of things. Likewise, honey adds a floral note to sweetness that sets it apart from cane sugar or maple syrup" (9). "Spiced aromatic" parallels Hay's "spice," with ingredients such as cinnamon, cloves, allspice, mace, coriander seed, cumin, saffron, and star anise. These produce aromas that *pull up* taste. Examples Kunz and Kaminsky give are: "Curry will bring out the subtle oceanic tones in shellfish. Cloves will focus the roundness of pork. Coriander seed and black pepper serve as messengers heralding the approach of substantial meaty dishes" (10). Perhaps the most interesting yet bizarre term is "funky" (but it is better than "stinky"), which denotes pungent cheeses like Camembert. This taste group includes some aged meats, cooked cabbage, and truffles that give off a smell akin to dirty socks. "While other ingredients such as fresh herbs and ground spices pull tastes up into more defined and ethereal areas of flavor," Kunz and Kaminsky assert, "funky ingredients pull all of them back into their basic organic origins" (11). They say: "We think of vegetables and flesh not so much as 'main ingredients' (although at times they certainly are); it is more accurate to call them platforms upon which other tastes can stand and interact" (12). Here is their phenomenological description of a lived culinary experience:

> If you think about it, the two strongest impressions you have with meat are texture and aroma. You bite down and it's a pleasing sensation as your teeth meet resistance from flesh. Then you breathe out and the mildly funky bouquet of the meat, which is the heart of its distinctive flavor, rises up into your nose, pulling with it all the fla-

vors that you have cooked into the meat with other ingredients. (13)

Agreeing with Chinese gastronomy, Kunz and Kaminsky think that taste has a narrative or temporal order (17). They use Aristotle's idea of dramatic unity: beginning (initial entry or immediate taste), middle (mid-taste), and end (aftertaste or finish). When they talk about "length" or "lasting," they are focusing on movement of qualities remaining essentially the same or subtly changing from beginning to end. This is another idiom for balance or harmony of the elements of taste. What that consists of tells us something about cultures and societies and their food ways. In other words, taste narratives are stories. "Texture," they say, for example, "helps you to 'read' longer taste messages and to make sense out of them" (15). Recipes are put together over time and experienced over time. Culinary experiences have a temporal sequence to them, and sorting them out is part of the fun of eating—to think about how a dish is composed and the perceptions that arise from it. To share these with others is one of the basic ways we communicate with one another in a culture. So with each of their recipes (*The Elements of Taste* is after all a cookbook), Kunz and Kaminsky give an accompanying taste narrative that makes their book unique and more experiential in nature. Chef Gray Kunz ends with these remarks: "I haven't finished learning the language of taste, that inner language that we all understand before we speak it. But I feel that now is as good a time as any to try to put the language into words" (250). He and Peter Kaminsky have done an admirable job of articulating phenomenologically the language of taste.

7. Conclusion

Historically, there are two thinkers that I have not mentioned who are important in the discussion of the elements of taste: Aristotle and Brillat-Savarin. In the West, Aristotle was the first to chart the elements of taste. Like Raghavan Iyer, he had a list of seven components of taste: sweet, sour, salty, bitter, astringent, pungent, and harsh.[18] (Iyer uses the terms "astringent" and "harsh" interchangeably, whereas Aristotle rightfully separates these out since they denote different sensations.) Aristotle was the only one who listed harshness among the elements. Horseradish, habanero, or any of the items on our chart under *Spicy, Sour, Salty*, and *Bitter*, if they are taken in excess, become harsh on the palate. We move from the agreeable to the disagreeable; such a negative sensation protects us from harmful reactions in the body. Indeed, this defense mechanism keeps us away from toxic substances. Thus we see the biological need for balance or harmony of the elements of taste; balance or harmony is a necessity of the human palate and it serves as a basis for our aesthetics.

Brillat-Savarin, on the other hand, believes that the number of tastes is infinite, since "every soluble body has a special flavor which does not wholly resemble any other."[19] He continues by saying that not a given taste has been adequately analyzed, "so that we have been forced to depend on a small number of generalizations such as *sweet, sugary, sour, bitter,* and other ones which express . . . the taste properties of the sapid body which they describe" (38). He concludes that without a doubt chemistry will reveal the causes and the basic elements of taste (38).

Now back to the original question: how many elements of taste are there? In doing research for their book, Kunz and Kaminsky at one time had as many as twenty-two, "but that became rather unwieldy" (5), so they settled on fourteen. They are primarily motivated in making a comprehensive list to cover the entire range of taste rather than a scientific one. The other lists are analytical and reductionistic, based on nutrition, physiology, or numerological association (like the Chinese five flavors). Contrary to most of our discussants, Goldstein concludes that "the four basic taste qualities of salty, sour, sweet, and bitter appear to be adequate to describe the majority of our taste experience" (444). Adequate? If we are talking about the range of culinary experience, these four qualities are woefully inadequate. We need a phenomenology akin to Kunz and Kaminsky's to describe our taste experiences of food with any specificity.

Since the release of the eighth edition of Goldstein's *Sensation and Perception*[20] in 2007, *umami* has been accepted by most of the scientific community as the fifth basic taste sensation because receptors were discovered that were specifically tuned to umami tastes, just as there were for sweet and bitter (371). The taste sensations for umami are frequently described as "meaty," "brothy," or "savory," and are often associated with the flavor-enhancing properties of MSG, monosodium glutamate (367).

There is some controversy as to whether or not water has taste; some physiologists say it does. Zotterman includes water in his list of the elements of taste, so he has five—including the basic four.[21] However, most who have addressed this issue think that water is tasteless. For instance, Brillat-Savarin believes that water has neither taste nor aftertaste (41). And Goldstein, like Aristotle, declares that water is tasteless and, if it has taste, it has some chemical in it that makes it have a taste (447). Others, whom we have discussed, do not address the issue.

Aside from water, what about fat? Do we *taste* fat? In *The Queen of Fats,* Susan Allport gives us the traditional take on fat:

Fat gives foods their distinctive aromas and tastes. It is the vehicle of what we think of as a cuisine. Whale blubber is every bit as connected with the Eskimos' sense of how foods should smell and taste as olive oil is for Italians, lard is for Mexicans, and sesame oil is for the Chinese.[22]

However, recent studies by Richard Mattes, a professor of nutrition science at Purdue University, challenges the current scientific dogma that fat has no taste because there is no mechanism to detect it.[23] His recent studies with rats show that fats are capable of causing electrical changes in taste cells, which indicates there is a chemical detection system there. So besides the four basic food tastes, and umami, which has been added as a fifth,[24] we may be adding the ability we have to taste fat, which could mean a sixth basic taste. Mattes conjectures that "this tells us that taste is a stimulus that causes the rise in blood fat levels. The taste, and not smell, is what the body is responding to."[25] Consequently, if his studies are confirmed, scientists will have to rewrite the textbooks (like Goldstein's) to add fat to the list of taste sensations. Most recently carbs (carbohydrates) have also been added to the ever-expanding list.[26]

Another puzzlement in this literature (the earlier puzzlement in section two) is that Kunz and Kaminsky omit umami from their list, although they have definite descriptions under "taste platforms" (meaty and oceanic), "tastes that pull," and "tastes that punctuate," but these categories together still do not capture what umami is all about (see section 3, above). However, their phenomenological description of eating meat that I cited earlier (section 6) definitely captures the essence of umami, so it is implicitly there in their account of taste.

Taste poses interesting questions and issues. In addition to texture, taste must normally be accompanied with smell, for it gives us our first clues as to what the food product is going to taste like. There is a saying that "we eat with our eyes first." Smell is just as central, for without it, things taste bland or all the same. (Recall Kennedy's olfactory descriptions of the habanero.) Another difficulty with tastes is that they are much more difficult to remember than sounds or sights. However, the temporal order or narrative order of tastes in great chef's dishes assists the memory because we think about what we are eating and how we experience food items.[26] Taste, like our other senses, can be refined and educated. So in spite of limitations, taste can be discriminatory, and the palate can be cultivated over a period of time. Kunz and Kaminsky have demonstrated this in their book, and thus we await the next development in the story of the elements of taste.

Notes

1. Corinne Trang, *Essentials of Asian Cuisine: Fundamentals and Favorite Recipes* (New York:

Simon & Schuster, 2003), 45.

2. Carolyn Korsmeyer, *Making Sense of Taste: Food and Philosophy* (Ithaca: Cornell University Press, 1999), ch. 4: "The Science of Taste," 68-102, esp. 71-74.

3. E. Bruce Goldstein, *Sensation and Perception* (Belmont, California: Wadsworth Publishing Company, 1980), ch. 13: "Touch, Smell, and Taste," esp. 442-453 on taste: "The surface of the tongue . . . contains many ridges and valleys due to the presence of structures called *papillae* of which there are four kinds: filiform papillae, shaped like cones, are found over the entire surface of the tongue; fungiform papillae, shaped like mushrooms, are found at the front and sides of the tongue; foliate papillae are a series of folds along the sides of the middle of the tongue; and circumvallate papillae, shaped like flat mounds surrounded by a trench, are found at the back of the tongue. . . . Since the filiform papillae contain no taste buds, stimulation of the central part of the tongue, which contains only filiform papillae, causes no taste sensations." (442)

4. Hsiang Ju Lin and Tsuifeng Lin, *Chinese Gastronomy* (New York: Pyramid Publications, 1972), 48.

5. For more information on Ann C. Noble and her wine aroma wheel, consult the Internet: http://en.wikipedia.org/wiki/Ann_C._Noble and http://www.winearomawheel.com/. These were accessed on 12/27/2008.

6. Jane and Michael Stern, "Hot Stuff: A Road Trip across New Mexico Unearths the State's Finest Chile Peppers," *Saveur* no. 140 (August/September, 2011), 30: "Not far from La Posta, at New Mexico State University, Paul Bosland, regents professor of horticulture and founder of the Chile Pepper Institute, is lobbying for chile heat to be recognized as the sixth sense, along with salty, sweet, sour, bitter, and umami." (See the next section for an explanation of *umami*.)

7. Diana Kennedy, *The Cuisines of Mexico* (New York: Harper & Row, Publishers, 1972), 37.

8. Diana Kennedy, *Nothing Fancy* (Garden City, New York: Doubleday & Company, 1984), 14.

9. Diana Kennedy, *The Art of Mexican Cooking* (New York: Bantam Books, 1989), 466.

10. Goldstein, *Sensation and Perception*, 442, emphasis added. See prefatory note: Olfaction [an act of smelling] + Taste = Flavor.

11. Elizabeth Andoh, *Washoku: Recipes from the Japanese Home Kitchen* (Berkeley: Ten Speed Press, 2005), 1-2.

12. Raghavan Iyer, *660 Curries* (New York: Workman Publishing, 2008), 8; emphasis added; see also 5.

13. Adrienne Lehrer, *Wine and Conversation* (Bloomington: Indiana University Press, 1983), 8.

14. Donna Hay, *Flavors* (North Vancouver, BC: Whitecap Books, 2000).

15. *Flavorings* refer to specific food items or products whereas *flavors* denote general terms associated with palate reactions. The Chinese make this distinction: there are *eight* flavorings— ginger root (or ginger juice), hot oil (or hot paste), rice vinegar, sesame oil, soy sauce, star anise, Sichuan pepper, and Chinese wine. With these, nearly any traditional dish can be prepared. See Linda Lew, Agnes Lee, and Elizabeth Brotherton, *Peking Table Top Cooking* (Laguna Beach, California: Gala Books, 1972), 17-18.

16. Gray Kunz and Peter Kaminsky, *The Elements of Taste* (Boston: Little, Brown and Company, 2001), ix.

17. The language of "push," "pull," and "platform" comes from painting and visual arts criticism; for example, blue and yellow push one another and red pulls them. Consult the abstract expressionist Hans Hofmann in *Search for the Real and Other Essays*, edited by Sara T. Weeks and Bartlett H. Hayes Jr. (Revised edition; Cambridge, Massachusetts: The MIT Press, 1967), 43-45. Kaminsky was probably not aware of this former use of "push" and "pull" coming from the art world. It has become commonplace in the language of criticism. However, it is interesting to see the transition of terminology from visual perception to gustatory experience.

18. Aristotle, "On the Soul" [*De Anima*] (422b10-16), in *The Complete Works of Aristotle*, edited by Jonathan Barnes (Princeton: Princeton University Press, 1984), I, 672.

19. Jean Anthelme Brillat-Savarin, *The Physiology of Taste or, Meditations on Transcendental Gastronomy* [1825], translated by M. F. K. Fisher (New York: Limited Editions Club, 1949), 36.

20. E. Bruce Goldstein, *Sensation and Perception* (Eighth Edition; Belmont, California: Wadsworth Cengage Learning, 2007), ch. 15, esp. 366-375 on the taste system that includes *umami*.

21. Goldstein (1980); and Y. Zotterman, "Species Differences in the Water Taste," *Acta Physiologica Scandinanivia* 37 (1956): 60-70.

22. Susan Allport, *The Queen of Fats: Why Omega-3s Were Removed from the Western Diet and What We Can Do to Replace Them* (Berkeley: University of California Press, 2006), 69.

23. Richard Mattes, "Fatty Food Triggers Taste Buds, New Research Finds," *ScienceDaily*, Purdue

University (2001, December 4); retrieved February 11, 2009, from http://www.sciencedaily.com/releases/2001/12/011204073223.htm.

24. We find more and more food writers and chefs incorporating the elements of taste into their discussion. For instance, in *Bon Appetit, Y'all: Recipes and Stories from Three Generations of Southern Cooking* (Berkeley: Ten Speed Press, 2008), Virginia Willis writes: "Mamas from both sides of the Atlantic have used fresh seasonal vegetables with a bit of hambone or cheese rind to prepare soulful, satisfying soups. We've long known that this combination tastes good. Now we have a name for why it does: umami. The Japanese term *umami* is now familiar to culinary professionals, chefs, and informed foodies, yet Asian cooks have appreciated the taste for centuries. It is the fifth taste after sour, salty, bitter, and sweet. Scientifically, umami is the distinctive flavor of amino acids, which are the building blocks of protein. Think about classic Caesar salad dressing, a combination of egg protein and salted anchovies. Or old-fashioned greens simmered with ham. Or this soup [Southern Minestrone], in which the rind of the Parmigiano-Reggiano cheese complements the vegetables in the tomato broth." (239)

25. Mattes, *Science Daily*.

26. "There is now a sixth taste—and it explains why we love carbs"—Jessica Hamzelou, quoting Associate Professor of Food Science & Technology Juyun Lim at Oregon State University. *Daily News*, Sept. 2, 2016.

27. Here is what Julia Child has to say about food and memory. In the Epilogue to *My Life in France*, with Alex Prud'homme (Anchor Books; New York: Random House, 2006), she writes: "In all the years since that succulent meal [*sole meuinere* she ate at La Couronne on her first day in France in November 1948], I have yet to lose the feelings of wonder and excitement that it inspired in me. I can still almost taste it. And thinking back on it now reminds me that the pleasures of the table, of a life, are infinite—*toujours bon appétit*" (333). Recall our discussion of The Duplication Problem in chapter 1.

4

Leibniz and Culinary Cognitions: A Speculative Journey

We eat not only because it is necessary for us to,
but also and much more because eating gives us pleasure.

GOTTFRIED WILHELM LEIBNIZ
New Essays, 92

* * *

In this chapter I develop a case for Gottfried Wilhelm Leibniz (1646-1716) as our first modern food philosopher. It is in his theory of perception and in his culinary examples that I find the most convincing evidence, especially when I contrast them with Locke and Hume's account of perception with reference to food. In the process, Leibniz expanded aesthetic perception to include nature (storms at sea) and food (sauces and relishes). He didn't draw a distinction between ordinary or regular perception and aesthetic perception; perceiving smells and tastes are similar to perceiving colors—both have structures,[1] but more on this later. In short, perception has ideational or conceptual content. This is also true of pleasure for Leibniz (see the epigraph above). The beginnings of modern food philosophy began with Leibniz because he senses that sauces are what elevate food to a level where serious reflection can take place. As Charlie Trotter (in note 16) says, sauces give dishes their character or essence and make them structurally interesting. "The history of dining is not the history of eating," Collingwood observes. "It is in virtue of his rationality that he not only eats but dines."[2]

Leibniz was a "foodie" of sorts; Roger Ariew, following Eckhart's biography, describes his daily routine:

> Leibniz was generally in good health, ate well, and seldom drank. He generally ate alone at irregular hours as his studies allowed. In his later years, he had gout and dined only on milk. He allowed himself a large supper and went to bed each night at one or two in the morn-

ing, often while reading, and slept the night in a chair; he would wake up at seven or eight in the morning and continue his work.[3]

His diplomatic travels throughout Europe gave Leibniz ample opportunity to sample the developing cuisines of the day.[4]

It is in his posthumous *New Essays on Human Understanding* (1765) that I find Leibniz's critique of Locke's theory of perception and the development of his own theory.[5] So it is in this philosophical context that I believe the origin of our ideas of food began to be seriously entertained. Locke, Hume, and Leibniz all thought that food was a complex idea, but their accounts of a complex idea were vastly different. Locke and Hume gave similar accounts: the complex idea of an apple (Hume's illustration) consists of its simple ideas—color, smell, size, ripeness (to the touch), and so on. What would happen to these qualities if apples were made into a sauce?[6] We don't know because they didn't address this issue, although Leibniz came the closest. However, it appears that both Locke and Hume thought that the qualities of an apple would be immediately present to the senses. If you were going to sense the qualities of an apple, all of them would appear together and at roughly the same time. As Locke put it, these qualities are imposed upon us and we don't have a choice in the matter, so if qualities are present in an object, like an apple, they are ones that we will involuntarily register by means of our senses. In other words, if they are there, we will perceive them (Leibniz agreed, but for a different reason). Hume seemed to concur with Locke on this matter when we examine the relevant passages in his *A Treatise of Human Nature*.[7] However, this view of qualities becomes problematic when we turn to the famous Cervantes wine parable in the essay, "Of the Standard of Taste," which I shall discuss below. Surprisingly, Leibniz had a better account of the perceptual process in regard to food than our two empiricists. I mainly draw on the passages on perception and ideas in the preface to Leibniz's *New Essays* and its early chapters in Book Two, "Of Ideas." But first, let me examine Locke's account, since it is background for what came later.

In *An Essay Concerning Human Understanding* (1689), Locke announced that *"External objects furnish the mind with the* ideas *of sensible qualities,* which are all those different perceptions they produce in us."[8] So the perceptions we have of food come from the sensible qualities that it has and not from us. On this last point, Locke is emphatic: *"In the reception of simple* ideas *the understanding* is merely *passive*; and whether or not it will have these beginnings, and as it were materials of knowledge, is not in its own power. For the objects of our senses do, many of them, obtrude their particular *ideas* upon our minds whether we will or not" (book II, chapter I, section 25). Here Locke mentioned "simple ideas." What are they? He answered in book II, chapter II, section 1: "And there is nothing can be plainer to a man than the clear and distinct perception he has of those simple *ideas* [among Locke's examples is the taste of sugar], which, being each in itself uncompounded, contains in it nothing but *one uniform appearance*, or conception in the mind, and is not distinguishable into different *ideas*." Likewise, "Simple perceptions or impressions and ideas," Hume declared (following Locke's lead), "are such as admit of no distinction nor separation" (7), although he later conceded that simple and uniform impressions are indefinable (182, 214), but not ideas. Through the interlocutor Theophilus, Leibniz gave the following explanation on the relativity of "simple":

> It can be maintained, I believe, that these sensible ideas appear simple because they are confused and thus do not provide the mind with any way of making discriminations within what they contain; just like distant things which appear rounded because one cannot discern their angles, even though one is receiving some confused impression from them. It is obvious that green, for instance, comes from a mixture of blue and yellow; which makes it credible that the idea of green is composed of the ideas of those two colours, although the idea of green appears to us as simple as that of blue, or as that of warmth. So these ideas of blue and warmth should also be regarded as simple only in appearance. I freely admit that we treat them as simple ideas, because we are at any rate not aware of any divisions within them; but we should undertake the analysis of them by means of further experiments, and by means of reason in so far as they can be made more capable of being treated by the intellect. (120)

Hume did not address any of the problems that Leibniz raised about simplicity. Furthermore, regarding "things which are uniform" (like Hume's simple impressions), Leibniz responded that they are "containing no variety, are always mere abstractions" (110). (This is what Alfred North Whitehead classified as the fallacy of misplaced concreteness.[9]) Hume's implication—that all sensory impressions, like color and taste, are simple—is simply false. The color green has a particular hue and intensity, which suggests that it is complex. Hume's difficulty (and Locke's too) probably stems from the Newtonian influence on his theory of impressions, that the simple ones were supposed to be the "atoms" of experience. But it is not clear from Hume's account that experience is atomistic—that impressions are discrete and independent of each other—nor is it clear what those postulated "atoms" of experience are.[10] Leibniz's caution and tentative stance on the concept of simplicity is admirable to say the least.

He reminds us that simplicity is analytic or conceptual in nature and not phenomenal. (Poor Hume digs a hole that he cannot get out of.) Leibniz, shying away from atomism in his analysis of perception is also admirable, especially since the doctrine was found persuasive for centuries before and after this period.

Another interesting point is that Locke and Hume saw no coordination between the senses and the understanding, whereas Leibniz did. (Leibniz is probably right on this issue.) For instance, what appears simple to a wine novice may be immensely complex to a wine connoisseur, or a sauce that goes unnoticed by an unreflective diner may occasion delight in a gourmand. In other words, perception is theory-laden, and Leibniz is the first to fully articulate that insight. This point will become more evident with the discussion of the following passages. The main passage from Locke we need to examine is in book II, chapter III, section 2. In detail:

> *Few simple* ideas *have names*. I think it will be needless to enumerate all the particular *simple ideas* belonging to each sense. Nor indeed is it possible if we would, there being a great many *more* of them belonging to most of the senses *than we have names for*. The variety of smells, which are as many almost, if not more, than species of bodies in the world, do most of them want names. Sweet and stinking commonly serve our turn for these *ideas*, [remember ideas and perceptions are the same thing for Locke, see book II, chapter I, section 9] which in effect is little more than to call them pleasing or displeasing, though the smell of a rose and violet, both sweet, are certainly very distinct *ideas*. Nor are the different tastes that we receive *ideas* of by our palates much better provided with names. Sweet, bitter, sour, harsh, and salt are almost all the epithets we have to denominate that numberless variety of relishes, which are to be found distinct, not only in almost every sort of creatures, but all the different parts of the same plant, fruit, or animal. The same may be said of colors and sounds.

An observation needs to be made concerning this passage. Locke identified one of the reasons description is so difficult in food situations, i.e., cooking and tasting or eating. Our language is impoverished in adequately depicting what our senses are able to detect. Even so, Locke's empiricist project—that complex ideas or perceptions can be divided (and identified) in terms of simple perceptions—dictates a language that can make this division and identification. An illustration is in order. Relish is a good food example because one can see the various ingredients that make up a relish—the onion, tomatoes, cucumbers, cabbage, peppers, celery seed, vinegar, mustard, and spices. "Mustard, peppercorns, vinegar and spices,"

Adrian Bailey remarks, "can transform many fresh fruits and vegetables into pickles or relishes ('chutneys' to the British) to accompany meats."[11] Relishes were a mainstay on the British table, and their familiarity led Locke to use relishes as an example when called upon.[12] In relishes all the ingredients are sensible according to our empiricists, and if we restrict our food example to this item, they are probably right. "A good palate," Hume claimed in "Of the Standard of Taste," "is not tried by strong flavours; but by a mixture of small ingredients, where we are still sensible of each part, notwithstanding its minuteness and its confusion with the rest."[13] He dramatically illustrated this point with Cervantes's noted wine story in *Don Quixote* (part 2, chapter 13):

> It is with good reason, says Sancho to the squire with the great nose, that I pretend to have a judgment in wine: this is a quality hereditary in our family. Two of my kinsmen were once called to give their opinion of a hogshead [a large barrel or cask holding from 63 to 140 US gallons], which was supposed to be excellent, being old and of a good vintage. One of them tastes it, considers it; and, after mature reflection, pronounces the wine to be good, were it not for a small taste of leather which he perceived in it. The other, after using the same precautions, gives also his verdict in favour of the wine; but with the reserve of a taste of iron, which he could easily distinguish. You cannot imagine how much they were both ridiculed for their judgment. But who laughed in the end? On emptying the hogshead, there was found at the bottom an old key with a leathern thong tied to it. (239-240)

Hume used this parable to exemplify what he called the delicacy of taste that a true, i.e., good, judge or critic has. The parable implies that not one true or good judge identifies all the sensible qualities of an object, like a wine, but that it takes at least two to get them all. So judging or identifying takes place in a social setting, like a tasting panel, and that contrary qualities or descriptions, like leather and metal, are really not in opposition to one another, but may well be complementary. In other words, judges, like the two kinsmen in the story, do not contradict or even disagree about what it is they are tasting. They are just tasting different things in or aspects of the wine, because their focus is not the same. But even here, Hume embraced Locke's project of complexity reducing to simples, and he did not contemplate that with some foods, not all parts are sensible and identifiable. For example, with a wine sauce or gravy, one cannot (or should not) do such a division or identification. A sauce is blended; the elements fuse together into a harmonious mixture. As our American culinary saint, Julia Child, often quipped, "If you taste nutmeg, there's too much nutmeg."

In other words, one should not be able to taste and identify the ingredients that make up a good sauce. Unlike a relish, the ingredients in a sauce are chemically transformed into something quite different as a whole.[14]

So the examples that suit Locke and Hume's theories of perception are food items, like relishes, where their components are discrete and identifiable. Leibniz, on the other hand, provides us with a theory of perception that can account for food items that have their elements transformed into something other than their taste components. This reflects a perennial debate among culinary experts and foodies as to whether the best cooking makes food "'taste of itself' or transmutes ingredients into something new and unrecognizable."[15]

For Locke, the primary qualities remain constant: "take a grain of wheat, divide it into two parts, each part has still *solidity, extension, figure,* and *mobility*; divide it again, and it retains still the same qualities" (book II, chapter VIII, section 9). But the secondary qualities—those of taste or smell—do diminish and become insensible. Hume seemed to take issue with this and suggested (by the Sancho story) that a true or good judge would detect these secondary qualities no matter how minute. Leibniz sided with Locke on this issue. In the preface to the *New Essays* (53-54), Leibniz writes:

> Besides, there are hundreds of indications leading us to conclude that at every moment there is in us an infinity of perceptions, unaccompanied by awareness or reflection; that is, of alterations in the soul itself, of which we are unaware because these impressions are either too minute and too numerous, or else too unvarying, so that they are not sufficiently distinctive on their own. But when they are combined with others they do nevertheless have their effect and make themselves felt, at least confusedly, within the whole.

Leibniz used the example of the roaring noise of the sea, which consists of numerous minute (*petites*) perceptions that we are unable to pick out from the whole sound. The roar impresses itself upon us when we stand on the shore. "To hear this noise as we do," he concluded, "we must hear the parts which make up this whole, that is the noise of each wave, although each of these little noises makes itself known *only* when combined confusedly with all the others, and would not be noticed if the wave which made it were by itself" (54; emphasis added). Then comes the food analogy: "These minute perceptions, then, are more effective in their results than has been recognized. They constitute that *je ne sais quoi*, those flavours, those images of sensible qualities, vivid in the aggregate but confused as to the parts" (55). So here is our description of a sauce: good sauces consist of flavors that are "vivid in the aggregate but confused as to the parts." This way of phrasing it fits perfectly with a sauce is supposed to be, "a thickened, flavored liquid designed to accompany food in order to enhance and bring out its flavor."[16] Consequently, Leibniz would dispute Hume's characterization of the delicacy of taste. For Leibniz, each part is not sensible; parts are insensible or confused and many of them we are not aware of, but taken together as a whole, they become a different taste sensation from what they are individually. These taste sensations we generally speak of as "flavors," and they are identifiable.

Leibniz mentioned "flavours," but what are they? Donna Hay has written a book on the subject,[17] but nowhere does she attempt a definition. However, from her chapters we get an idea of where to start: vanilla, lemon + lime, ginger, chili [chile], garlic + onion, chocolate, salt + pepper, basil + mint, and cinnamon + spice. All of these are derived from plants (with the exception of salt) and usually are concentrated by drying, cooking, or distilling. They usually deliver a powerful impact on foods without adding excess volume or changing the consistency (with the exception of chocolate)—an impact Leibniz described as "vivid."

In the early modern era, sauces had a bad name; in the days before refrigeration, sauces were more often than not used to mask the taste of foods that had begun to spoil. Locke echoed this sentiment—a typical British attitude towards the French cuisine of the time—when he announced: "Sauces and ragouts and food disguised by all the arts of cookery 'to tempt palates when their bellies are full' are not to be preferred to a plain and simple diet."[18] (Locke had a fragile constitution.) Be that as it may, let us return to the theory of perception.

For Locke and Hume perceptions are clear and distinct (Descartes's criteria for a true idea) and are things we are conscious of. For Leibniz "distinct" applies only to aggregates of perceptions in that one is different from other aggregates of perceptions; "distinct" does not apply to perceptions themselves. Ideas of sensible qualities can be "clear, because we recognize them and easily tell them from one another; but they are not distinct, because we cannot distinguish their contents" (255). And aggregates of perceptions can be confused in terms of what makes them up—the multitude of perceptions are indistinguishable because of their numbers or our lack of attention. (By "confused," Leibniz means, "a running together" [132].)

These perceptions may also be unconscious, so Leibniz parted company with Descartes, Locke, and Hume on this point. For them, if you have a perception, you must be aware of it. So we have perceptions at times and at other times we don't. "We are never without perceptions," Leibniz countered, "but necessarily we are often without *awareness* [apperception], namely when none of our perceptions stand out" [i.e., are distinct] (162). Because of what they thought of the perceptual process, it determined the examples they chose to write about: relish for Locke and sauce for Leibniz. As for Hume, we have a crucial question: How can complex impressions be derived from simple ones when the latter are discrete (distinct), clear, and atomistic in nature, *and* when in the former they appear to be blended and indistinct, like in a good sauce? For Locke, complexity enters the picture only on the level of ideas. (Did Locke's "plain and simple diet" condition his view?) With Hume, complexity appears at both levels, impressions and ideas. (Hume's acquaintance with French cuisine probably contributed to his view.[19]) Leibniz backed off from a distinction between impressions and ideas, or at least said that complexity is relative to whatever it is applied to. Complexity, for Leibniz, starts at a level that our empiricists thought was simple—our immediate sensations.[20]

In fact, "sensations," Leibniz observed, "also involve action, in as much as they present us with perceptions which stand out more, and thus with opportunities for observation and for self-development, so to speak" (211). So when you taste, for instance, a sauce, you begin inquiring, "What are the ingredients?" and "How was this prepared?" if you are a taster; or, "Does it need anything?" and "Does this complement what it is served with?" if you are preparing it. Such questions led to situations where, as Philalethes (Locke's spokesman in the dialogue) says, "Men may and should correct their palates, and make them appreciate things. The soul's tastes can be altered too, by 'a due consideration, practice, application, and custom.' That is how one becomes accustomed to tobacco, which eventually becomes enjoyable through use and familiarity" (208). Theophilus nods in agreement. Leibniz's main point here is that "the senses provide us with materials for reflections: we could not think even about thought if we did not think about something else, i.e., about the particular facts which the senses provide" (212). This is especially true of food. Hence, he has a better account of food than our empiricists do. This is rather surprising, because we expect Locke and Hume to have the upper hand when it came to an explanation of the perceptual process involved with food. But Leibniz saw the senses and the understanding working in concert with most experiences, and this is certainly true of food.

Another idea that factors into our conclusion is his distinction between sensible and insensible perceptions. This works especially well with refined foods, like sauces. The insensible perceptions that you don't readily perceive play a part in that which you can perceive and detect. "Perceptions which are at present insensible," Leibniz foresees, "may *grow* some day" (242; emphasis added). So what is imperceptible to the wine novice may some day be perceptible to her. This kind of development or refinement of the senses is absent in Locke's account. Hume even speaks of the delicacy of taste as hereditary (239), although later in the essay he speaks of taste as "educable." For them, taste is something you simply have or you don't; good taste, for Hume, is a matter of judgment. But taste and judgment, for Leibniz, are interactive from the very beginning of the perceptual process. Leibniz's view is not "atomistic," so foods like baked products, e.g., breads, that involve chemistry, where elements are transformed into something different from what one starts with, have a better explanation of what is going on than what the atomistic view of Locke and Hume provides. In fact, baked goods go unaccounted for under their view.

An analogy can be drawn between children's cognitions and those of food novices. They lack "order" (Kulstad's translation, 141) and attention to detail (*New Essays*, 86). Also they lack the experience of the items in question to make them orderly; with acquaintance, Leibniz thinks there is "self-development" (211). There is nothing like this in Locke or Hume's theory of perception. One is fully aware, under their view, of the elements or not—there is no growth (242) or learning. The only exception is in Hume's "The Standard of Taste," where he describes the true critic: "Strong sense, united to delicate sentiment, *improved by practice*, perfected by comparison, and cleared of all prejudice, can alone entitle critics to this valuable character; and the joint verdict of such, wherever they are to be found, is the true standard of taste and beauty" (241; emphasis added). But given Hume's theory of perception, it is not clear how such an improvement is possible. Hence, Leibniz captures the rudiments of the perceptual process involved in culinary practices.

Leibniz thinks we have a twofold handicap when it comes to our ideas of sensible qualities. First, "we cannot define these ideas: all we can do is to make them known through examples; and, beyond that, until their inner structure has been deciphered we have to say that they are a *je ne sais quoi*" (255). The exchange between Philalethes and Theophilus on the taste of pineapple makes for a nice illustration:

> We are in agreement, then, that our simple ideas cannot be nominally defined. We cannot know the taste of pineapple, for example, by listening to travellers' tales, unless we can taste things by the ears . . . . You are right. All the travellers in the world could not have given us through their narratives what we have been given by a single one of our own countrymen—a gentleman who grows pineapples at a place near the banks of the Weser three leagues from Hanover. He has found out how to propagate them, so that some day we may have home-bred pineapples as plentifully as Portuguese oranges, though we could expect pineapples grown here to have lost some of the flavour. (298)

But those who have the acquaintance, the "expert people . . . can name and tell apart . . . the many varieties of oranges, limes and lemons" (293). "And since some connoisseurs," Leibniz adds, "make finer discriminations than others, the whole affair [of judging] is relative to men and appears to be arbitrary" (327). However, "arbitrary" does not suggest wholesale relativism on the part of Leibniz in regard to taste. Like Hume, he thinks that disputes about matters of taste are legitimate or worthwhile:

> It is also true that men's tastes differ, and it is said that one should not argue about matters of taste. However, since tastes are only confused perceptions, we should rely on them only when their objects have been examined and are acknowledged to be insignificant and harmless. If someone acquired a taste for poisons which would kill him or make him wretched, it would be absurd to say that we ought not to argue with him about his tastes. (201)

Second, "We are not to blame for the confusion which reigns among our ideas, for this is an imperfection in our nature: to be able to pick out the causes of odours and tastes, for instance, and the content of these qualities is beyond us" (256). In other words, Leibniz noted, "We also lack senses which are sharp enough to sort out the confused ideas and comprehensive enough to perceive them [particular facts] all" (389).

Where do these ideas fit into the scheme of things in the perceptual process? We start with sensation: it occurs "when one is aware of an outer object" (161) and that awareness is what the body senses. In other words, "the sensations of sweet and bitter come from the outer senses" (83), and "the ideas that come from the senses are confused; and so too, at least in part, are the truths which depend on them" (81). So strong sensations (ones that have our attention) are simply conscious perceptions, and reflection upon them turns them into ideas, and truths are formulated on the basis of both mini processes: the former physical, and the latter, mental. Truth, the intellectual mini process pertaining to taste or sensible qualities, is an alignment of sensations and ideas, which is what we expect of, say, recipes. But this account is too tidy; Leibniz appears to be ambivalent, especially in regard to "ideas of sensible qualities."

Following Robert McRae's analysis (127), Leibniz lapses into language expressing the very thing he condemns Locke of—using "idea" and "image" interchangeably. But Leibniz does not mean quite the same thing that Locke and Hume meant by "image"; they had vision as a model for their use, where Leibniz has touch or taste in mind. By "image" he means sensations making an appearance or being present to the senses. Images are expressions of sensations. So tactile images or appearances are the distinctness of a sensation or several sensations on the palate. Let us use a wine sauce as an example again. The sensation or feel of a wine sauce, for the educated, experienced palate, is one that is rich, complex (or has depth), robust, yet supple: these qualities are the minute perceptions which are insensible (i.e., they cannot be sensed individually by themselves) in terms of the sauce's specific, individual ingredients. Most of the sensible qualities of wine, like its alcohol and tannin, evaporate in cooking and the fruit is intensified. Consequently, the sensation of taste is a confused idea or image because we do not know how the wine produces those secondary qualities of richness, robustness, suppleness, and complexity, but it does, and we come to expect these when we are told (or we figure out on our own) that it is a wine sauce. The main point here is that sensations never exist independently of ideas or concepts. (This is the main reason I use the term "cognitions" instead of "perceptions" in the title of the essay.) These concepts are capacities we have to recognize tastes when confronted with them. In other words, we can identify a sauce as a wine sauce from the taste. This taste, Leibniz claims, is really only "illusory images" or "sensory images" (404), "for the truth is that these ought to be called 'images' rather than 'qualities' or even 'ideas'" (404). But he does say that "the truth about contingent singular things is grounded in the outcome that sensory phenomena are linked together in just the way required by truths of the intellect" (392). So sensations and ideas or concepts are "linked" or connected, and this is clearly seen in cooking that is guided by a recipe. Images, and Leibniz also labels them as "impressions" (487), "result from various minute ideas which are distinct in themselves though we are not distinctly aware of them" (487). And more importantly, he stated:

> The role of these impressions is to provide us with natural inclinations [what we called "capacities" above], and to provide a grounding for observations of experience, rather than to furnish materials for reasoning—except in so far as distinct perceptions come with them. So what holds us back is primarily the inadequacy of our knowledge of these distinct ideas concealed within the confused ones; and even when everything is revealed distinctly to our senses or our minds, the multiplicity of things which must be taken into account sometimes confuses us. (487)

From this passage, it appears that Leibniz thought that sensations and images contain ideas but that we are not aware of them; however, we could be, under the right conditions—like identifying a sauce as a wine sauce. Flavors are images or appearances and expressions of sensations. Leibniz's discussion along these lines is what has suggested to us that he has the superior theory of perception when it comes to accounting for food.

To be considered our first modern food philosopher, one has to be able to give an adequate account of sauces, among other things. As Charlie

Trotter reminds us, "Sauces are not just an afterthought in gourmet cooking; they serve a major function in the composition of a dish. . . . They give a dish its character" (91). Leibniz appreciated this idea and this is probably the reason he selected "flavours" (55) as his primary example. Consequently, he is our first modern food philosopher.

Notes

1. For background on this, consult Emily Brady, "Sniffing and Savoring: The Aesthetics of Smells and Tastes," in *The Aesthetics of Everyday Life*, edited by Andrew Light and Jonathan M. Smith (New York: Columbia University Press, 2005), Part III: Finding the Everyday Aesthetic, pp. 177-193. Seeing structure in smells and tastes is decidedly anti-Kantian and stands against traditional aesthetics. This also denies Mill's distinction between higher and lower pleasures.

2. R. G. Collingwood, *The Principles of History*, edited and with an Introduction by W. H. Dray and W. J. van der Dussen (Oxford: Oxford University Press, 1999/2003), 46.

3. Roger Ariew, "G. W. Leibniz, Life and Works," in *The Cambridge Companion to Leibniz*, edited by Nicholas Jolley (Cambridge: Cambridge University Press, 1995), 38.

4. There were notable culinary occasions: Leibniz attended a Swedish wedding banquet in 1707, dined with the Russian ambassador in 1709, while in Russia for a royal wedding in the fall of 1711 dined at the Czar's table, and dined with King George I in the summer of 1716. See, for details, E. J. Aiton, *Leibniz: A Biography* (Bristol: Adam Hilger, 1985), 271, 275, 309, 325. For the developing cuisines of the day, see Ken Albala, *Food in Early Modern Europe* (Westport, Connecticut: Greenwood Press, 2003), and Gilly Lehmann, *The British Housewife: Cookery Books, Cooking and Society in Eighteenth-Century Britain* (Devon, Great Britain: Prospect Books, 2003).

5. G. W. Leibniz, *New Essays on Human Understanding* (1765), edited by Peter Remnant and Jonathan Bennett (Cambridge: Cambridge University Press, 1996); parenthetical references are to page numbers. When Leibniz heard of Locke's death (1704), he withheld publication of the *New Essays* since Locke couldn't reply.

6. This is not just a conceptual question, but a historical one. Sauces were well developed by French chefs long before Marie-Antoine Carême in the nineteenth century. For instance, wine sauces were established and in use in French cooking by the seventeenth century; see, e.g., Maguelonne Toussaint-Samat, *History of Food*, translated by Anthea Bell (Oxford: Blackwell, 1992), 276. Alma Lach declares: "To cook in the French manner is to know your sauces. They are individualistic, logical, and follow a scheme of organization." In the *Hows and Whys of French Cooking* (Chicago: The University of Chicago Press, 1970/1974), 14.

7. David Hume, *A Treatise of Human Nature* (1739-40), edited by David Fate Norton and Mary J. Norton (Oxford: Oxford University Press, 2000), 19; parenthetical references are to page numbers.

8. John Locke, *An Essay Concerning Human Understanding*, edited by P. H. Nidditch (Oxford: Clarendon Press, 1975), bk. II, ch. I, sec. 5; references are to book, chapter, section. Locke's italics unless otherwise noted.

9. A. N. Whitehead, *Science and the Modern World* (London: Macmillan, 1925), ch. III; and *Process and Reality* (London: Macmillan, 1929), ch. II, sec. I.

10. Garrett Thomson, *Bacon to Kant: An Introduction to Modern Philosophy* (Second Edition; Prospect Heights, Illinois: Waveland Press, 2002), 215. Hume's atomism can be seen in the following passage: "For in order to form a just notion of these [tiny] animals [mites], we must have a distinct idea representing every part of them; which, according to the system of infinite divisibility, is utterly impossible, and according to that of indivisible parts or atoms, is extremely difficult, by reason of the vast number and multiplicity of these parts" (24). So Hume accepts a *minima sensibilia*, a minimum sensibility, or "atoms of sense."

11. Adrian Bailey, *The Cooking of the British Isles* (Foods of the World series; New York: Time-Life Books, 1969), 105.

12. Locke's interest in food, eating, and diet has been recorded by Jean S. Yolton, "Locke's Coquinaria," in *A Locke Miscellany: Locke Biography and Criticism for All*, edited by Jean S. Yolton (Bristol: Thoemmes, 1990), 153-160. Here's his "To Pickle Wallnutts" recipe: "Gather the Wallnutts in June about midsummer and let them lye in water 3 weeks or a month shifting the

water once a day then take them out and dry them with cloth then put your nutts into a strong earthen pot well glazed laying first at the bottom of the pot a handfull of dill seeds then putt in your nutts and cover them with the best vinegar you can get putting in a handfull of salt a little whole peper cloves and mace and a head of Garlick then strew on a handfull of dill seeds on the top of them you must proportion your spice and Garlick according to the quantity of Walnutts you doe cover them close and keep them close for your use some put in a little mustard seed" (160).

13. David Hume, "Of the Standard of Taste" (1757), in *Essays Moral, Political and Literary* (Oxford: Oxford University Press, 1963), 241.

14. I am aware that the terms "relish" and "sauce" are used interchangeably at times, as in a "picante sauce" or "dipping sauce," but for my purpose here I am making a sharp distinction to contrast some claims about taste. The distinction is made, for example, in *The Professional Chef's Techniques of Healthy Cooking*, edited by Mary Deirdre Donovan for The Culinary Institute of America (New York: Van Nostrand Reinhold, 1993), ch. 11 "Basic Hot Sauces," and ch. 12 "Cold Sauces and Relishes." What guides the making of a good relish or sauce is that the end product must have a pleasing balance of flavors and an even consistency. The same distinction is seen in James Peterson's classic work, *Sauces: Classical and Contemporary Sauce Making* (Second Edition; New York: John Wiley & Sons, 1998), where *sauces* consist of ingredients and a liaison which binds them, like almond butter or bread, and *relishes* usually have no binding agent that would change the ingredients as in a sauce. Concerning relishes or salsas, Peterson writes: "The concept of chopping ingredients and then serving the mixture as a sauce opens up a whole range of possibilities for sauce making. The ingredients retain their color, texture, and individual flavor but are cut small enough for the mixture to take on an identity of its own. It can then be spread over foods and eaten like a sauce." (421)

15. Barbara Ketcham Wheaton, *Savoring the Past: The French Kitchen and Table from 1300 to 1789* (A Touchstone Book; New York: Simon & Schuster, 1983/1996), 53; she continues: "To satisfy its advocates, food that tastes of itself should be locally produced and in season, served at the peak of its natural ripeness; in contrast, transmuted food is a compound of the rare, the exotic, and the difficult, made from ingredients belonging to other places and seasons and produced by techniques that require special skills or equipment." And Wheaton adds: The cook's time was limited, so the "result was likely to be dishes in which individual ingredients were readily recognizable—those foods that taste of themselves. But fashion preferred greater complexity, so people had elaborate food when they could afford it." (101)

16. Sharon Tyler Herbst, *Food Lover's Companion* (Hauppauge, New York: Barron's 1990), 408. Herbst is helpful above in our discussion of "flavour." The renowned Chicago chef, Charlie Trotter, the advocate of sauces who expanded their use, says: "Sauces are not just an afterthought in gourmet cooking; they serve a major function in the composition of a dish. Not only do sauces complement the flavor of a dish, but they also add succulence, visual interest, and texture. They give a dish its character." Charlie Trotter, with Judi Carle and Sari Zernich, *Gourmet Cooking for Dummies* (Foster City, California: IDG Books, 1997), 91.

17. Donna Hay, *Flavours* (North Vancouver, B.C.: Whitecap Books, 2000). For a discussion of flavors and the elements of taste, see chapter 3.

18. Yolton, "Locke's 'Coquinara'," 155. "The fact that fresh meat was readily available," in the fifteenth century (and thereafter) Lehmann, in *The British Housewife*, argues, "counters the argument that spices [and sauces] were used to disguise the flavour of tainted or salted meat." (25) However, as a medical doctor, Locke's remark is probably based on his experience of treating people with food poisoning, so her claim is questionable.

19. For details, see chapter 6.

20. My discussion of Leibniz has profited from Alison Simmons's study, "Changing the Cartesian Mind: Leibniz on Sensation, Representation and Consciousness," *The Philosophical Review* 110 # 1 (January 2001): 47-75; Mark Kulstad, *Leibniz on Appreception, Consciousness, and Reflection* (Analytica series; Munich: Philosophia Verlag, 1991), esp. ch. 4 on "Consciousness, Reflection, and Apperception in the *New Essays*"; and Robert McRae's classic examination, *Leibniz: Perception, Apperception, and Thought* (Toronto: University of Toronto Press, 1976), esp. ch. 3 on perception.

5

Taste and Food in Rousseau's *Julie, or The New Heloise*

* * *

What are the historical origins of aesthetic education? Two of these origins come from the eighteenth century. These became important themes in a novel of the times. Published in 1761, Jean-Jacques Rousseau's *Julie, or the New Heloise: Letters of Two Lovers who Live in a small Town at the Foot of the Alps*[1] was an instant success in eighteenth-century Europe. Widely read, the novel made European culture self-conscious and forced it to pay attention to aspects of living that had gone unnoticed or underappreciated, including taste and food.[2] These aspects—taste and food—became concrete manifestations of aesthetic education. The voices of Julie and her tutor turned lover, Saint-Preux, provided a lively critique of French (and Swiss) society and its values. This critique was vigorously debated by those who read it at the time. During this time French haute cuisine was developing and was enthusiastically embraced by the upper class and the bourgeoisie. Primarily through the character of Julie, we find a criticism of the emerging French (Parisian) cuisine and a defense of the country cuisine it was displacing, and these two themes are the focus of this article. Below, we give a brief historical survey of the emerging French haute cuisine that occurred during Rousseau's stay outside Paris at the Hermitage and in the Montmorency district (1756-62). Based on Julie's remarks and his description of her, we find an interesting argument against elite, urban French food and manners, and an argument embracing country life and its cuisine. An assessment of these arguments concludes our discussion.

At the outset, I will state the conclusions of this study. They center on Jean-Claude Bonnet's claim that Rousseau's corpus (including *Julie*) is not a document on the manners of the day (which I think it is), but portrays a specific *system* that Rousseau espouses (which I doubt). (See note 32 for more details.) Each work (especially *Julie*) provides a different avenue for details about life and living, so we find different descriptions of life and living in *Julie* because of its literary format that allows food, meals, and taste preferences to be a theme which is not in, say, the *Confessions*. Rousseau's works, I think, cannot be reconciled or rendered consistent, so speaking of them as forming a system does not make any sense; *Reveries of the Solitary Walker* (1782) makes this abundantly clear. However, we can say that he had a very general theory about the state of nature and modern civilization; that is, modern society is corrupt and the natural state of man was free, virtuous, and happy. Therefore we can easily see that what Rousseau has to say about taste and food will be played out in these terms. Consequently, he would obviously condemn the exaggerated refinery of fine, courtly cuisine and prefer simple country cuisine and the values of a life withdrawn from the corruption of city life. Rousseau contrasted the simplicity and healthiness of country life with the pomp and false pride of the court, a theme that no doubt would remind his readers of classical literature—of Hesiod or of Horace. This contrast is centered on the introspective curiosity about taste and food that guarantees Rousseau (through the characters in *Julie*) an exceptional place in intellectual history. The details of this situation in *Julie* are fascinating and without parallel in his other works, so we shall examine these details below.

I

In *Food in History*,[3] Reay Tannahill speaks of the French becoming assured of their superiority in all matters of taste from about 1660 on. In his *Nouveau Traite de la Cuisine* (1739), M. Menon scorned "third-class persons," but in later years included them and even spoke positively of third-class cuts of meat in his book, *La cuisinière bourgeoise* (1746). Along with Menon, François Marin, in his *Les Dons de Comus, ou L'Art de la Cuisine* (1739), proclaimed that the bourgeoisie, if they had the proper pots and pans, went to the market daily, and knew how to make good bouillon, could eat like princes and princesses.[4] But it was Menon's 1746 cookbook, *La cuisinière bourgeoise*, "which was the most popular cookbook of the latter eighteenth century," Ken Albala declares, "and is clear proof that professional chefs were trying to appeal to middle class audiences rather than stay aloof from them" (164). So some of the meals that Rousseau speaks fondly of were probably ones that came from this cookbook,[5] and from François Massialot's *Le Cuisinier roial et bourgeois* (1691), of which "100,000 copies of such works were in print."[6] Menon was the first cookbook writer to consciously distinguish the *haute cuisine* of the court from the *cuisine bourgeoisie* produced in country kitchens.[7] However, some of the food practices in *Julie* do not come from this cookbook literature.

The eighteenth century was a period of transition in which professional chefs were on the rise. "This is the first time that we see a clear distinction being made," Jean-François Revel observes, "between the cuisine of the female cook, transmitted by a tradition of manual skills and instruction within the family, and the cuisine of the chef, based on invention and reflection."[8] The cuisine of the female cook appears in Saint-Preux's description of the domestic economy of the Wolmar household (Part Four, Letter X):

> The three women are, the chambermaid, the children's governess, and the cook. The latter is a most proper and clever peasant who Madame de Wolmar has taught to cook; for in this still simple country young ladies of all stations learn to perform themselves all the tasks that the women in their service will one day perform in their house, so they will know how to direct them as needed and not be pushed around by them.[9] (369)

Consequently, the food in the Wolmar estate is prepared by a female cook and not by a chef.[10] "What is a chef?" Revel answers, "For this new class of financiers or aristocrats who resided in cities and were given over entirely to life in worldly circles, a chef is a man capable of inventing what has not yet been eaten in the houses of others" (180). Rousseau romanticized the cooks and implicitly attacked the chefs, but his argument was sexist in nature. In detail:

> The very choice of dishes helped to make them [the sexes] interesting. Milk products and sugar are one of the [fair] sex's natural tastes and as it were the symbol of the innocence and sweetness that constitute its most endearing ornament. Men, on the contrary, usually seek strong flavors and spirits, foods more suited to the active and laborious life that nature requires of them; and when it happens that these diverse tastes are perverted and confounded, it is an almost infallible mark of a disorderly mingling of the sexes. Indeed I [St. Preux] have observed that in France, where women live all the time in the company of men, they have completely lost the taste for dairy products, the men largely that for wine, and in England where the two sexes are less confounded, their specific tastes have survived better. In general, I think one could often find some index of people's character in the choice of foods they prefer. The Italians who live largely on greenery are effeminate and flaccid. You Englishmen, great meat eaters, have something harsh that smacks of barbarity in your inflexible virtues. The Swiss, naturally cold, peaceful, and simple, but violent and extreme in anger, like both kinds of food, and drink both milk and wine. The Frenchman, flexible and changeable, consumes all foods and adapts to all characters. Julie herself could serve as my example: for although she is sensual and likes to

eat, she likes neither meat, nor stews, nor salt, and has never tasted wine straight. Excellent vegetables, eggs, cream, fruit; those are her daily fare, and were it not for fish of which she also is very fond, she would be a true Pythagorean [a vegetarian who abstains from drinking wine].[11] (372-73)

Rousseau apparently believed that differences of taste and appetite originated in nature. The quality of a dish depended upon the temperament and taste of the person who ate it. After Rousseau, people began to accept the idea that the quality of a dish is an intrinsic quality of the dish itself. And following this logic, "national cuisines were similarly divorced from national characters."[12] So instead of laying out numerous, unrelated dishes at a dinner table so people could find dishes to suit their tastes, a harmonious meal with dishes relating to one another could be laid out for guests.[13] Furthermore, this sexist argument goes back to Rousseau's idea that our natural state is solitude. "His natural man and woman walk alone through the fertile forests," Peter France suggests, "not speaking and meeting only for as long as is necessary for procreation" (18). But this solitary view is compromised by family life, especially as it was portrayed in *Julie* "where a household lives in relative isolation from the wicked cities and . . . [in] loving interdependence" among its members, as Peter France puts it. Hence, there is a deep conflict in Rousseau's thought between solitude and communal life, but in *Julie*, we find his grandest statement of social living. Let's face it: man or woman in solitude will not eat well. The conditions for eating well are clearly social, and Rousseau realized this (451), where a baker and dairyman are needed as well as a hunter or fisherman, in addition to a gardener and a butcher, let alone the cook.

All this discussion raises an important issue: whether Rousseau, who believed that tastes were natural and not the result of cultivation, was inconsistent in writing a novel that tried to educate or cultivate the tastes of his readers. However, Rousseau did espouse the idea that a work of imaginative literature could serve as a means for educating its readership.

"This was the era," Revel narrates, "when King Louis XV himself fixed omelettes, eggs *en chemise a' la fanatique*, lark pates, and chicken with basil" (171), and "the French nobility attached its names to sauces or combinations of food" (172)—a practice Rousseau frowned upon; "all the dainty and refined dishes, the whole value of which lies in their rarity and which have to be named to seem good" (444). This is probably the reason that we find the absence of named dishes like "*soupe a la reine*" or "soup after her majesty or the queen" in Rousseau's writings.[14]

II

Rousseau labeled his philosophical position as "the epicureanism of reason" (*Julie*, 544) rather than as an epicureanism of the senses; he referred to advocates of the latter as "vulgar epicureans" (444). "It is a poor philosophy," Julie announces, "always to go as far as desire leads us" (444) rather than being led by reason and severity. By "severity" she means that "they abstain on a daily basis from certain things they reserve to lend to a few meals a festive air that makes them more agreeable though not more expensive" (444), or more succinctly, "abstaining the better to enjoy" (544). How she does this "abstaining" she describes as follows:

> Sometimes I break off an outing for the sole reason that I enjoy it too much; by resuming it later I enjoy it twice. However, I work at maintaining the control of my will over myself, and I would rather be accused of capriciousness than allow myself to be governed by my fancies. (444)

In other words, ". . . her manner of savoring them [pleasures] resembles the austerity of those who abstain from them, and for her the art of enjoyment is that of privations" (443) " . . . but passing and moderate privations, which preserve the empire of reason, and by serving as seasoning to pleasure prelude its distaste and abuse" (443); accordingly, she would " . . . deny them to herself twenty times for the once she enjoys them" (443). So the question arises: Why "break off" doing something when you enjoy it so much? Rousseau's tacit answer is that it shows the exercise of reason in addition to the enjoyment occurring twice rather than just once.

Moreover, Rousseau rhetorically questions: "The idea of taste? Does not taste appear a hundred times better in simple things than in those that are smothered in riches?" (447). One of the dominant characteristics of the new bourgeois cuisine was its simplicity, and Rousseau gives this a favorable nod in his food descriptions. For instance, he writes:

> Julie has a liking for fine food, and in the attention she devotes to all the parts of her household, food above all is not neglected. The table reflects the general plenty, but this plenty is not ruinous; in it prevails a sensuality without refinement; all dishes are common, but each excellent in its kind, their preparation is simple and yet exquisite. . . . Some excellent local vegetable, some one of the savory greens that grow in our gardens, certain lake fish prepared in a certain manner, certain cheeses from our mountains, some German-style pastry, to which is added some piece of game brought in by the household servants; that is all the special fare to be noticed; that is what covers and decorates the table, stimulates and satisfies

our appetite on days of celebration; the service is modest and rustic, but tidy and cheerful, grace and pleasure are in evidence, joy and appetite give it spice. . . . (444-45)

Fine food can be common and simple—this is a premise of the new bourgeois cuisine of the times.[15] One is to cultivate "a taste for the innocent pleasures that moderation, order, and simplicity enhance" (443). This idea is nicely illustrated by the scene when Julie is on her death bed:

> The supper was even more agreeable than I [Monsieur de Wolmar, Julie's husband] had expected. Julie, seeing that she could bear the light, had them move the table forward, and, inconceivable as it seemed in her condition, she had an appetite. The Doctor, who saw no reason not to satisfy it, offered her a chicken breast; No, she said, but wouldn't mind some of this Ferra [Rousseau's note: "an excellent fish particular to Lake Geneva, found only at certain times"]. She was given a small morsel of it; she ate it with a little bread and found it good. (599)

This passage also exemplifies Rousseau's epicureanism of reason. Julie's "natural instincts" are a part of what Rousseau means by the epicureanism of reason and they—the natural instincts—being good for her is indeed part of the motivating force behind this death scene. But passages like this, mentioning specific foods, e.g., chicken (136), were objected to by critics, and Voltaire twice quoted in mockery the phrase "I sent for a chicken" (136; 668). So Rousseau was one of the first novelists to elevate food to an important aspect of human life and living. We find it puzzling that Voltaire would ridicule such inclusions, since he was a literary innovator himself and should have been tolerant, if not enthusiastic, of such innovations.[16]

Besides offering a positive portrait of country life and its cuisine, we also find a negative critique of urban life and its cuisine. This penetrating critique is primarily aimed at Parisian life, some of which is unusually interesting. For instance:

> City people do not know how to like the Country [because] inhabitants of Paris who think they go to the country do not go there at all; they take Paris with them. [That is,] their table is set as in Paris; they eat at the same times of day, they are served the same dishes, with the same pomp, everything they do is the same; they might as well have stayed there.[17] (493)

Such ridicule and sarcasm runs through much of Rousseau's critique of the exaggerated refinery of courtly cuisine and the fact that they wish to exercise it in the country.

III

What are we to make of all this? Are Rousseau's arguments concerning taste and food cogent? First, taste, for him, is something—a faculty—not cultivated or educated as it is in Hume;[18] Rousseau thought that taste is something natural and unassisted by social and cultural conventions, and in fact, it is corrupted by them; e.g., in *Reveries* ("Seventh Walk"), he claimed, "he [man] gradually loses . . . taste as he grows more corrupt" (113). Is this right? We side with Hume on this issue on taste, because, as Hume points out, taste is malleable and subject to change and influenced by perception and thought, e.g., wine preferences change with experience and age. The novelty of Rousseau's idea of taste lies in the notion of severity or abstainment of its use in order to heighten its sensitivity. Associated with this restriction by reason is the sense of moderation: "Here [at Julie's table] they [her guests] know not the art of feeding the stomach through the eyes; but they know the art of adding charm to good fare, eating plenty without reaching the point of discomfort, making merry with drink without impairing their reason, staying long at table without becoming bored, and rising always without distaste" (445). So this sense of moderation is probably a reaction to the seventeenth century practice of overeating and gluttony that was prevalent during the reigns of Henri IV, Louis XIII, and Louis XIV.[19] "[T]hose vulgar epicureans," Rousseau says disapprovingly, "always . . . go as far as desire leads us, without considering whether we will not come to the end of our faculties sooner than to the end of our life span, and whether our exhausted heart will not die before we do" (444). Temperance of the senses by reason is Rousseau's prescription for health. This notion parallels the Chinese idea of the proper amount of consumption which is *chi fen pao* or "70 percent full."[20] And while we are on Chinese parallels, the following remark sounds as if it could come from the *Tao Te Ching*: "If true happiness belongs to the sage, that is because he is of all men the one from who fortune can take the least away" (444). And in speaking of Julie's sense of taste, Saint-Preux remembers that "her taste does not go flat; she never needs to revive it through excess, and I often see her savor with delight a child's pleasure that would be insipid to anyone else" (443). Here we have another Taoistic parallel of "taste without tasting"[21] or tasting the tasteless. (Incidentally, Rousseau describes Chinese gardens in one letter [397] and in another letter Saint-Preux writes "After the supper, I set off rockets I had brought from China, which made quite an impression" [491], so like many Enlightenment thinkers, he was taken with what Europe was learning about Asia and China in particular.)

Nonetheless, what is important here is the idea of taste without tasting or tasting the tasteless. The claim that Julie's taste doesn't go flat and that her sensitivity is heightened by abstaining is counterintuitive to most of French gastronomy. For instance, Jean-Robert Pitte believes that eating well or gastronomy "is a form of aestheticism acquired by constant, intensive cultivation of the senses, the most important, in this case, being taste."[22] And he continues: "For the average person, the sense of taste is long left lying fallow and widely cultivated short of its potential during big dinners and occasional banquets over the course of which, through lack of good judgment, quantity and pretense prevail over quality."[23] Pitte and many others would argue fiercely against Rousseau on this point and would undoubtedly challenge some of the premises of his epicureanism of reason. So the issue surrounding taste is abstaining versus exercising. The debate gets even more complicated if we interject "supertasters"[24] into the picture. Supertasters may not need practice the way we normal folks need it; maybe Julie could be viewed as a supertaster.

Secondly in regard to food, Rousseau distinguishes between two different types of cuisine: the royal or upper class (urban) and the bourgeoisie (country), and as we have seen in section I, this distinction was in the cookbook literature and mirrored in French food practices at the time. So as introduced by Rousseau in *Julie*, this is not anything new. Ken Albala's comments, in speaking of *Emile*, would apply even more so to *Julie*: "Indirectly Rousseau spawned what we now know as the health food movement. Now simpler foods, unprocessed, unrefined, and unspoiled at the hands of over-zealous chefs, were to be sought out" (208). Here is one of the many descriptions of Julie's country table: "Our commodities alone grace our table, . . . nothing is scorned for being common, nothing is valued for being rare . . . . we limit ourselves, out of discrimination as much as moderation, to the choice of the best things nearby, the quality of which is not suspect. Our food is simple, but select" (450). So, in a significant sense, Rousseau is the precursor of the organic food movement and of aspects of the slow food movement.

Is the table populated with food that reflects the new bourgeois cuisine or is it simply a product of a female country cook? Probably a little of both, given the food lists that are found in *Julie*. There are parallels between what is given in *Julie* and what we find in Massialot and Menon. But much of this remains enigmatic. We cannot, however, *equate* the new bourgeois cuisine with the country cuisine. No doubt Rousseau had experienced the full range of French and Swiss cuisines of his time, and this is certainly reflected in his writings, especially in *Julie*.[25] Be this as it may, he still gives us insight into what the cuisines were like at the time and the attitudes towards them.

In some ways, Julie is a portrait of the tastes of the eighteenth century; e.g., her dislike of salt and her avoidance of so-called masculine foods (stews, meat, and undiluted wine). Even though the Wolmar estate represented the elite, and especially Julie, who "ate only 'delicate' fowl, relatively 'light' fish, and soft wheat bread,"[26] we find instances of equality between the elite class and its servants: "We [the Wolmar clan] dine with the peasants . . .

just as we work alongside them. We eat with good appetite their somewhat coarse, but good and healthy, soup, full of excellent vegetables" (496). And "Domestics eat at the same table with their masters" (66). Is Rousseau attempting to break down rigid social barriers with remarks like these? Perhaps so; he was critical of most French social organization, especially pertaining to food practices. This situation represents a liberation of the eater from diets tied to gender to the sharing of dishes where men and women alike taste and eat the same food. Now they have something in common to converse about. All this is implicit in his dining descriptions. For instance:

> The supper is served on two long tables. The luxury and pomp of feasts are absent, but plenty and joy are present. Everyone takes a seat at the table, masters, day-workers, domestics; each rises to serve indiscriminately, without exception, without preference, and the service is always performed with grace and pleasure. One drinks at will, liberty having no limits but those of propriety. The presence of masters so respected acts as a restraint on everyone and does not inhibit informality and merriment.[27] (498)

The depiction of the Wolmar private dining room and its ambience is worth quoting in detail:

> On the first storey is a small dining room separate from the one where we ordinarily dine, which is on the ground floor. This partic-ular room is in the corner of the house and lighted on two sides. On one it faces the garden, beyond which you can see the lake through the trees; from the other you see that great hillside of vineyards which is beginning to display the riches that will be harvested there in two months. This room is small but decorated with everything that can make it pleasant and cheerful. This is where Julie gives her little banquets for her father, her husband, her cousin, and me [Saint-Preux], for herself, and sometimes for her children. . . . Mere visitors are not admitted there; never do we eat there when we have strangers present; it is the inviolable sanctuary of trust, friendship, freedom. The companionship of hearts there binds the table com-panions; it is a sort of initiation to intimacy, and never are assembled there any but people who would wish never again to be separated. . . . The absence of domestics invited me to dispense with the reserva-tions in my heart, and it is there that at Julie's behest I resumed the practice relinquished years earlier of drinking straight wine with my hosts at the end of the repast.[28] (445)

In this passage Rousseau mirrors what Louis XV did when he ascended the throne: "Formality was replaced by vivacity, grandiosity by intimacy, and magnificence by delicacy."[29] For example, "Louis XV's hunting lodge at Choisy contained a mechanism that enabled a fully set table to be elevated into the dining room from the kitchen below, eliminating the need for servants and permitting the king and his friends to enjoy complete intimacy. It was the custom in Versailles for the servants to be dismissed and for the king himself to serve his guests after supper parties when the company retreated into the salon for coffee."[30] And speaking of coffee, it "changed more than just eating habits—it changed social and political habits as well," writes Linda Civitello. "For the first time, people had a public place and a reason to congregate that did not involve alcohol."[31] Coffee became the rage during the eighteenth century, and as Civitello noted, it changed the social landscape. It even has a place in *Julie* and it illustrates Julie's epicureanism of reason:

> The privations she imposes on herself through that temperate sensuality I [Saint-Preux] have mentioned are at the same time new means of pleasure and new opportunities to economize. For example she is very fond of coffee; at her mother's she took some every day. She has given up that habit in order to heighten her taste for it; she has limited herself to taking coffee only when she has guests, and in the Salon d'Apollon, so as to add this token of festivity to all the others. It is a touch of sensuality that gratifies her more, costs her less, and by which she sharpens and disciplines her craving at the same time. Contrariwise, her attention to anticipating and satisfying her father's and her husband's tastes is unstinting, a natural and gracious prodigality which makes them savor what she offers them better because of the pleasure she derives from offering it to them. Both of them like to prolong the end of a meal somewhat, in the Swiss manner: she never fails after supper to have a bottle of finer wine served, older than their everyday stock. (451-52)

Enlightened epicureanism was at its heyday during the reign of Louis XV and this was Rousseau's contribution to it. However, these last few passages display a deep paradox in Rousseau's thought. On one hand, he thought solitude and separation of the sexes to be the benchmark of authentic human existence (modeled after certain animal behavior); and on the other hand, he appreciated the communal bond that is present in family life and symbolized in rituals of food and eating. He never seemed to reconcile these two opposing ways of thinking about human beings. "I was never completely satisfied with others or with myself," Rousseau surmises in *Reveries* ("Eighth Walk"). "I was deafened by the tumult of the world and bored by solitude, I was always wanting to move and never happy anywhere" (124). Be that as it may, food and taste are not incidental to his philosophy, but rather an integral part of it; and *Julie* is an immense part of what has been substantially overlooked by historians of French philosophy. I have attempted to correct that here.[32]

Notes

1. Jean-Jacques Rousseau, *Julie, or the New Heloise: Letters of Two Lovers who Live in a small Town at the Foot of the Alps*, translated and annotated by Philip Stewart and Jean Vaché, in *The Collected Writings of Rousseau*, edited by Roger D. Masters and Christopher Kelly, Vol. 6 (Dartmouth College; Hanover: University Press of New England, 1997). Usually parenthetical references are by page numbers after citation.

2. For a notable example, Leo Tolstoy was taken with *Julie* and it was influential on *War and Peace* (1865), translated from the Russian by Richard Pevear and Larissa Volokhonsky (New York: Alfred A. Knopf, 2007), Vol. I, Part One, ch. XXII, pp. 89/1228n.

3. Reay Tannahill, *Food in History* (New York: Stein and Day, Publishers, 1973), 286.

4. Ibid., 285. For a good overall view of this historical period, see Ken Albala, *Food in Early Modern Europe* (Westport, Connecticut: Greenwood Press, 2003), 151-164 on France in ch. 4, "Cuisine by Region."

5. For example, see Jean-Jacques Rousseau, *Reveries of the Solitary Walker* (1782), translated by Peter France (London: Penguin Books, Ltd.,1979), 87, "Fifth Walk." Numerous examples appear in *The Confessions of Jean-Jacques Rousseau*, translated by A.S.B. Glover (New York: The Limited Editions Club, 1955), where he gave vivid descriptions of picnic dinners and great suppers and spoke of scenting "a good chervil omelette" (394) as he passed through a hamlet.

6. Felipe Fernández-Armesto, *Near a Thousand Tables: A History of Food* (New York: The Free Press, 2002), 123. See Philip Hyman and Mary Hyman, "Printing the Kitchen: French Cookbooks, 1480-1800," in *Food: A Culinary History from Antiquity to the Present*, English Edition by Albert Sonnenfeld (New York: Penguin Books, 1999/2000), 394-402.

7. Anne Willan, *Great Cooks and Their Recipes: From Taillevent to Escoffier* (London: Pavilion Books Ltd., 1995/2000), 88.

8. Jean-François Revel, *Culture and Cuisine: A Journey through the History of Food*, translated by Helen R. Lane (Garden City, New York: Doubleday & Company, Inc., 1979/1982), 180.

9. This passage is at odds with Gilly Lehmann's claim: "If women did become confined to a purely domestic role, one might expect advice literature and cookery books to emphasize the importance of culinary knowledge for the mistress of a family. This is far from being the case. All the evidence points to the ladies' desire to play a managerial role from a distance: conduct-books warned against active participation in the kitchen, and by the middle of the [eighteenth] century cookery books made a selling-point of the fact that a book could relieve the mistress of the need to teach her servants to cook. Whether such an ideal could be attained in real life was another matter." *The British Housewife: Cookery Books, Cooking and Society in Eighteenth-Century Britain* (Devon, Great Britain: Prospect Books, 2003), 67. Rousseau's fictional account probably mirrors real life. A few pages later (70), Lehmann does add an opinion that is reflected in Rousseau's domestic remark: "But even so vigorous an author [John Essex] as this does not suggest that girls should return to the kitchen: they should merely acquire enough knowledge to be able to direct their servants." (See also 71ff.)

10. Another instance of a cook and not a chef in *Julie*: "Julie seeing we had little appetite found the way to make us eat some of everything, now on the pretext of instructing her cook, now to see whether she would dare take some herself, now motivating us with our own health which we needed in order to assist her, always manifesting the pleasure we could give her in such a way as to preclude any means of declining, and mingling with all this a playfulness meant to distract us from the sad business [her impending death] that occupied us" (584).

11. Professor Lehmann echoes the feminine-masculine associations in her discussion of "Meals and Meal-Times" from a British perspective: ". . . sweet dishes and innocuous drinks [like tea] could have been seen as feminine, whereas meat and hard liquor had masculine connotations. (Such imagery also influenced perceptions of cookery itself, and contributed to the English rejection of French *nouvelle cuisine* as too insubstantial and thus too feminine, when compared to English macho roast beef.)" (321). Consequently, "[s]uch associations led to the differentiation of the various meals, which offered their discrete forms of social intercourse . . . breakfast were

predominantly male (a shared breakfast preceding sport or business), that dinner was most likely to bring sexes together, and that tea parties were largely, but not exclusively, feminine (with inferiors such as tradeswomen invited, as well as social equals)" (322).

12. Jean-Louis Flandrin, "From Dietetics to Gastronomy: The Liberation of the Gourmet," in *Food: A Culinary History*, 431.

13. Ibid., 420.

14. For a variation of this soup, see the recipe and its discussion of "The Queen's Pottage," in Ivan Day, *Cooking in Europe: 1650-1850* (Westport, Connecticut: Greenwood Press, 2009), 26-27.

15. Lehmann draws the contrast between country food and court-city food this way: "Country food was seen as rustic and natural: court and city food as refined and elaborate, a product of culture. [A later echo of Rousseau's dichotomy.] This opposition is a fundamental and recurrent theme in gastronomic discourse, and the tension between nature and culture, between the impulse to simplify and that to elaborate, is an important factor in culinary creativity" (356). And, "[t]he underlying demand is for a return to a mythical golden age, before innocence had been contaminated by luxury" (357), a remark which could have come from Rousseau himself.

16. For example, M. de Voltaire, *The History of Zadig; or, Destiny* (1748), translated by R. Bruce Boswell (Paris: Priester Freres, 1952), an Oriental tale.

17. This was a common practice that goes back to the Middle Ages; see Maggie Black, *The Medieval Cookbook* (New York: Thames and Hudson, 1992), 13-15.

18. David Hume, "Of the Standard of Taste" (1757), in *Essays Moral, Political and Literary* (Oxford: Oxford University Press, 1963), essay 23. For a discussion of this essay, see S. K. Wertz, *Between Hume's Philosophy and History: Historical Theory and Practice* (Lanham, Maryland: University Press of America, 2000), ch. 6; and his "Hume's Aesthetic Realism," *Southwest Philosophy Review* XXII # 2 (July, 2006): 53-61.

19. See Fernández-Armesto, 122-23 on the eating habits of Henri IV, Louis XIII and XIV.

20. Corinne Trang, *Essentials of Asian Cuisine: Fundamentals and Favorite Recipes* (New York: Simon & Schuster, 2003), 46.

21. Lao Tzu, *Tao Te Ching*, translated by Stephen Addiss and Stanley Lombardo (Indianapolis: Hackett Publishing Company, 1993), verse 63. For a brief discussion of Rousseau and Lao Tzu on taste, see chapter 2.

22. Jean-Robert Pitte, *French Gastronomy: The History and Geography of a Passion*, translated by Jody Gladding (New York: Columbia University Press, 2002), 5.

23. Ibid.

24. Carolyn Korsmeyer, *Making Sense of Taste: Food and Philosophy* (Ithaca: Cornell University Press, 1999), 87, and 73: supertasters are people who have an unusually large number of taste buds or papillae who are especially sensitive to sweet and sour and who are about 20 percent of the population.

25. Rousseau was a frequent patron of Café Procope, which was the first Parisian café that became a rendezvous for intellectuals of the late seventeenth and early eighteenth centuries. See Willan, 89.

26. J.-L. Flandrin, "Introduction: The Early Modern Period," in *Food: A Culinary History*, 363.

27. This democratic idea of everyone eating together, regardless of social class or status, is out of the mainstream of eighteenth century food practices; Lehmann's whole study is premised on social hierarchies for meals, meal-times, and culinary styles. So Rousseau's egalitarian notion of food practices stands unique in eighteenth century literature and actual historical domestic situations in France and Britain. And if the novel advances an important idea to come to fruition later in European history, it would be this one.

28. This description of the private dining room is much like what the Romans (actually Cicero) called "*aedicula*" that was a small room for those who used it which gave them privacy and intimacy, and apparently the French independently discovered these rooms without knowing that the early Romans had them for the same reasons.

29. Witold Rybczynski, *Home: A Short History of an Idea* (New York: Penguin Books, 1986), 83.

30. Ibid., 86.

31. Linda Civitello, *Cuisine and Culture: A History of Food and People* (Hoboken, New Jersey: John Wiley & Sons, Inc., 2004), 149.

32. One can easily see what Rousseau has to say about taste and food as an extension of his very general hypothesis that modern civilization is corrupted and that in the natural state man was free, virtuous, and happy, so he would obviously condemn the exaggerated refinery of

fine, courtly cuisine and prefer simple country cuisine and the values of a life withdrawn from the corruption of city life. For a brief survey of Rousseau's life and thought, see Sally Scholz, *On Rousseau* (Belmont, California: Wadsworth/Thomson Learning, Inc., 2001). Besides Ken Albala's *Food in Early Modern Europe*, there is also a discussion of Rousseau in Jean-Robert Pitte, *French Gastronomy*; this latter work contains a citation (186) of what appears to be the most detailed study yet on this topic: Jean-Claude Bonnet, "Le systeme de la cuisine et du repas chez Rousseau," appendix to Serge Theriault, *Jean-Jacques Rousseau et la medicine naturelle* (Montreal: L'Aurore, 1979), 117-150. This work is much more comprehensive than mine; Bonnet is attempting to give an overall view of Rousseau's particular ideas on food and society–the appetite, eating in society (as opposed to alone, as in the natural state), simple, country meals that are basically vegetarian, his critical stance toward meat, the lack of detailed descriptions of fancy dishes, preference for small meals, such as breakfast and snacks. Bonnet's main thesis is that Rousseau's works (including *Julie*) are not a document on the manners of the day (which I think it is), but portray a specific system that Rousseau espouses (which I doubt).

However, the Rousseauian general hypothesis of the opposition between society and nature fails to capture what is going on in *Julie*. Rousseau is exploring new territory here by synthesizing the best traits of social and familial life with the natural country living. In other words, *Julie* is his attempt to move beyond the dichotomy of society and nature to find some middle ground for authentic living. Consequently, *Julie* is not part of a Rousseauian system, but a movement away from his earlier (and later in *Reveries*, "Eighth Walk") opposition of society and nature— trying to discover something more grand, a more enlightened way of living; this is something he wished for, but couldn't find in his own life, but found in a dream which he shared with us in *Julie*.

6

Hume's Culinary Interests and the Historiography of Food

* * *

n the early 1940s, Ernest Campbell Mossner was the first to write about "the forgotten Hume." Professor Mossner hypothesized that the personal Hume was forgotten because he lacked the contemporary Boswell that Samuel Johnson had.[1] So Hume scholars have had to piece together the forgotten Hume from numerous letters and sources. A significant part of that forgotten Hume is his culinary interests. I shall focus on those in this chapter. It is very rare that we find Hume boasting about anything, but his culinary skills are among the very few instances. Usually he is humble and modest in his claims and outlook, but not here. First I will look at the letters and his essays, then I shall examine *The History of England,* which will make up a substantial part of my study. (Unfortunately, his culinary interests are conspicuously absent in the *Treatise* and the *Enquiries,* which raises interesting questions about his philosophy proper,[2] like, why weren't they included?—given the other displays.) Some of Hume's culinary remarks and claims will be compared to recent studies in the history of food.

My general thesis is that knowledge of Hume's culinary interests leads us to understanding another dimension of his historiography and historical narrative, in addition to some of the essays. Without this knowledge, a subtext goes unappreciated. In the section that follows, his culinary interests are manifested in the correspondence (and some of the essays), so this account is largely biographical. The remaining sections reflect a more scholarly account of these interests and are the most interesting historically. In other words, Hume's history of the British Isles contains a history of European food and this would go unnoticed if one were not cognizant of his culinary interests. Consequently, I shall turn to these.

Correspondence and Essays

In Letter XXXVI about Hume in Edinburgh, October 25, 1769, in a note to his reference about keeping "a plentiful table for myself and my friends," Birkbeck Hill narrates:

> On Oct. 16, 1769, nine days earlier than the date of the letter in the text, Hume had written to Sir Gilbert Elliot:--'I live still, and must for a twelvemonth, in my old house in James's Court, which is very cheerful, and even elegant, but too small to display my great talents for cookery, the science to which I intend to addict the remaining years of my life! I have just now lying on the table before me a receipt [recipe] for making *soupe a la reine,* copied with my own hand; for beef and cabbage (a charming dish), and old mutton and old claret nobody excels me. I make also sheep-head broth in a manner that Mr. Keith speaks of it for eight days after, and the Duc de Nivernois [ambassador in England in 1762] would bind himself apprentice to my lass [a cook-maid] to learn it.' Stewart's *Robertson*, p. 361. . . . Boswell writing on June 19, 1775, says:--'On Thursday I supped at Mr. Hume's, where we had the young Parisian, Lord Kames, and Dr. Robertson, an excellent supper, three sorts of ice-creams. What think you of the northern Epicurus style? I can recollect no conversation. Our writers here are really not prompt on all occasions, as those of London.' *Letters of Boswell,* p. 203. The 'three sorts of ice-creams' were in those days a great luxury; for Lord Cockburn, writing of Edinburgh twenty or thirty years later, says:--'Ice, either for cooling or eating, was utterly unknown, except in a few houses of the highest class.' Hume's old claret would not have been so costly as in England, for in Scotland claret was exempted from duty till about 1780. Cockburn's *Memorials,* p. 35.[3]

Hume's lass or cook-maid was Peggy Irvine, whom he personally trained as a chef or in "the art of sophisticated cookery," to prepare his meals and those of his company.[4] (Alexander Carlyle said of her that she was "much more like a man than a woman,"[5] which I take to mean in temperament.)

Where and from whom did Hume receive this culinary expertise? The note above shows that he was acquainted with French cuisine. This was at the beginning of French cuisine, so cookbooks were not that prevalent, and the culinary traditions were personally handed down from generation to generation by receipts or recipes. In fact recipes had just made an appearance at this time as a conventional means of culinary communication.[6] Was it while he was in France, specifically in Paris and La Fleche, when he was composing the *Treatise* (1730s), that he received culinary instruction? Probably, as Mossner accounts. "In France, Hume had acquired a choice stock of personally selected and tested recipes . . ." (TFH,

198). From whom did Hume copy the recipe for *soupe a la reine*? What is *soupe a la reine*? "*A la reine*" refers to the manner of the queen. The closest recipe I have found is "Her Majesty's Chicken and Almond Soup" (*potage puree de volaille a la reine*), which James Peterson describes as follows:

> This luxurious soup captures the essence of chicken and delicately teams it with almonds. Puree a la reine is traditionally a luxury soup because it contains cooked chicken breasts worked into a fine puree. At one time this meant hours bent over a motor and pestle, but a blender or food processor works almost as well in about one-fiftieth of the time.
>
> In my home library, I have recipes for *puree a la reine* that date back to the 17th century. The recipes change little over the centuries except that early versions are garnished with pistachios and pomegranate seeds—typical medieval touches. Most earlier versions contain bitter almonds to give this soup its characteristic flavor, but in this recipe sweet almonds and almond extract are used, since bitter almonds contain traces of cyanide and are illegal in the United States.[7]

What Peterson is probably alluding to historically are recipes for *soupe a la reine* from *Massialot's Le Cuisinier roial et bourgeois* (1691), which became *Le Nouveau Cuisinier royal et bourgeois* (1712-1730), Vincent La Chapelle's *Le Cuisinier moderne* (1733, three English volumes, and 1735, four French volumes), and Menon's *Nouveau Traité de cuisine* (1739/1742) and *Soupers de la Cour* (1755).[8] Hume may have consulted these early cookbooks, and who knows, his recipe for *soupe a la reine* may have come from one of these. Hume's "*soupe a la reine*" is probably a variation of *puree a la reine*. Where it came from and from whom are lost in the forgotten annals of history.

In 1763 Hume returned to France, in particular to Lord Hertford's embassy in Paris, as its secretary, and remained there until 1766. In "My Own Life" he makes observations about life in Paris, which surely included the Parisian cuisine.

> Those who have not seen the strange Effect of Modes will never imagine the Reception I met at Paris, from Men and Women of all Ranks and Stations. The more I recoiled from their excessive Civilities, the more I was loaded with them. There is, however, a real Satisfaction in living at Paris from the great Number of sensible, knowing, and polite Company with which the City abounds above all places in the Universe. I thought once of settling there for Life. (LDH, 614)

In all likelihood, Hume acquired more recipes for his collection during this time. In the summer of 1766, he briefly returned to Edinburgh and then finally settled there in 1769 for the rest of his life.

In the essay "The Sceptic," Hume addresses the issue of the relative subjectivity of taste: "There is something approaching to principles in mental taste; and critics can reason and dispute more plausibly than cooks or perfumers" because "what seems the most delicious food to one animal, appears loathsome to another."[9] His most famous discussion of taste comes from the essay "Of the Standard of Taste," where Hume gives a noted story from Cervantes's *Don Quixote* (part 2, ch. 13), which is discussed in chapter 4. In that passage, Sancho reveals that two of his kinsmen were ridiculed because one tasted a trace of leather in a hogshead of wine, while the other tasted a trace of iron. What was discovered at the bottom of the barrel was an iron key with a leather thong.

Even though Hume holds that taste, but especially mental taste, belongs "entirely to the sentiment, internal or external; it must be allowed, that there are certain qualities in objects, which are fitted by nature to produce those particular feelings" (E, 235).[10] This allowance is especially true of wine tasting, but not in, say, poetry or drama, so maybe cooks are better off than critics after all, because they are tasting qualities in objects, and their taste is a reflection of their palates and not just a reflection of their sentiments. If one detects almond in a soup, it is mainly because of a substance in the soup that is almond or almond-like. The moral of the story is that the two kinsmen are not contradicting one another with their remarks as those who ridiculed them thought, but that each kinsman contributed to an understanding of the wine. So two tasters are better than one—more the better so as to come to a consensus of what the wine really is. Likewise with the soup: one taster may detect almond and another chicken, so together they provide a better understanding of the soup than separately. (It goes without saying that a chef or a diner could, and often does, taste both almond and chicken. However, one may taste neither almond nor chicken because when they are cooked together, the ingredients are transformed into a new, completely different flavor.) Given Hume's culinary prowess, I am surprised that he gives critics an edge over cooks in matters of taste.

Hume notes cooks, along with musicians, painters, players, and tailors, as professionals equal in number in Camillus's time as well as Augustus's days (citing Livy) in "Of Commerce" (E, 258). In the note above, he speaks of claret, and in "Of Populousness of Ancient Nations" he mentions the city of Bordeaux (E, 448), but he knew more about wine than what comes from the Bordeaux region. In "Of Commerce," he speaks of "the fine vineyards of Champagne and Burgundy" (E, 266). And from the note above, we can conclude that Hume must have had some fine wines, for "the Rev. Alexander Carlyle writes glowingly of 'warm suppers and excellent claret'" (TFH, 197). Mossner adds: "His [Hume's] *petits souper fins* [small refined suppers], embellished with rare old claret, were the source of genuine pride" (TFH, 198). It is clear from the several references to "claret" that it was the favorite wine of Hume's circle of friends. There is a remote chance that Hume and his friends are using the term "claret" in the generic sense, as Jancis Robinson describes, "for a vaguely identified class of red table wines supposedly drier, and possibly higher in tannins, than those wines sold as generic burgundy."[11] But I don't think so for two reasons: (1) from the passages above, we can infer that they knew a great deal about the wine of their time, and (2) the term "claret" had been used to denote red Bordeaux wine since the sixteenth century.

As for the first reason, a document that clearly demonstrates this is: "On that same day [6 August, 1776] Hume drew up the codicil to his will . . . 'I leave to my Friend, Mr. John Home of Kilduff, ten dozen of my old Claret at his Choice; and one single Bottle of that other Liquor call Port. I also leave to him six dozen of Port, provided that he attests under his hand, signed *John Hume,* that he has himself alone finished that Bottle at two Sittings'" (LDH, 599). Anyone who has ten dozen of claret and six dozen of port to bequeath has a fairly large cellar, especially in those days, and probably knows a great deal about those wines—even by today's standards. Apparently Hume had some of the early vintages in bottles because this was the time of the rediscovery of the cork, so bottles began to be used for storing wine instead of casks or barrels (before this time, bottles, if used at all, were for serving wine at the table).[12] However, wine corks go back at least as far as Oliver Cromwell (1650s).[13]

As for the second reason, Tim Unwin states that:

> The word claret does not appear to have been used at all extensively in England until the 16th century. In the second half of the 17th century a new type of wine, of much higher quality and deeper colour, began to be produced in the Graves and on the sands and gravels of the Medoc to the north west of Bordeaux. These wines, the provence of specific properties, where close attention was paid to grape selection, improved methods of vinification, and the use of new oak barrels, became known by the beginning of the 18th century as New French Clarets, and the earliest and most famous of them were Haut-Brion, Lafite, Latour, and Margaux.[14]

The "warm suppers" were "an especial feature of the Edinburgh literary life [which] was the informal exchange of suppers from home to home" (TFH, 198). Furthermore these meals were "never merely gastronomic" (TFH, 198), but were "the intimate—as distinguished from the grand— *salon* [*salon intime*] [which] was the society of a few choice spirits, warm in friendship and mutual respect, animated in intellect, and appreciative of good food and good wine" (TFH, 197). James Boswell gives an account of an after-dinner libation he had with Hume and his family:

The philosopher was just finishing dinner with his sister and nephew. "He had on a White nightcap and a hat above it. He called for a fresh bottle of port, which he and I drank, all but a single glass that his Nephew took. I indeed took the largest share." (TFH, 180)

Hume best sums up his life and living in "My Own Life"; he describes the early 1760s activities (in Edinburgh writing the early volumes of his history) as "opulent" (LDH, 614), and the late 1760s on as "very opulent" (LDH, 615).

The Early History

The History of England also displays Hume's culinary interests—not to the extent that it contained a minihistory of food like it did a minihistory of British literature[15] and a minihistory of science,[16] but there is a bona fide chronology. For example, prior to the reign of Charles II (in the part on "Manners and arts"), Hume reports: "The first mention of tea, coffee, and chocolate, is about 1660. Asparagus, artichoaks, colliflower, and a variety of sallads, were about the same time introduced into England" (H, Six, LXII, 148). Hume is actually wrong about asparagus and artichokes here—they appeared much earlier.[17] And "the usual bread of the poor was at this time [early 1600s] made of barley" (H, Five, Appendix IV, 139). Several times at the end of a reign, Hume announces: "It may not be improper, at this period, to make a pause: and to take a survey of the state of the kingdom [during the reign of James I], with regard to government, manners [including food], finances, arms, trade, learning. Where a just notion is not formed of these particulars, history can be little instructive, and often will not be intelligible" (H, Five, Appendix IV, 124).

The first food reference is not what one would expect from the annals of early Britain. In his narration of Prince Alfred the Great (ca. 875 CE), Hume gives the following humorous story:

> The wife of the neat-herd was ignorant of the condition of her royal guest; and observing him one day busy by the fire-side in trimming his bow and arrows, she desired him to take care of some cakes, which were toasting, while she was employed elsewhere in other domestic affairs. But Alfred, whose thoughts were otherwise engaged, neglected this injunction; and the good woman, on her return, finding her cakes all burnt, rated the king very severely, and upbraided him, that he always seemed very well pleased to eat her warm cakes, though he was thus negligent in toasting them. (H, One, II, 67)

So in the midst of reading of wars, battles, invasions, murders, and other barbarous behavior in general, we encounter this humane domestic tale that exhibits a sense of humor and gives us a sense of (comic) relief. And later in the chapter Hume remarks, "We wish to see him [Alfred] delineated in more lively colours, and with more particular strokes, that we may at least perceive some of those small specks and blemishes, from which, as a man, it is impossible he could be entirely exempted" (H, One, II, 75). Indeed, the food incident accomplishes this historiographical aim.

From this barbarous age, one would expect a more dine-and-die scene; for instance:

> Edmund was young when he came to the crown, yet was his reign short, as his death was violent. One day, as he was solemnizing a festival in the county of Glocester, he remarked, that Leolf, a notorious robber, whom he had sentenced to banishment, had yet the boldness to enter the hall where he himself dined, and to sit at table with his attendants. Enraged at this insolence, he ordered him to leave the room; but on his refusing to obey, the king, whose temper, naturally choleric, was inflamed by this additional insult, leaped on him himself, and seized him by the hair: But the ruffian, pushed to extremity, drew his dagger, and gave Edmund a wound, of which he immediately expired. This event happened in the year 946, and in the sixth year of the king's reign. (H, One, II, 89)

Edmund's grandfather was Alfred the Great, and his epoch was as violent as the earlier one. During this time, some kings' and officers' fates ended in a similar fashion.[18] And speaking of dining and dying, Hume includes this morsel of information about King Henry I (1135): "He was preparing for the journey [returning to England from Normandy], but was seized with a sudden illness at Saint-Denis-le-Ferment, from eating too plentifully of lampreys,[19] a food which always agreed better with his palate than his constitution" (H, One, VI, 276).

Lampreys, along with other food items, were used as currency; here, in detail, is an amusing listing that Hume found entertaining:

> There were no profits so small as to be below the king's [John's] attention. . . . Roger, son of Nicholas, gave twenty lampreys and twenty shads [herring] for an inquest to find, whether Gilbert, son of Alured, gave to Roger 200 muttons to obtain his confirmation for certain lands, or whether Roger took them from him by violence: Geoffrey Fitz-Pierre, the chief justiciary, gave two good Norway hawks, that Walter le Madine might have leave to export a hundred weight of cheese out of the king's dominions.
>
> It is really amusing to remark the strange business in which the king sometimes interfered, and never without a present: The wife of Hugh de Neirle gave the king 200 hens, that she might lie with her husband one night; and she brought with her two sureties, who answered each for a hundred hens. It is probable that her husband

was a prisoner, which debarred her from having access to him. . . .
The bishop of Winchester gave one tun [a large cask] of good wine
for his not putting the king in mind to give a girdle to the countess
of Albemarle. [Hume ends this list with the following comment.]
There are in the records of exchequer many other instances of a like
nature. (H, One, Appendix II, 480-82)

Then, at this point, Hume was not finished with culinary instances in that
he has this footnote: "*We shall gratify the reader's curiosity by subjoining a
few more instances from Madox,* p. 332. . . . Roger, son of Nicholas, promised all the lampreys he could get, to have the king's request to Earl William Mareshal, that he would grant him the manor of Langeford at Ferm.
The burgesses of Glocester promised 300 lampreys, that they might not be
distrained to find the prisoners of Poictou with necessaries, unless they
pleased" (H, One, Appendix II, 482n; Hume's italics).

The economic value or cost of food products especially interested
Hume. In Note [R] (to p. 404), he conjectures: "Commodities [cows, bulls,
sheep, oxen, mares, and hogs] seem not to have advanced in their price
since the [Norman] conquest, and to have still been ten times cheaper
than at present" [1770s] (H, One, X, 496-7). At the end of each volume
there is a section he calls "Miscellaneous transactions of this reign," and
it is usually in there and in the notes where we will find such references. However, appendices contain such references too: "The price of corn
[grain], during this reign [James I], and that of the other necessaries of
life, was no lower, or was rather higher, than at present" (H, Five, Appendix IV, 138). It was not until the late sixteenth century when corn or
maize became a familiar staple for the table, and even later for the British
Isles; maize was referred to as "Indian corn" and not as "corn." "'Corn'
being, then as now," Tannahill says, "a general-purpose European name
for any kind of grain."[20] Throughout *The History of England* there are numerous discussions of agriculture, or the lack thereof; for example, in the
reign of James I, Hume at the beginning of a long discussion announces: "Agriculture was anciently very imperfect in England," and concludes
"It was not till the fifth [year] of Elizabeth, that the exportation of corn
[grain] had been allowed in England; and Camden observes, that agriculture, from that moment, received new life and vigour" (H, Five, Appendix IV, 148-9). "And as the improvements of agriculture were also much
checked," Hume earlier observes, "by the immense possessions of the nobility, by the disorders of the times, and by the precarious state of feudal
property; it appears, that industry of no kind could then have place in
the [Feudal and Anglo-Norman] kingdom" (H, One, Appendix II, 484).

In the course of the reign of Henry II, Hume mentions Thomas Becket's "table" three times in his description of his life style as "splendid and
opulent": "the luxury of his table," "the gentlemen, who paid court to him,

and who could not by reason of their great number, find a place at table, should soil their fine cloaths by sitting on a dirty floor," and "the greatest barons were proud of being received at his table" (H, One, VIII, 307-8). But then: "No sooner was Becket installed in this high dignity [Archbishop of Canterbury], which rendered him for life the second person in the kingdom, with some pretensions of aspiring to be the first, than he totally altered his demeanor and conduct, and endeavoured to acquire the character of sanctity. . . . His usual diet [now] was bread; his drink water, which he even rendered farther unpalatable by the mixture of unsavoury herbs" (H, One, VIII, 309). He still continued to serve his guests at his table the finest dishes he could offer.[21] Given his culinary interests, it is surprising that Hume didn't discuss what was on the table; it must have been special from the remarks he makes about the barons and gentlemen.

Within the character narration of Henry (his maternal grandfather was Henry I), Hume includes this statement: "He preserved health, and kept himself from corpulency, to which he was somewhat inclined, by an abstemious diet, and by frequent exercise, particularly hunting" (H, One, IX, 370). And of the number of courses served at a meal during this time, Hume reports:

> We are told by Gyraldus Cambrensis, that the monks and prior of St. Swithun threw themselves one day, prostrate on the ground and in the mire before Henry, complaining, with many tears and much doleful lamentation, that the bishop of Winchester, who was also their abbot, had cut off three dishes from their table. How many has he left you, said the king? Ten only, replied the disconsolate monks. I myself, exclaimed the king, never have more than three; and I enjoin your bishop to reduce you to the same number. (H, One, IX, 375)

Hume probably took delight in showing the abstinence of the king and opulence of the monks—we would assume the reverse for these two stations in life. But more importantly, Hume's satire on the monks is connected to a larger theme of the *History*: its anti-clericalism.

The number of dishes (three) as a meal became a law during the reign of Edward III (ca. 1375). Hume accounts "that no one should be allowed, either for dinner or supper, above three dishes in each course, and not above two courses" (H, Two, XVI, 282), although Hume criticizes "that such ridiculous laws must prove ineffectual, and could never be executed." It was not uncommon during the medieval period that twenty or more dishes in a given course of a meal would be spread out on a large table—smorgasbord style—and people would either eat what was in front of them or select what they wanted. Usually a meal—like dinner or supper—consisted of two courses.

In discussing the horrific treatment of the Jews during the reign of

Richard I (ca. 1190), Hume includes this incident within a long passage: "The king had issued an edit, prohibiting their appearance at his coronation; but some of them, bringing him large presents from their nation, presumed, in confidence of that merit, to approach the hall in which he dined: Being discovered, they were exposed to the insults of the bystanders; they took to flight" (H, One, X, 379). So even while dining, where hospitality is usually in effect, we find that Jews were persecuted. This is not a single incident in Hume's narrative; he writes about the plight of the Jews throughout the early volumes of *The History of England* with sympathy and compassion (e.g., H, Two, XIII, 76-78).

The Nobility

Kitchens and wine cellars were immense in the country estates of the nobility. For instance, "the greater part of [the elder] Spenser's vast estate," Hume reports, "was farmed by the landlord himself, managed by his stewards or bailiffs, and cultivated by his villains [feudal tenants]. Little or none of it was let on lease to husbandmen: Its produce was consumed in rustic hospitality by the baron or his officers" (H, Two, XIV, 179). This produce consisted of "28,000 sheep, 1000 oxen and heifers, 1200 cows with their breed for two years, 560 cart horses, 2000 hogs, together with 600 bacons, 80 carcasses of beef, and 600 muttons in the larder; ten tuns of cider." Because there was "no sown grass, little hay, and no other resource for feeding cattle, the barons, as well as the people, were obliged to kill and salt their oxen and sheep in the beginning of winter, before they became lean upon the common pasture" (H, Two, XIV, 180). This state of affairs signals "the wretched state of ancient husbandry." Another account along the same lines but with expenditures is:

> Stowe, in his survey of London, gives us a curious instance of the hospitality of the ancient nobility in the period: It is taken from the accounts of the cofferer or steward of Thomas earl of Lancaster, and contains the expences of that earl during the year 1313, which was not a year of famine. For the pantry, buttery, and kitchen, 3405 pounds. For 369 pipes of red wine,[22] and two of white, 104 pounds, &c. The whole 7309 pounds; that, is near 22,000 pounds of our present money; and making allowance for the cheapness of commodities [especially the wine], near a hundred thousand pounds. (H, Two, XIV, 181)

Not a year of famine indeed. The enormous cost of this noble hospitality is clearly seen in Queen Elizabeth's country outings two hundred years later. "The expence of hospitality, she [Elizabeth] somewhat encouraged," Hume tells us, "by the frequent visits she paid her nobility, and the sumptuous feasts, which she received from them." He enumerates:

> The earl of Leicester gave her an entertainment in Kenilworth Castle, which was extraordinary for expence and magnificence. Among other particulars, we are told, that three hundred and sixty-five hogsheads of beer were drunk at it. . . . The earl of Derby had a family consisting of two hundred and forty servants. . . . Burleigh, though he was frugal, and had no paternal estate, kept a family consisting of a hundred servants. He had a standing table for gentlemen, and two other tables for persons of meaner condition, which were always served alike, whether he were in town or in the country. . . . Burleigh entertained the queen twelve several times in his country house; where she remained three, four, or five weeks at a time. Each visit cost him two or three thousand pounds. . . . But though there were preserved great remains of the ancient customs, the nobility were, by degrees, acquiring a taste for elegant luxury; . . . the ancient hospitality was the source of vice, disorder, sedition, and idleness. (H, Four, Appendix III, 381-83)

But even before Elizabeth, we find such opulence with Richard II one hundred years earlier (1399).

> This prince lived in a more magnificent manner than perhaps any of his predecessors or successors. His household consisted of 10,000 persons: He had 300 in his kitchen; and all the other offices were furnished in proportion. It must be remarked, that his enormous train [entourage] had tables supplied them at the king's expence, according to the mode of that age. (H, Two, XVII, 332)

If other households were this size, this helps explain the 369 pipes of red wine at the estate of Thomas Earl of Lancaster a generation earlier (1313). The household book of the earl of the family of the Duke of Northumberland shows "that he has eleven priests in his house, besides seventeen persons, chanters, musicians, &c. belonging to his chapel: Yet he has only two cooks for a family of 223 persons, p. 325. [Footnote: *In another place, mention is made of four cooks, p. 388. But I suppose, that the two servants, called in p. 325 groom of the larder and child of the scullery* [back kitchen where dishes are washed, &c.], *are in p. 388. comprehended in the number of cooks.*]" (H, Three, Note [C], 471; Hume's italics).[23] This is certainly a more modest household than that of Richard II.

Even on the battlefield we find exhibited the magnificence of the age: "Henry [VIII] erected a spacious house of wood and canvas, which had been framed in London; and he there [in the plains of Picardy] feasted the French monarch" (Francis). And "In these entertainments, more than in any serious business, did the two kings pass their time, till their departure"

(H, Three, XXVIII, 85, 131). Henry's extravagance is perhaps unparalleled in British history; for instance: "He was so profuse in these liberalities, that he is said to have given a woman the whole revenue of a convent, as a reward for making a pudding, which happened to gratify his palate" [source: *Fuller's Church History*] (H, Three, XXXI, 255). Under "Miscellaneous transactions," Hume lists:

> It was not till the end of this reign [Henry VIII] that any sallads, carrots, turnips, or other edible roots were produced in England. The little of these vegetables, that was used, was formerly imported from Holland and Flanders. [source: Anderson, vol. i, p. 338] Queen Catherine, when she wanted a sallad, was obliged to dispatch a messenger thither on purpose. The use of hops and the planting of them, was introduced from Flanders about the beginning of this reign, or the end of the preceding. (H, Three, XXXIII, 327)

Aside from Italy, Hume rightfully considers Flanders the culinary mecca of Europe during this time. In discussing the fourteenth century, he remarks that "all trade and manufactures indeed were then at a very low ebb. The only country in the northern parts of Europe, where they seem to have risen to any tolerable degree of improvement, was Flanders" (H, Two, XIV, 178). On the same subject, he later adds: "Guicciardini tells us, that the Flemings in this century [fifteenth] learned from Italy all the refinements in arts, which they taught the rest of Europe. The progress, however, of the arts were still very slow and backward in England" (H, Two, XVIII, 351). In speaking of Italy, he had this to say: "If we consider the magnificent and elegant manner in which the Venetian and other Italian noblemen then lived . . . we shall not wonder that they considered the ultra-mountaine nations as barbarous. The Flemish also seem to have much excelled the English and even the French" (H, Three, Note [C], 472). And in the same vein, he wrote: "Italy was, during that age [Henry VIII], the seat of religion, of literature, and of commerce; and as it possessed alone that luster, which has since been shared out among other nations, it attracted the attention of all Europe, and every acquisition, which was made there, appeared more important than its weight in the balance of power was, strictly speaking, entitled to" (H, Two, XXVIII, 120). I take these quotations to include food, and the one from Note [C] has food as its context, so Hume is in line with what recent food historians take to be the origins of cuisine: Italy, then France, and then it spread elsewhere in Europe, although Spain and Portugal followed Italy in strict chronological order.[24] Hume discussed Spain and its royalty, but not its cuisine (H, Four, XLI, 215).

One other thing worth noting about the reign of Henry VIII is the statute prices of "flesh-meat," i.e., beef, mutton, pork, and veal, but prices were also fixed on poultry, cheese, and butter. Hume enumerates:

> Beef and pork were ordered to be sold at a halfpenny a pound: Mutton and veal at a halfpenny half a farthing, money of that age. The preamble of the statute says, that these four species of butcher's meat were the food of the poorer sort. This act was afterwards repealed. [source: 33 Hen. VIII. c.11] (H, Three, XXXIII, 330)

What the nobles and the ladies dined on and what time of day Hume listed from the earl's household book:

> The drinking . . . was tolerable, namely, ten tuns and two hogsheads of Gascogny wine,[25] at the rate of four pounds thirteen shillings and four-pence a tun . . . . The family rose at six in the morning, dined at ten, and supped at four in the afternoon . . . . My lord and lady have set on their table for breakfast at seven o'clock in the morning a quart of beer; as much wine; two pieces of salt fish, six red-herrings, four white ones, or a dish of sprats.[26] In flesh days half a chyne of mutton, or a chyne of beef boiled. (H, Three, Note [C], 470)

A "chyne" or "chyme" is the backbone with ribs. From the use of the term, it appears that it was also a unit of measurement or weight.

There were some unusual things that happened in the name of food. For example, Oliver Cromwell was a man with a strange sense of humor: "He frequently gave feasts to his inferior officers; and when the meat was set upon the table, a signal was given; the soldiers rushed in upon them; and with much noise, tumult, and confusion, ran away with all the dishes, and disappointed the guests of their expected meal" [source: Bates] (H, Six, LXI, 90). This anecdote about Cromwell presenting food to his officers and then having it snatched away says something about Hume's attitude toward the "manners" of Cromwell and his movement. Given the importance of refined manners to Hume, the incident can be read as an indictment of the excesses of the Parliamentary causes, the Protectorate, etc. In other words, the anecdote testifies to the perversion of manners at this point in English history.

The Common People

By contrast with the culinary spread of the nobility, we find the common people, the servant, and the soldier just barely above the level of subsistence.

> Their whole equipage consisted of a bag of oat-meal, which, as a supply in case of necessity, each soldier carries behind him; together

with a light plate of iron, on which he instantly baked the meal into a cake, in open fields. But his chief subsistance was the cattle which he seized; and his cookery was as expeditious as all his operations. After fleaing the animal, he placed the skin, loose and hanging in the form of a bag, upon some stakes, he poured water into it, kindled a fire below, and thus made it serve as a caldron for the boiling of his victuals. (H, Two, 184, ca. 1327)

In 1512 at the Battle of Guinegate, "Fontrailles [a French officer] appeared at the head of 800 horsemen, each of whom carried a sack of gunpowder behind him, and two quarters of bacon" (H, Three, XXVII, 103). But these were good conditions—many times soldiers were left to pillage and fend for themselves wherever they were: provisions were slim to none. Sometimes a soldier's diet had disastrous consequences.

The plague creeped in among the English soldiers; and being encreased by their fatigue and bad diet [for they were but ill supplied with provisions (source: Forbes, vol. ii, p. 377, 498.)] it made such ravages, that sometimes a hundred men a day died of it, and there remained not at last fifteen hundred in a condition to do duty. . . . To encrease the misfortune, the infected army brought the plague with them into England, where it swept off great multitudes, particularly in the city of London. Above twenty thousand persons, there, died of it in one year. (H, Four, XXXIX, 64-65)

"The native Irish were so poor," Hume writes, "that their country afforded few other commodities than cattle and oatmeal, which were easily concealed or driven away on the approach of the enemy; and as Elizabeth was averse to the expence requisite for supporting her armies, the English found much difficulty in pushing their advantages, and in pursuing the rebels into the bogs, woods, and other fastnesses, to which they retreated" (H, Four, XLIV, 316). And during a skirmish with the English in 1643, the Irish soldiers "for want of food . . . had been obliged to eat their own horses" (H, Five, LVI, 425). But the city dwellers had it better—here is one instance which involves food symbolism of the politics of the times. There was joy and exultation displayed throughout London when general George Monk declared a free parliament and dissolution of the old:

The populace, more outrageous in their festivity, made the air resound with acclamations, and illuminated every street with signals of jollity and triumph. Applauses of the general were every where intermingled with detestation against the [old] parliament. The most ridiculous inventions were adopted, in order to express this latter passion. At every bonfire rumps were roasted; and where these could no longer be found, pieces of flesh were cut into that shape: And the funeral of the parliament (the populace exclaimed) was celebrated by these symbols of hatred and derision. (H, Six, LXII, 133)

During the rise of Protestantism (including independents, Presbyterians, anti-royalists, fanatics, zealots, millenarians, and Deists), fasting put a damper on feasting and elegant dining. In 1645 parliament ordered a fast on the last Wednesday of every month, and King Charles I, "that he might combat the parliament with their own weapons, appointed likewise a monthly fast, when the people should be instructed in the duties of loyalty and of submission to the higher powers; and he chose the second Friday of every month for the devotion of the royalists" (H, Five, LVII, 445-46). Parliament countered with "a new and more solemn fast" by the independents. "But these institutions," Hume notes, "they [parliament] found great difficulty to execute; and the people were resolved to be merry when they themselves pleased, not when the parliament should prescribe it to them" (H, Five, LVII, 452n-53n). He then adds: "Even minced pyes,[27] which custom had made a Christmas dish among the churchmen, was regarded, during that season, as a profane and superstitious viand by the sectaries; though at other times it agreed very well with their stomachs" (H, Five, LVII, 453n). The development of cuisine in the British Isles was retarded because of religious prescriptions such as these. At the beginning of the English commonwealth (1643), the impact of Protestantism is seen on food practices: "Even in a feast, which the city [London] gave to the parliament and council of state, it was deemed a requisite precaution, if we may credit Walker and Dugdale, to swear all the cooks, that they would serve nothing but wholesome food to them" (H, Six, LX, 13). Such was the chilling affect of Protestantism on British cuisine for this century.

As for servants, Hume again relies on the earl's household book (1509):

If a servant be absent a day, his mess is struck off: If he go on my lord's business, board wages are allowed him, eight-pence a day for his journey in winter, five-pence in summer: When he stays in any place, two-pence a day are allowed him, beside the maintainance of his horse. Somewhat above a quarter of wheat [eight bushels] is allowed for every mouth throughout the year; and the wheat is estimated at five shillings and eight-pence a quarter: Two hogsheads are to be made of a quarter; which amounts to about a bottle and a third of beer a day to each person, p. 4. and the beer will not be very strong. . . . The other servants, as they eat salted meat, almost through the whole year, and with bad and unhealthy diet: So that there cannot be any thing more erroneous, than the magnificent idea formed of the *Roast Beef of Old England*. (H, Three, Note [C], 470)

This passage is corroborated by Doris Mary Stenton: "If he [the villain; feudal tenant] worked all day the lord generally gave him food at mid-day, ale, or in some parts cider, bread and cheese, more occasionally meat or fish, or a sort of soup of which the main ingredients were beans and peas."[28] So not much had changed diet-wise in the span of four hundred years for the servant.

Conclusion

The previous three sections demonstrate that *The History of England* has a subtext of the history of food, in particular, food of the British Isles. However, this history is primarily the social setting of food and food commodities. The narratives of contemporary food historians—like Tannahill and Albala—are accounts of early recipes and unusual cooking methods or techniques. We do not find recipes in Hume's narrative, but we do find some discussion of cooking procedures; for example, the makeshift caldron made from cow hide of a field soldier or "chyne" of mutton or boiled beef from the earl's household book. But not all food historians are recipe-driven in their narratives; one example is Colin Spencer's brief history of food of the British Isles.[29]

In the first section, we found recipes mentioned, but no actual recipes given, so Hume was not at that level of culinary communication with his readers or audience. In spite of this omission, we do find an intense interest in food and its related matters. The earlier volumes of *The History of England*, which contain more food references than the later ones,[30] were written in the 1760s when Hume was entertaining people with his "warm suppers," and probably working his way through his recipe collection.

Hume again reminds us: "At this aera [era], it may be proper to stop a moment, and take a general survey of the age, so far as regards manners, finances, arms, commerce, arts and sciences. The chief use of history is, that it affords materials for disquisitions of this nature; and it seems the duty of an historian to point out the proper inferences and conclusions" (H, Six, LXII, 140). Included in this general survey is: "The first mention of tea, coffee, and chocolate, is about 1660. Asparagus, artichoaks, colli-flower, and a variety of sallads, were about the same time introduced into England" [source: Anderson, vol. ii, p. 111.] (H, Six, LXII, 148). Actually, coffee's appearance was before 1660, because the first coffeehouse in England was at Oxford University in 1650 and two years later in London.[31] Hume talks about the coffeehouses as scenes of political conversation and about Charles's administration issuing a proclamation to suppress these places of rendezvous. "The king," Hume subsequently adds, "observing the people to be much dissatisfied, yielded to a petition of the coffee-men, who promised for the future to restrain all seditious discourse in their houses; and the proclamation was recalled" (H, Six, LXVI, 296). As Linda Civitello infers: "Coffee changed more than just eating habits—it changed social and political habits as well. For the first time, people had a public place and a reason to congregate that did not involve alcohol."[32] Prior to this, hardly anyone was ever sober! (Even though the wine was diluted with water, they started drinking beer and wine with breakfast and continued throughout the day; see the earl's household book passages cited above.) One of the more important developments in the history of food is the spice trade. Hume acknowledges this with mention of the spice trade several times in the *History*.[33] Battles and wars were fought over the spice trade. Hume finds that:

> The passage to the East-Indies had been opened to the English during the reign of Elizabeth; but the trade to those parts was not entirely established till this reign, when the East-India company received a new patent, enlarged their stock to 1,500,000 pounds [source: Journ. 26th Nov. 1621.], and fitted out several ships on these adventures. . . . Impatient to have the sole possession of the spice-trade, which the English then shared with them [the Dutch], they assumed a jurisdiction over a factory of the latter in the island of Amboyna. (H, Five, Appendix IV, 145)

Hume slips in a spice reference in a list of loans that Charles I had made (1640): "All the pepper was bought from the East-India company upon trust, and sold, at a great discount, for ready money" [source: May, p. 63.] (H, Five, LIII, 278). Charles was reduced to such financial extremes as this to raise money for his projects.

One noticeable deficiency of Elizabeth's marvelous reign was patents for monopolies on commodities that she granted to her servants and courtiers who in turn sold them to others and soon the inflated prices "put invincible restraints upon all commerce, industry, and emulation in the arts" (H, Four, XLIV, 344). Among the items were currants, salt, aniseed, vinegar, bottles, pots, brushes, saltpeter, oil of blubber, dried pilchards,[34] and beer. "These monopolists were so exorbitant in their demands," Hume comments, "that in some places they raised the price of salt, from sixteen-pence a bushel, to fourteen or fifteen shillings" [source: Sir Simon D'Ewes, p. 648] (H, Four, XLIV, 345). In 1601, "the queen, who perceived how odious monopolies had become, and what heats were likely to rise, sent for the speaker, and desired him to aquaint the house, that she would immediately cancel the most grievous and oppressive of these patents" (H, Four, XLIV, 346). So Elizabeth ended her reign with the removal of some of the oppressive measures that "preserved the affections of her people" (H, Four, XLIV, 347). This action was carried further by her successor (H, Five, XLV, 20), but it was not until the reign and administration of James II before monopolies came to a complete end. They are one reason that England lagged behind the other European nations in the development of their cuisines. Hume appreciated this constraint on food and the impact on its development. In other words, the monopolies on spices in the reign of Elizabeth I restricted the development of English cuisine, and it can be viewed as an instance of a major theme of *The History of England:* restrictive economic practices retard cultural development.

He first utilized some of the sources for the history of food in the British Isles that recent food historians also used; for instance, the record made by William Fitzstephen, Thomas Becket's secretary and historian,[35] was employed by Bridget Ann Henisch in her narrative.[36] And there are other sources that today's food historians of the British Isles might profit from by examining; for example, the earl's household book (H, Three, Note [C], 469-72), which I have used several times in some of the above sections.

When we look at these above sections that deal with the *History*, we find a fairly detailed account of the history of British food practices and products that is substantial and impressive. It is my hope that today's food historians will take a serious look at Hume's historical narrative as a source and inspiration for further studies. It is remarkable to find this written in the eighteenth century; however, given Hume's culinary interests, it makes sense. All of this was initially reflected in the correspondence and essays, but it is the historical narrative that demonstrates the depth of his culinary interests.

Notes

1. Ernest Campbell Mossner, *The Forgotten Hume: Le bon David* (New York: Columbia University Press, 1943), 208; hereafter cited with page numbers as TFH.

2. For a discussion of this, see chapter 4.

3. G. Birkbeck Hill, ed., *Letters of David Hume to William Strahan* (Oxford: The Clarendon Press, 1888), 112, 116. This is referred to as "the note above" in the body of the paper.

4. Ernest Campbell Mossner, *The Life of David Hume* (Second Edition; Oxford: Clarendon Press, 1980), 559-60, with slight alterations, gives the same quotation from Hill; hereafter cited with page numbers as LDH.

5. Hill, *Letters*, 291. This characterization helps explain why Hume probably didn't have an amorous relationship with Ms. Irvine as did Descartes with his live-in.

6. See the pioneer of food history, Reay Tannahill, *Food in History* (New York: Stein and Day, 1973), ch. 15, which discusses eighteenth century Europe.

7. James Peterson, *Splendid Soups* (New York: Bantam Books, 1993), 446-47.

8. Philip Hyman and Mary Hyman, "Printing the Kitchen: French Cookbooks, 1480-1800," in *Food: A Culinary History from Antiquity to the Present*, under the direction of Jean-Louis Flandrin and Massimo Montanari, English Edition by Albert Sonnenfeld (New York: Penguin Books, 2000), 394-402, see 398.

9. David Hume, "The Sceptic," in his *Essays Moral, Political and Literary*, edited by Eugene F. Miller (Revised Edition; Indianapolis: Liberty Classics, 1987), 163, 162; hereafter cited parenthetically with an "E," followed by page numbers.

10. For a discussion of this concession, see S. K. Wertz, "Hume's Aesthetic Realism," *Southwest Philosophy Review* XXII # 2 (July, 2006): 53-61.

11. Jancis Robinson, ed., *The Oxford Companion to Wine* (Oxford and New York: Oxford University Press, 1994), 242.

12. See John Hailman, *Thomas Jefferson on Wine* (Jackson: University Press of Mississippi, 2006), Introduction and Chapter One: "Early Wines."

13. David Hume, *The History of England from the Invasion of Julius Caesar to The Revolution in*

1688, edited by William B. Todd (In Six Volumes; Indianapolis: Liberty Classics, 1983), vol. Six, ch. LXI, p. 90, where Hume accounts the protector opening a bottle of wine with a corkscrew. Hereafter citations are to "H," followed by volume, chapter or appendix, and page numbers.

14. In *The Oxford Companion to Wine*, 242. For more on the term "claret," see Hailman, *Thomas Jefferson on Wine*, 36-37.

15. E. C. Mossner, "An Apology for David Hume, Historian," *Proceedings of the Modern Languages Association* LVI (1941): 657-690; 679 and 687.

16. S. K. Wertz, *Between Hume's Philosophy and History: Historical Theory and Practice* (New York: University Press of America, 2000), ch. 8.

17. See Maguelonne Toussaint-Samat, *History of Food*, translated from the French by Anthea Bell (Oxford: Blackwell Publishers, 1992), 701-07. I will discuss coffee later in the last section.

18. For Hume's accounts, see H, One, X, 400; H, Four, XLIV, 313; H, Two, XXII, 470; H, Six, LX, 17.

19. Sharon Tyler Herbst, *Food Lover's Companion* (Hauppauge, New York: Barron's Educational Series, Inc., 1990): "Varieties of this long (about 21 inches), eel-shaped fish are found in both fresh and marine waters. It is a delicately flavored but extremely fatty fish, which makes it indigestible for many people" (252). Apparently this included King Henry I.

20. Tannahill, *Food in History*, 246.

21. For what those dishes might have been, consult, e.g., Maggie Black, *The Medieval Cookbook* (New York: Thames and Hudson, 1992), for things like *Stekys of venson or bef, Samon roste in Sauce, Leche lumbarde, Payn ragoun, Caboches in potage*, and *Capouns in councy*; for a complete list of dishes and recipes, see 141.

22. The origin of the wine term "pipe" is unknown, but it obviously predates this period; a pipe of wine is about 600 liters. So 369 pipes would be 221,400 liters of wine! The earl must have had many thirsty guests and "family" to say the least. The earliest reference to "pipes of wine" is 1090 (H, One, V, 232). For a discussion of the term, see *The Oxford Companion to Wine*, 738-39.

23. Hume's eye for historical detail is amazing. His quibble with the discrepancy of the number of cooks in the household book testifies to the depth of his culinary interests.

24. Ken Albala, *Food in Early Modern Europe* (Westport, Connecticut: Greenwood Press, 2003), ch. 4.

25. For a brief discussion of Gascogny wine, see *The Oxford Companion to Wine*, 423. And for a more detailed account, see "The wine trade with Gascony," by Frank Sargent, *British History Online* (accessed in April, 2008).

26. "A close relative of the herring, the sprat is a small (about 6 inches in length) fish that can be found off the European Atlantic coast. Because of its high fat content, sprats are perfect for broiling or grilling. They're also available either in salted or smoked" in *Food Lover's Companion*, 442.

27. "Pye" or "pie" meant *a dish of meat or fruit covered with paste* (or dough) and not something necessarily sweet or dessert-like, in *The Little Oxford Dictionary of Current English*, compiled by George Ostler, revised and supplemented by J. Coulson (Third Edition; Oxford: The Clarendon Press, 1941), 369. "A wager of a hundred pounds was laid, and stakes made" [by the closest royalists], Hume writes, "that the king [Charles II.] should eat no more Christmas pyes" (H, Six, LXVII, 336). Food historian Sandra Sherman says: "In eighteenth-century cookbooks, pies are a cornerstone of culinary art. Hannah Glasse, for example, offers an astonishing 'Yorkshire Christmas Pie' in which a pigeon is wrapped in a partridge, which is wrapped in a fowl, then a goose, and finally a turkey, before the layers are baked in a huge crust packed with hares, woodcocks, game, and 'at least four Pounds of Butter'" in *Fresh from the Past: Recipes and Revelations from Moll Flanders' Kitchen*, by Sandra Sherman, with collaboration of Henry and Karen Chotkowski (New York: Taylor Trade Publications, 2004), 167. Sometimes wine, beer, and cream were added after it was served so those ingredients could pouch in the mixture to give a custard-like consistency, then people would gather around with spoons or bread and partake. Indeed, this was a dish fit for a king. "From Cumberland came 'standing pie' or 'sweet pie,'" Adrian Bailey reminisces, "filled with chopped mutton, apples and raisins, the grandfather of the mince pie" in *The Cooking of the British Isles* (Food of the World series; New York: Time-Life Books, 1969), 194; and "[t]hree centuries ago mince pie was a huge dish called 'Christmas pye,' and described as 'a most learned mixture of Neats-tongues [ox tongues], chicken, eggs, various kinds of Spicery, etc.'" (195). Nowadays, the pies are quite small and contain dried fruit (previously marinated in brandy), spicies, and suet; for a recipe, see 200-01.

28. Doris Mary Stenton, *English Society in the Early Middle Ages (1066-1307)*, (Fourth Edition; Baltimore, Md.: Penguin Books, 1967), 141.

29. In *The Cambridge World History of Food*, edited by Kenneth F. Kiple and Kriemhild Coneé Ornelas (Cambridge: Cambridge University Press, 2000), II, 1217-26.

30. The breakdown of food (including beer and wine) references in the *History* is: One (37), Two (40), Three (25), Four (25), Five (33), and Six (31); of those my paper utilized 53 of the 191, so I have only given you a glimpse of what there is, but I think I have shown you the most interesting passages that pertain to the history of food.

31. Linda Civitello, *Cuisine and Culture: A History of Food and People* (Hoboken, New Jersey: John Wiley & Sons, Inc., 2004), 150. Her coffee chronology indicates that in 1616 the Dutch smuggled a coffee tree from Aden to Holland.

32. *Cuisine and Culture: A History of Food and People*, 149.

33. Other mentions of the spice trade are: H, Three, XXVI, 80; Four, XLI, 215; Appendix III, 375 ("In the year 1600, the queen granted the first patent to the East-India company."); Five, XLVI, 39; Six, LXI, 67, 79, 81-82; LXII, 148; LXXI, 501, 538; and LXIV, 208.

34. "A small, high-fat saltwater fish found in abundance off the European Atlantic coast from Scandinavia to Portugal. Though Europeans can buy fresh pilchard from July to December, it's usually canned in oil or tomato sauce like sardines" in *Food Lover's Companion*, 349.

35. William Fitzstephen, *The Life and Death of Thomas Becket*, translated by G. Greenaway (London: Folio Society, 1961), 42.

36. Bridget Ann Henisch, *Fast and Feast: Food in Medieval Society* (University Park: The Pennsylvania State University Press, 1976), 191, 198.

7

Revel's Conception of Cuisine: Platonic or Hegelian?

The chef's art is precisely the art of knowing what he can borrow from various traditions without betraying them.

JEAN-FRANÇOIS REVEL

* * *

In *Culture and Cuisine*,[1] Jean-François Revel draws a distinction between different kinds of cuisine—popular (regional) cuisine and erudite (professional) cuisine. Revel is the first philosopher to take food seriously and to offer a topology for food practices. His contribution has been acknowledged by Deane Curtin, who offers an interpretation of Revel's conceptual scheme along Platonic lines.[2] In this chapter I review his interpretation, find it wanting in certain respects, and develop an alternative reading of Revel along Hegelian lines. My interpretation, I conclude, is a more sympathetic and comprehensive reading of his text. But first let us examine Professor Curtin's interpretation of Revel.

A Platonic Interpretation

Curtin thinks that if Plato had written a philosophy of food, it would have been very similar to Revel's. Curtin describes Revel's philosophy as essentially dualistic and concludes:

> Revel perfectly replicates Plato's distinction between practices that involve knowledge (erudite cuisine, which has intellectual rules that can be taught and applied elsewhere), and knacks or routines (popular cuisine, which is practical, must be shown rather than explained, and cannot be exported outside those craft traditions). Perhaps it is not intended as dismissively as Plato's, but Revel's distinction is, nonetheless, hierarchical. International cuisine is regarded as the

summit of gastronomic experience. (CET,125.)

On one hand, popular cuisine is linked to the land and regional traditions. It is usually prepared by the women in the family who use the produce of a region and the different seasons in close accord with nature. Popular cuisine is "based on age-old skills, transmitted unconsciously by way of imitation and habit, of applying methods of cooking patiently tested and associated with certain cooking utensils and recipients prescribed by a long tradition." (CET,125/148;CAC,19) Popular cuisine aims at perfecting nutrition.[3]

On the other hand, erudite cuisine, Revel says, "is based by contrast on invention, renewal, experimentation." (CET,125;CAC,19) Chefs are trained or educated in this cuisine; it is an end in itself that is dedicated to food for food's sake. It knows no boundaries, like land or custom, yet "it is a striking fact that truly great erudite cuisine has arisen principally in places where a tasty and varied traditional cuisine already existed, serving it as a sort of basis." (CAC,20) So "a chef who loses all contact with popular cuisine," Revel adds, "rarely succeeds in putting something really exquisite together." Hence, these two cuisines actually interact with one another, and it is mainly in international cuisine where that takes place. The Platonic interpretation of the cuisines gives no account of their interaction—only their difference. Platonic interaction runs only from the world of forms to the world of appearance—what reality the secondary world has is only in participation in the formal world. But with an empirical practice, like cuisine, the participation is *in reverse*—the regional cuisines dictate the involvement. So a Platonist reading is counterintuitive when it comes to food practices. Curtin seems to treat international cuisine as under erudite cuisine—a final development of erudite cuisine—which he described earlier as "the summit of gastronomic experience." This is in keeping with his dualistic (admittedly Platonic) interpretation of Revel. But when we look beyond this discussion (CAC, ch. 2) to his later chapter (8) on international cuisine, we find that a third category of cuisine has emerged from the others. This situation calls for an alternative reading, and Hegel's dialectic of opposition or negativity and its resolution provides a useful one.

A Hegelian Interpretation

Our model from Hegel is first a leading idea or starting point (Spirit)—popular cuisine, x, which arrives initially on the cultural (world) scene. Then opposition of that point emerges, like moving from the rooted, regional cuisine that is not exportable to a cuisine that is exportable. So a negation develops which is the erudite cuisine, y—the opposite qualities of those found in popular cuisine. When these two opposing concepts are confronted (*aufheben*),[4] they give way to a resolution, which in this case is international cuisine. This dialectical interpretation of the history of cuisine becomes persuasive when we examine Revel's characterization of international cuisine. Here is his clarification of the term:

> I mean by "international cuisine" not a corpus of recipes, but a body of *methods*, of *principles* amenable to *variations*, depending on different local and financial possibilities, just as this body of methods and principles is conducive to variations within a given country, depending on seasonal possibilities. The expression "international cuisine" takes on a pejorative connotation when it designates a certain false grand cuisine also known as "hotel cuisine," a cuisine that retains the outward features and, above all, the vocabulary of the Grand Cuisine of the nineteenth century, but that limits itself to drowning various foods in all-purpose sauces with pretentious names and to engaging in certain types of spectacular presentation for the mere sake of display. (CET, 245; CAC, 214.)

Erudite cuisine is essentially a corpus of recipes, but it also includes "a number of such erudite gastronomic revolutions," (I count three), that "have taken place, the two most important of which, at least insofar as European cuisine is concerned, occurred at the beginning of the eighteenth century [the 'bourgeois' cuisine] and at the beginning of the nineteenth [the international cuisine or the Grand Cuisine]." (CET, 148-49; CAC, 20) Both of these can represent a step backward in culinary advancement. Now we have undergone the third revolution—a negation of these two cuisines. Notice that these later cuisines are corruptible, whereas the popular cuisine and the erudite cuisine are not corruptible. The latter two do appear to have conditions—conditions of sincerity and accuracy, respectively. As the above passage indicates, Grand Cuisine can be corrupted and become "*bad* international cuisine that *transports the picturesqueness* of a regional dish without *transporting its principles*, because they have not been understood." (CET, 247; CAC, 218) This quotation is followed by one which is distinctly Hegelian: "When such comprehension [resolution] exists, on the other hand, real Grand Cuisine can sometimes give the diversity of local registers an interpretation that is at once faithful [starting point: popular cuisine] and new" [opposition or negation: erudite cuisine].

So the "bourgeois" cuisine of the urban middle class is a growth or development of erudite cuisine just as international cuisine was a century later. The "bourgeois" cuisine, Revel thinks, is a "marriage" of the two cuisines, the popular and the erudite, "the cuisine unconsciously transmitted *and* the cuisine deliberately created" (emphasis added). (CET, 149; CAC, 20) International cuisine is a marriage of sorts, too, but only to the extent that it never loses contact with the popular—that the latter serves as a basis for the former. This service is never unconsciously transmitted as it is in "bourgeois" cuisine. Hence, the difference between the two more recent cuisines.

Revel sums up by stating "that cuisine that from the beginning of the nineteenth century came to be known as Grand Cuisine, the invariable expression after [Antoine] Carême, is international by vocation. It consists, certainly, of knowing how to make various dishes [erudite cuisine] but even more of knowing *the conditions allowing them to be made.*" (CET, 247; CAC, 223) So this is the distinction between erudite cuisine and international cuisine or Grand Cuisine—the depth of knowledge employed in food preparation and food making or food production. As he later amends: "It is not the time spent in preparation nor the amount of money that make the difference here, but rather *the conception,* and this is as true of simple recipes as it is of complex ones" (emphasis added). (CET, 249; CAC, 225)

Consequently the evolution from popular cuisine and erudite cuisine produced a new and different kind of cuisine that combined elements of both in diverse contributory ways: the base from popular cuisine and the knowledge of recipes from erudite cuisine. The knowledge in international cuisine becomes a conception or understanding of the conditions for food making. So this is not just an extension of erudite cuisine, but a transformation of it (*aufheben*), where elements of both basic cuisines contribute. That contribution, it seems to me, is more adequately captured in a Hegelian model than a Platonic one. The culinary evolution is not "hierarchical," as Curtin suggests, but dialectical in nature.

Craft/Art Distinction

Another way we can make the contrast between international cuisine and the regional or erudite cuisines is to use the art/craft distinction. Regional and erudite cuisines are crafts: regional cuisine is skilled manual work made with the purpose of nurturing that is handed down from generation to generation, and erudite cuisine is craft because a cook carefully follows a recipe in order to produce a preconceived result by means of consciously controlled and directed actions.[5] Both cuisines satisfy Collingwood's conception of craft: they involve a distinction between means (the agricultural products, like plants, meats, spices, and the actions concerning them, i.e., preparing and cooking them) and end (food, like a dish, a meal, a menu and their respective actions—eating). Other obvious distinctions are planning and execution, raw material and finished product or artifact, and form and matter. (These distinctions are related to one another.) Some of these ideas are seen at work in Revel; e.g., "there are certain skillful touches to improve the dish [*bouillabaisse marseillaise*] that depend not on the recipe but on its execution." (CET, 147; CAC, 15)

International cuisine is craft too, but it is a craft that has evolved into an art. "Art is a personal creation," Revel comments, "but this creation [cuisine] is impossible without a base in traditional craftsmanship." (CET, 149; CAC, 22) This artistic implication is clearly seen in the following passage:

> In its attempt to assimilate the greatest number of regional dishes possible, international cuisine must be very attentive to the methods of cooking and the sources of the elements that give them their scent and flavor. If this condition is respected, it can absorb a very great number of ideas, because it alone is capable of comprehending the *creative principle* behind this or that local knack of preparing a dish and of applying consciously what was executed unconsciously and mechanically. For international cuisine has curiosity as its motivating force, unlike regional cuisine, which for its part is *obliged* to remain routine and exclusive, finding its salvation purely and simply in the refusal to take into consideration any other register of flavors than its own. (CET, 246; CAC, 216)

International cuisine is, in other words, flexible, experimental, creative, and original in its outlook. "The production of something new in creation" is (according to Tolstoy) "real artistic activity."[6] An excellent recent example of this cuisine is chef Stephan Pyles of Dallas, Texas, who has transformed regional/erudite cuisines (Western, Mexican, Tex-Mex) into the new Southwestern cuisine (an international cuisine).[7] His sweet potato tamales and brown butter-mango custard tart are testimonials to Pyles's creativity and originality. His legacy is from Carême, and Revel speaks of this cuisine as art (which means both craft and fine art).[8] Revel narrates:

> Like classic art, the result of Carême's art is always very simple and immediately obvious. What is complicated is the process for arriving at this result, a process whose aim is not to superimpose flavors but, quite the contrary, to isolate them and set them in relief. . . . Carême introduced into cuisine what in painting are called "values"; that is to say, he was the first to put across the fact that flavors and odors must be judged not in the absolute but according to their mutual relationships. (CAC, 258)

"Following in Carême's footsteps, several masters of international cuisine," and Stephan Pyles is a prime example I might add, "were to invent new dishes, to create a recognizable personal style, but they did not change the basic principles [and methods] of cuisine." (CAC, 263) "The importance of artistic activity," Tolstoy reminds us, "is properly attributed to creation—that is, to artistic production." He gives this condition of novelty such a strong interpretation that we wonder what would satisfy it: "something that is perfectly new to him, which he has never heard of from anybody." (*op.cit.*) Very few things would qualify as creativity under such a definition, but the realm of food is one good possibility. Frequently chef Pyles amazes his audiences with gastronomical creations that satisfy Tolstoy's condition of novelty. Such a radical transformation is captured by a Hegelian interpretation of the historical process. This is cuisine—to use a Hegelian phrase—becoming conscious of itself. The Platonic reading misses the mark.

Notes

1. Jean-François Revel, *Culture and Cuisine: A Journey through the History of Food*, translated from the French by Helen R. Lane (Garden City, New York: Doubleday & Company, 1979/1982); hereafter referred as CAC, followed by page number(s). Also reprinted in CET (see the next note), 145-52, 244-50.
2. Deane W. Curtin, "Recipes for Values," in *Cooking, Eating, Thinking: Transformative Philosophies of Food*, edited by Deane W. Curtin and Lisa M. Heldke (Bloomington: Indiana University Press, 1992), 124-26. Hereafter referred to as CET, followed by page number(s). Lisa Heldke also is suggestive of such an interpretation; see her "Foodmaking as a Thoughtful Practice," in CET, 213-14.
3. Leo Tolstoy, in *What Is Art?* (1896/1898), makes a similar point in regard to peasant food; that it is nutritious; see the next chapter (8).
4. In his "The World Spirit," *Southwestern Journal of Philosophy* II #1 & 2 (Spr. & Sum., 1971): 153-61, Rex Martin gives the following characterization of *aufheben*: "The literal meaning of the [German] term is *to lift up*: by this it is suggested that the x/y otherness is moved to a new context under another heading. A second sense is *to abolish*: what is abolished is the 'opposition' or appearance of incompatibility of the pair. Finally, we have the meaning *to preserve*: their otherness, their distinctions are preserved at the same time that their apparent opposition is annulled. The leading idea of philosophical dialectic is, by lifting up, 'to integrate and reorder.' One chooses a new concept (one relatively more complete) and a new organizing point of view (under some new superordinate concept)." (154) In the domain of cuisine, we have international cuisine as our new superordinate concept, the x is regional cuisine and the y otherness is erudite cuisine. They are integrated and reordered into international cuisine where certain things are "preserved" (a chef continues to return to regional cooking for ideas and inspiration) and are "abolished" (the reliance of knack or unconscious skills in regional cooking and the sole preoccupation with recipes in erudite cooking). What remains is "lifted up" into the new concept, international cuisine. (See note 8.)
5. See R. G. Collingwood, *The Principles of Art* (1938), Book I, Part II, section 1.
6. Leo Tolstoy, "On Art" (1896), sec. III.
7. Consult Stephan Pyles, *The New Texas Cuisine* (New York: Doubleday, 1993), and *New Tastes from Texas (as Seen on Public Television)* (New York: Clarkson Potter/Publishers, 1998). I'm sure we will see another book on the new tastes from Mexico, since we have seen a series on that theme on PBS (public broadcast system).
8. Revel assumes, and does not argue for, international cuisine as art: "the summits of this *art* are reached in precisely those periods when the refinement of recipes *allies* complexity of conception with lightness of touch in execution" (CET,145;CAC,13; emphases added—a unity of opposites of sorts) and "*the real art* lies neither in products in their natural state nor in heaviness and complexity: a great chef glorifies natural elements, uses them in ways that enhance their essence, knows how to extract their aromas and flavors and set off their consistencies—but he does so by transposing them into a new register, *where they disappear only to be reborn as a whole that owes its existence to intelligence*" (ibid., emphases added). This latter statement sounds dialectical and Hegelian to me; for a definitive discussion of Hegel's dialectic, see Gustav E. Mueller, "The Hegel Legend of 'Thesis-Antithesis-Synthesis,'" *Journal of the History of Ideas* XIX #3 (June, 1958): 411-14, who objects to a linear, mechanical interpretation, and who

suggests an "ever growing development" based on a biological paradigm. For one of Hegel's accounts of "*aufheben*," see *The Encyclopaedia Logic (Part I of the Encyclopaedia of Philosophical Sciences with the Zusätze)*, a new translation with Introduction and notes by T. F. Geraets, W. A. Suchting, and H. S. Harris (Indianapolis: Hackett Publishing Company, 1991), 153-57 (sec. 96). In the *Introduction to The Philosophy of History*, translated by Leo Rauch (Indianapolis: Hackett Publishing Company, 1988), Hegel writes (in chapter 4): "The determinate form of Spirit does not merely pass away naturally in time, but is negated (*aufgehoben*) in the self-activating, self-reflecting activity of self-consciousness. Since this negation is an activity of thought, it is (at once and the same time) a preservation and a transfiguration." (81) (Also see note 4.) The marriage of craft and art, by the way, is uncharacteristic of Collingwood's discussion (see note 5), but then he did not entertain food as a possibility.

8

The Analogy between Food and Art: Tolstoy and Eaton

* * *

In her discussion of consequential theories of aesthetic value, Marcia Eaton presents Tolstoy's food analogy to explain "a confusion he thought accounted for the prevalence of counterfeit art and a misunderstanding about what constitutes real value."[1] In the end, Eaton concludes that "the analogy is not very helpful." I find her argument wanting, and this has prompted me to reexamine the Count's analogical argument. Below I will review and analyze Tolstoy's argument, look at Eaton's analysis and criticism, and suggest (with her assistance) an alternative interpretation that centers around her definition of art.

Tolstoy starts out with a generalization against inherent theories of aesthetic value—ones which Monroe Beardsley[2] and Professor Eaton (129, 143) wish to defend. "If we say that the aim of *any* activity is merely our pleasure, and define it solely by that pleasure, our definition will evidently be a false one."[3] If this is true of any human activity, surely it is true of art and food; so one commonality is established for the analogy, at least in Tolstoy's mind. He tells us what an adequate definition must consist of: "In order to define any human activity, it is necessary to understand its sense and importance. And in order to do that it is primarily necessary to examine that activity in itself, in its dependence on its causes and in connection with its effects, and not merely in relation to the pleasure we can get from it" (116). Tolstoy sets up the first half of the analogical argument this way:

> But this [defining an activity by our pleasure in it] is precisely what has occurred in the efforts to define art. Now, if we consider the food question, it will not occur to anyone to affirm that the importance of food consists in the pleasure we receive when eating it. Everybody understands that the satisfaction of our taste cannot serve as a basis for our definition of the merits of food, and that we have therefore

no right to presuppose that dinners with cayenne pepper, Limburg cheese, alcohol, etc., to which we are accustomed and which please us [he is speaking of the Russian diet here!], form the very best human food. (116)

Tolstoy at this juncture makes the inferential move from the food question to art: "In the same way, beauty, or that which pleases us, can in no sense serve as the basis for the definition of art; nor can a series of objects which afford us pleasure serve as the model of what art should be" (116-17). There is no connection made among objects that would give the series definitive power by pleasure—it is a reflection upon *us* rather than the objects. The central portion of his extended argument is given in the following passage:

Just as people who conceive the aim and purpose of food to be pleasure cannot recognize the real meaning of eating, so people who consider the aim of art to be pleasure cannot realize its true meaning and purpose, because they attribute to an activity the meaning of which lies in its connection with the other phenomena of life, the false and exceptional aim of pleasure. People come to understand that the meaning of eating lies in the nourishment of the body, only when they cease to consider that the object of that activity is pleasure. And it is the same with regard to art. People will come to understand the meaning of art only when they cease to consider that the aim of that activity is beauty, i.e., pleasure. . . . And since discussions as to why one man likes pears and another prefers meat do not help towards finding a definition of what is essential in nourishment, so the solution of questions of taste in art (to which the discussions on art involuntarily come) not only does not help to make clear what this particular human activity which we call art really consists in, but renders such elucidation quite impossible until we rid ourselves of a conception which justifies every kind of art, at the cost of confusing the whole matter. (117-18)

Now let us put Tolstoy's argument from analogy into standard form. The model (or one version of it)[4] is:
X and Y are alike. [An assumed premise that leads to the others.]
Things of type X have the properties of p, q, r, etc., and z.
<u>Things of type Y have the properties of p, q, r, etc.</u>
∴ Things of type Y also have property z.
Instantiated, the argument of Tolstoy looks like this:
Food and art are alike.
Food has the properties of not being solely pleasurable, pleasing, the best, but also offering nourishment.

Art has the properties of not being solely pleasurable, *pleasing (enjoyable), the best (true art)*.

∴ Art also has real value like nourishment (an internal, defining component) of the soul, which Tolstoy later calls "spiritual food" (250): the communication of sincere feeling.

Eaton comments on the conclusion when she remarks: "Art, like food, is *really important*, and it could not be, Tolstoy reflected, if all it did were to give us pleasure. Its real value must lie in the contribution it makes to a healthy individual and a healthy society" (130; her emphasis). After a promising account of Tolstoy's analogical argument, she ends with this brief criticism:

> Tolstoy failed to realize—or to admit—that even people who are forced to eat only nutritious food usually prefer something "tasty," at least occasionally. What is true of food may well be true of art. Thus the analogy is not very helpful. (130)

Now, I do not think Tolstoy would have distinguished the two—tasty from nutritious. Obviously food can (and probably should) be both, and the food of the peasant or lower class was usually both nutritious *and* tasty. There are numerous descriptions of peasant food in Tolstoy's major fiction, and one episode that comes to mind is from *Anna Karenina,* where Levin had been out mowing with the peasants and they had taken a break.

> The peasants got ready for dinner. Some washed, the young lads bathed in the stream, others made a place comfortable for a rest, untied their sacks of bread, and uncovered the pitchers of kvass. [For an explanation of this beverage, see note 5.] The old man crumbled up some bread in a cup, stirred it with the handle of a spoon, poured water on it from his whetstone-case, broke up some more bread, and . . . seasoned it with salt. . . . "Come, master, taste my sop," said he, kneeling down before the cup. The sop was so good that Levin gave up the idea of going home for dinner.[5]

By this quote I do not mean to imply that we are to identify Tolstoy with his character Levin. What I do suggest by this kind of passage (of which this is only one example) is that Tolstoy did entertain the nutritious and the pleasurable (or tasty) with respect to food. So Eaton's claim about people preferring tasty to nutritious is unfounded because both attributions can be made to food; hence, her conclusion does not follow or is at least poorly supported. Tolstoy was aware of these issues in regard to food, and his fiction testifies to this circumstance. But this is just the tip of the iceberg.

The most telling description of food that is both nutritious and pleasurable comes from Aylmer Maude's paraphrase of Tolstoy in "Tolstoy's View of Art" (1900), where the Count predicts: "The good art of the future should be superior to our present art in 'clearness, *beauty*, simplicity, and compression,' for one penalty of forgetting the primary aim of art is that we greatly lose that which is *a natural accompaniment of art—the pleasure given by beauty*. We are like men who, living to eat, eventually lose even *the natural pleasure food affords to those who eat to live*."[6] Such a remark clearly casts doubt on Eaton's first premise. Tolstoy objects to pleasure as the aim or object of an activity—whether food or art—and not to pleasure per se.

It is regarding the other half of the distinction in the analogy that I have questions—the nourishment part. Does peasant food have real or nutritional value? The Russian diet seems to be wanting in this regard; after all, how nutritious is the old man's sop, which Levin found so good that he gave up the idea of going home for dinner? What was Levin's dinner menu? In a passage (I, 177-78) where dinner is served to a guest at Levin's country estate, the preliminary course consisted of bread and butter, salt goose and salted mushrooms, and herb brandy. The nettle soup was next, followed by chicken in white sauce and white Crimean wine. Elsewhere (I, 189) fried eggs are mentioned for supper, served with herb-brandy. One may have doubts about the old man's sop, but "sops" were really "soups" when it came to the cuisine of the people:

> In the old [pre-revolutionary] days, the peasant returning from a long day of labor in the fields joined his family around a crude wooden table in a tiny—sometimes a one-room—wooden cottage. Their repast, illuminated by weak oil lamps or flickering candles, consisted of a single nourishing course. It was simple and cheap, but hearty and flavorful. The head of the house cut the loaf of sour, dark Russian bread [the most important food staple] into thick slabs and a steaming bowl of *borshch* (beet soup) or *shchi* (cabbage soup) or *ukha* (fish soup) was passed around. When the soup was thin, as it often was, plates heaped high with the coarse cooked grain called *kasha* helped fill the diners' stomachs. The food was lightened—and the spirits of the family lifted—by glass after glass of *kvas[s]*.[7]

Such a description is frequently found with literary variation in Tolstoy's fiction. In a Moscow restaurant (the *England*), Tolstoy (I, 41-44) describes the dinner options: turbot (a fish snack), vodka (an aperitif), fresh oysters (Flensburg, not Ostend), cabbage soup, porridge á la Russe, white bread, clear soup with vegetables, roast beef with capons, white seal, stewed fruitage, Parmesan cheese, Champagne, nuits, and Chablis. The soup and the porridge appealed most to Levin (since it is the food of the people). In the course of the dinner Stepan Arkadyevich remarks that the aim of culture is to make everything a source of enjoyment, and Levin responds, "Well, if that's its aim, I'd rather be a savage" (I, 44). Levin was horrified at the meal's cost—over 26 roubles (I, 51). "Levin belonged to the second class" (I, 59) of Russian high society. An example of the sort of thing that Tolstoy despised in the Czars' dietary habits is:

> "They [the Schützburgs] asked my husband and myself to dinner, and I was told that the sauce at that dinner cost a thousand roubles," Princess Miaghkaia said, speaking loudly, conscious that all were listening; "and very nasty sauce it was—some green mess. We had to ask them, and I made a sauce for eighty-five kopecks, and everyone was very much pleased with it. I can't afford thousand-rouble sauces." (I, 150)

Eaton's premise in her criticism is curious for another reason, because Tolstoy's instances of peasant art are usually those of people who are enjoying themselves. In *What Is Art?* he writes of a choir of peasant women who sang with "a definite feeling of joy, cheerfulness, and energy . . . expressed . . .without noticing how it infected me" (221). This incident found its way into *Anna Karenina* where he narrates: "The women, all singing, began to come close to Levin, and he felt as though a storm were swooping down upon him with a thunder of merriment . . . and the whole meadow and distant fields all seemed to be shaking and singing to the measures of this wild merry song, with its shouts and whistles and clapping. Levin felt envious of this health and mirthfulness; he longed to take part in the expression of this joy of life" (I, 302). So, of course, Tolstoy realized and admitted true art—real or genuine art—could be pleasurable, just like food could be; consequently, contrary to Eaton, the analogy, I think, *is* very helpful and moreover appropriate.

One of the reasons this is so is that the nutrition/pleasure confusion in food is also seen in art, in the confusion of real value and instrumental value (i.e., pleasure). "The art of commoners communicates sincere feeling, according to Tolstoy," Eaton reasons, "and hence has genuine value" (130), much like a "hungry animal eagerly clutches every object it can get, hoping to find nourishment in it" (*Anna*, II, 33), not seeking pleasure in it; and although pleasure may accompany it, pleasure is not to be confused with its real value (see note 6). One of the marks of a good analogy is that the Xs and Ys have essential or characteristically shared attributes or features; the food analogy does possess these. And we expect something like this of someone of the literary stature of Tolstoy who had such masterful fictional skills and imagination. Writers like Tolstoy are masters of metaphor, description, and analogy, and their works of fiction are exquisite blends of these linguistic elements.

To drive this point home, we can use food as a test case for Eaton's definition of art:

> X is a work of art if and only if X is an artifact and X is discussed in such a way that information concerning its history of production brings the audience to attend to intrinsic properties considered worthy of attention in aesthetic traditions (history, criticism, theory).[8]

For X within the domain of food, I will talk about bread, A Daily Loaf, *pain ordinaire Carême*. Here is what Bernard Clayton has to say about Carême (1784-1833) and his bread:

> The great eighteenth-century French cook and founder of *la grande cuisine*, Antonin Carême, wrote of grand dishes for princes and kings, yet he created an ordinary loaf of bread that has been passed down from one generation of bakers to the next for more than 175 years.
>
> Carême, who has been called the cook of kings and the king of cooks, wrote: "Cooks who travel with their gastronomically minded masters can, from now on, by following this method, procure fresh bread each day."
>
> This excellent bread is made with hard-wheat bread flour to give the dough the ability to withstand the expansion it undergoes when it rises more than three times its original volume. Baking at high heat provides the oven-spring that makes possible the formation of a large cellular structure, the distinguishing characteristic of *pain ordinaire*.[9]

First of all, our *pain ordinaire* is an artifact—something created from a recipe by a baker (a skilled craftsman)—much like a particular musical performance by musicians following a score. The particular loaf will vary with weather conditions, room conditions, who is making it, and so on, much like the musical performance will vary by who is playing it, where, when, and so on. But the essential defining characteristics of the loaf do not vary, so it is identifiable as *pain ordinaire*. Identity and repeatability are necessary conditions for something to be considered one of the languages of art (see Eaton, BIA, ch. 4).

Pain ordinaire, our X, is also discussed by Bernard Clayton and many others,[10] in such a way that information (the type of flour used, the dough's expansion, the baking, and so on) concerning its history of production (Carême's life and times, his method and writings) brings the audience (numbering into the thousands, if not millions, of cooking fanatics) to attend to intrinsic properties (the bread's shape, color, weight, smell, taste, and "large cellular structure") considered worthy of attention in aesthetic traditions (history, criticism, theory). For this last condition—the aesthetic—we have been witnessing the revising of views about what constitutes the canon of art in addition to technological changes in cooking that bring us to attend to qualities that are finally being recognized as worthy of serious aesthetic attention (see BIA, 95). (Think of all the refined cookbooks, choice magazines, gourmet cooking shows on TV, and fine restaurants that pay attention to these details.) The way food is made, presented, and appreciated can elevate it to an art form. Indeed, in some cases it is or has been a work of art.[11] My test case can be further augmented, but I think my claim has been established.

So if food satisfies Eaton's definition of "art" (and I have shown that in the previous paragraph), then food has the essential properties (necessary and sufficient conditions) to be regarded as art—whether from the standpoint of identity (Eaton or my interpretation of Eaton) or analogy (Tolstoy). In fact, given some of the activities Tolstoy includes as genuine art (triumphal marches, utensils, jest, dress, the ornamentation of houses), he probably would be amenable to the inclusion of food on this list. Cooking and eating could be ways of communicating sincere feelings toward one another (as *gestures* perhaps) in a family or a group, e.g., our (American) Thanksgiving dinner, which is as much a celebration of certain traditional values as it is a meal. Symbolism is present here.

Toward the end, Eaton argues for a position which is remarkably close to Tolstoy's: "If by 'inherent' one means 'separable from all other areas of our experience,' then aesthetic value is consequential. If 'consequential' means 'independent of the pleasure or displeasure the object itself gives us,' then aesthetic value must be inherent. Both factors, I think, are part of aesthetic experiences" (145). Given what I have presented above, Tolstoy would probably agree. He could have even made the following statement by Professor Eaton: "The consequences of engaging in aesthetic activity are often as important as the inherent pleasure obtained from them" (144). She combines these two theories in much the same way she combines the moral and the aesthetic—something Tolstoy would have certainly approved of.

The analogy, as I claim above, is a good one, but that does not mean it is not without faults. As the passages from *Anna* indicate, Tolstoy romanticizes the peasants and their food through the eyes of Levin. This is clearly a shortcoming, but by itself this criticism is not devastating. Tolstoy sees a connection between the peasant cuisine and the cuisine of the upper classes. Elite cuisine becomes corrupted and loses sight of its purpose when it no longer has peasant (or regional) cuisine as its base. Expert or erudite cuisine (of the upper classes for Tolstoy), as Jean-François Revel describes it,[12] is "*bad* international cuisine that *transports the picturesqueness* of a regional dish [i.e. peasant or popular cuisine] *without transposing its principles*, because they have not been understood. When such comprehension exists, on the other hand, real [or good] Grand Cuisine can sometimes give the diversity of local registers an interpretation that is at once faithful and new" (247; his emphases). He adds that "a chef who loses all contact with popular cuisine rarely succeeds in putting something really exquisite together. Furthermore, it is a striking fact that truly great erudite cuisine has arisen principally in places where a tasty and varied traditional cuisine already existed, serving it as a sort of basis" (149). Tolstoy anticipates the dialectical relationship between these two cuisines in his discussions of food.

Perhaps I should, in closing, heed the advice of the poet A. R. Ammons: "argument is like dining: mess with a nice dinner long enough, it's garbage."[13] Maybe I messed too long with the food analogy.[14]

Notes

1. Marcia Muelder Eaton, *Basic Issues in Aesthetics* (Belmont, California: Wadsworth Publishing Company, 1988), 130. Hereafter, references or citations will be made by page number within parentheses in the body of the chapter; this includes Eaton's BIA plus those listed below.

2. Monroe Beardsley, *Aesthetics* (New York: Harcourt Brace Jovanovich, 1958), 531.

3. Leo Tolstoy, *What Is Art? and Essays on Art*, translated by Aylmer Maude (New York: Oxford University Press, 1962), 116; emphasis added.

4. See, for example, Robert D. Boyd, *Critical Reasoning: The Fixation of Belief* (Bessemer, Alabama: Colonial Press, 1992), 124-26; and his *Critical Reasoning and Logic* (Pearson Education, Inc.; Upper Saddle River, NJ: Prentice-Hall, 2003), 127.

5. Leo Tolstoy, *Anna Karenina*, translated by Constance Garnett (Two Volumes; Moscow: State Publishing House for Fiction and Poetry, 1933), I, 279. *Kvass* is a beer of slight alcoholic content and mildly acid flavor that the Russian people usually made at home pouring warm water over a mixture of rye, barley, and other cereals and allowing it to ferment. See John Ayto, *The Diner's Dictionary: Food and Drink from A to Z* (New York: Oxford University Press, 1993), 186.

6. Aylmer Maude, *Tolstoy on Art* (London: Oxford University Press, 1924), 368-69; emphases added. A later critic, John Bayley in *Tolstoy and the Novel* (Chicago; University of Chicago Press, 1966/1988), believes: "Tolstoy's central conviction that bad art is an affair of the will is expressed more powerfully in the narration of *Anna* than in his theoretical statements. Such artistic activity—whether as producer or spectator—means that one's life is not proceeding along natural, simple and inevitable lines. To amuse oneself with art is like amusing oneself with food, or with sex, and making a diversion out of something that should be an essential" (235). Obviously Bayley is persuaded by the analogy and primarily for the reasons that Maude and I have cited.

7. Helen and George Papshvily, *Russian Cooking* (Foods of the World series; New York: Time-Life Books, 1969), 65. See ch. III for recipes and cultural details that surround them (65-99).

8. BIA, 94, and in Professor Eaton's earlier book, *Art and Nonart: Reflections on an Orange Crate and a Moose Call* (East Brunswick: Associated University Presses, 1983), 99-122.

9. Bernard Clayton Jr., *The Complete Book of Breads* (Revised Edition; New York: Simon and Schuster, 1987), 253.

10. See Reay Tannahill, *Food in History* (New York: Stein and Day Publishers, 1973), 333-42; Maguelonne Toussaint-Samat, *A History of Food*, translated from the French by Anthea Bell (Oxford: Blackwell Publishers, 1992), 535, 731-34; and almost every cookbook devoted to bread.

11. As Laura Esquivel relates in her novel, *Like Water for Chocolate*, translated by Carol and Thomas Christensen (New York: Doubleday, 1992), 230: "Esperanza and Alex spent many afternoons following these recipes to the letter so they could make invitations that were unique, and in that they had succeeded. Each was a work of art. They were the product of crafts that have, unfortunately, gone out of style, like long dresses, love letters, and the waltz." And in "On Food and Happiness," Charles Simic recalls, "Like pizza today, it's [*burek*] usually good no matter where you get it, but it can also be a work of art" (*Not for Bread Alone: Writers on Food, Wine, and the Art of Eating*, edited by Daniel Halpern [Hopewell, NJ: The Ecco Press, 1993], 19).

12. Jean-François Revel, *Culture and Cuisine* (New York: Bantam Doubleday Dell Publishing Group, 1982) and excerpts in *Cooking, Eating, Thinking: Transformative Philosophies of Food*, edited by Deane W. Curtin and Lisa M. Heldke (Bloomington: Indiana University Press, 1992), 145-152 and 244-250, from which my references are taken.

13. A. R. Ammons, *Garbage: A Poem* (New York: W. W. Norton & Company, 1993/1994), 68.

14. For more on the food/art question, see Marienne L. Quinet's interesting study, "Food as Art: The Problem of Function," *British Journal of Aesthetics*, XXI #2 (Spring 1981): 159-71; and for philosophical hints, see M. F. K. Fisher, *The Art of Eating* (Vintage Books; New York: Random House, 1976), e.g., 265: "eating meat [when herbal butters are added] becomes not a physical function, like breathing or defecating, but an agreeable and almost [?! what about it is an] *intellectual satisfaction of the senses*" (emphasis added). Quinet quotes this passage in the conclusion of her study; it would make a good beginning for an exploration between food and philosophy; see the previous chapters and the ones that follow this one.

9

Maize: The Native North American Legacy of Cultural Diversity and Biodiversity

* * *

Recent research, for example by Darrell A. Posey (1999), has established an intimate connection between cultural diversity and biodiversity—they mirror each other; i.e., one enhances the other and to threaten one is to threaten the other. And to date, diverse natural habitats and indigenous cultures have coexisted without one overwhelming the other (Gary Paul Nabhan, 1997: 4). This relationship is especially true of indigenous and traditional peoples, like the Native North American. In this chapter, I show that Native North Americans understood that an important way to preserve biodiversity in our ecosystem is to preserve cultural diversity. This valuable insight is captured in the phenomenon of corn or maize. This phenomenon forms a text which can be "read" by the rules of interpretation that pervade Native North American culture. A Native American philosophy would be an articulation of the discoveries and habits of thought which give rise to the conceptions that lie behind maize. Maize constitutes a value and knowledge system—not just a plant or a seed, but an entire complex of techniques, technology, and processing skills.

The myths and stories group themselves into three natural categories: world (nature/cosmos), self (person, clan, tribe, nation), and the relationship(s) between world and self. These three conceptions form an agenda for Native American philosophy. Maize actually involves all three conceptions, so it can serve as a paradigm of Native American thinking. In addition to an examination of the particular cultural and agricultural forms associated with maize in diverse tribes, most Native North American groups had a central place for maize in ceremonies, stories, and everyday life. As a result, the subject area provides one of the few areas from which common philosophical conceptions can emerge. But first, let me supply some historical and scientific background on maize.

I

Wild maize is extinct;[1] only domesticated forms exist today. But maize management or domestication began at the dawn of civilization in Native America; see Pope et al (2001). "Evidence from central Mexico indicates that, perhaps as long ago as 9,000 years," Kopper (1986: 49) suggests, "people began to manipulate the ancestral stocks of today's corn (maize) to produce a larger 'ear.'" And "by A.D. 700 there were locally adapted strains of maize, from pod corn through sixteen-, fourteen- and twelve-row varieties to the larger-kerneled eight-row variety" (Kopper, 1986: 226). However, maize diversity took a tumble in the modern period. Of one of the twentieth century's nightmares, Visser (1986: 47) laments:

> Reid's Yellow Dent [an accidental strain discovered in 1893] was so good, so obviously preferable, that other corns were forgotten, simply not planted. And "not planted," when we speak of "man-created" *Zea mays*, means nonexistent forever after. Thousands of kinds of corn, varieties reverently preserved and kept separate by the Indians, as well as many carefully improved by American farmers, disappeared off the face of the earth.

Nor is this the end of it, according to Visser (1986: 53):

> Worst of all, varieties of corn are disappearing by the dozen even as these words are being written. A corn not being planted is a corn which ceases to exist; man alone can keep *Zea mays* alive. Hybrid corns have been created, and continue to be crossed and improved and adapted to various circumstances, but hybrids are *combinations* only. Their ancestral lines are germ-plasm from corn varieties. Which lines are used is in fact largely a matter of chance. Reid's Yellow Dent was itself an accident. And often corn types which have extraordinarily valuable traits have come to light in obscure traditional corn cultures. Who knows what possibilities lay in the genetic material of the thousands of corns we have rejected and therefore lost in the last hundred years?

These are sobering thoughts which prompt us to ask the same question in regard to genetic engineering manipulation and chemical "enhancement" of meats, vegetables, and fruits. Alteration of our food products without adequate research into the long-term effects appears to be very dangerous behavior for human beings to be engaged in. No one has done any long-term testing on any genetically engineered food products. "Given that an estimated sixty to sixty-five percent of all the produce on American market shelves is likely to contain material from genetically modified plants, and that even organic foods (especially corn)," warns Marc Lappé (2001: 25), "may contain cross-pollinated gene products, these choices [for the consumer] are more than academic." An example of where this situation has gone awry is the recent recall of Mission Foods taco shells that were sold by the Tom Thumb supermarket chain because test results showed that they might contain genetically engineered "corn" (called StarLink corn) that is not approved for use in human food. (Nearly 300 products were recalled by the FDA.) StarLink "corn" is allowed for use in animal feed, but not permitted in human food products because it contains a protein that can cause allergies (AP, 2000). Is there not a potential problem here, too? What about the animals? And even if one is not concerned about the welfare of the animals, what about those animals that are potential food products for humans? Nearly everyone is concerned about genetically modified foods—foods that contain genetically modified organisms (GMOs)—but they do not know enough to compare these with those from conventional or organic production, so making informed decisions about what to eat is not easy. But it has gotten easier, since Alan McHughen (2000) has brought out his excellent, informative book, *Pandora's Picnic Basket*. He brings much-needed scientific information to the public debate about GMOs and explains the science behind them with the general reader in mind. (For further discussion of GMOs, see the next chapter.)

If these stormy clouds have a silver lining, it would be the recent "corn" creation by Mexican scientists, Surinder Vasal and Evangelina Villegas, at the International Maize and Wheat Improvement Center in Texcoco, Mexico. The pair won the World Food Prize for developing a "corn" that contains fifty percent more usable protein than normal corn, and it yields ten percent more grain per plant. (The $250,000 prize, established by Norman Borlaug, a Nobel Prize winner, honors people who have made vital contributions to improving food availability, quality, and quantity.) Villegas, a cereal chemist, is the first woman to receive the prize (AP, 2000). The Western technological attitude— some of which I have sketched above—is strikingly different from the Native North American attitude that I will sketch below. At least we have one to compare ours with, even if the Native North American attitude is on the verge of becoming extinct. But there is also some good news on this front. The situation underlying the Western technological attitude is slowly changing from a paradigm of exploitation and manipulation of specific plants and animals in isolation in the name of "scientific progress" to one of "agrobiodiversity" [Kristina Plenderleith's term in Posey (1999: 287)] and traditional subsistence farming systems. The Green Revolution, in her words, has "not only failed to live up to its promise, it also destroyed much of the skills and knowledge of traditional farmers" and has made food production and distribution even worse today than before. Furthermore, it is not just the diversity of the seed and the plant of corn for which recovery efforts have been made, but there has also been an organized effort by Virginia D. Nazarea (1998 and 1999) and others to record the skills and knowledge of traditional farmers that Plenderleith spoke about. Ethnoecology is a new field that documents and analyzes human-environment interactions. It is not enough to save genetic material in isolation; it is also necessary to understand why local people conserve the particular plants they do. Nazarea (1998: 5-6) puts it this way:

> Without this [the parallel collection and documentation of indigenous knowledge and technologies, including uses, preferences, and evaluation criteria associated with traditional varieties of crops—what I refer to as *memory banking*], the genetic information preserved in gene banks will be decontextualized in the sense that the cultural and ecological forces that shaped their selection will be largely ignored.

And I would add that they would be *lost forever*, if memory banking is not vigorously pursued. Ford (Nazarea, 1999: 71-87) has done an ethnoecological case study of the Zuni Pueblo which mentions corn, but there is no detailed treatment of it. My study here will fill in the details pertaining to maize.

Ecology and the environmental movement have been a driving force behind the paradigm shift from a Western technological attitude to one of agrobiodiversity. In the United States, Gary Nabhan (1989), an environmental biologist, has been instrumental in this change of attitude with his collective efforts. First is his organization, Native Seeds/SEARCH, and his continuing work to save native seeds by locating people who are willing to grow the seeds and return them for distribution. Second is his Forgotten Pollinators Campaign at the Arizona-Sonora Desert Museum, which brings about awareness of one of the world's most vital processes linking plants and animals. Nabhan and Stephen L. Buchmann (1996: 5) declare

> That ecological process is *pollination*—linking plants and animals. In fact, the range of animals active in moving pollen from one plant to another is bewildering in its diversity. In turn, many families of seed plants have diversified into their present array of species under the evolutionary influence of the myriad animal pollinators on this planet. And all these transactions between pollen-producing plants and pollen-moving animals make up a significant portion of what biological scientists are now calling *biodiversity*.

Man is the primary pollen-moving animal for corn. Corn is one of the hundred species out of a million species of organisms that have received intensive study, and the Native North Americans have contributed to this study with their stories. The stories of corn all have a structure to them: some superhuman figure gives corn to a people or tribe, who tells them how to grow or care for it, and how to prepare or cook it. Furthermore, these stories give us accounts of cultural diversity centered on one food staple.

II

One of the many "stories" or accounts of corn is from the Hidatsa Indian, Buffalo Bird Woman.[2] Preparing the land (in the same hills by a river, in this case the Missouri), soaking the seed and planting the field, hoeing, and watching (for thieving young boys and birds) were "women's work." This is how she begins her narrative:

> Corn planting began the second month after sunflower-seed was planted, that is in May; and it lasted about a month. It sometimes continued pretty well into June, but not later than that; for the sun then begins to go back into the south, and men began to tell eagle-hunting stories. We knew when corn planting time came by observing the leaves of the wild gooseberry bushes. This bush is the first of the woods to leaf in the spring. Old women of the village were going to the woods daily to gather fire wood; and when they saw that the wild gooseberry bushes were almost in full leaf, they said, "It is time for you to begin planting corn!" (Wilson, 1987: 22)

Corn planting is an integral part of many Native American calendars[3] and mirrors a belief in the interrelatedness of nature and a corresponding socially structured process. Corn is not merely a plant. Corn is a cluster of institutions and these institutions necessarily carry with them a set of images, dreams, tastes, choices, and values. Women made scarecrows to frighten away the birds, and "a platform, or stage, was often built in a garden, where the girls and young women of the household came to sit and sing as they watched that crows and other thieves did not destroy the ripening crop" (Wilson, 1987: 27). Buffalo Bird Woman (Wilson, 1987: 27) draws the following analogy: "We cared for our corn in those days as we would care for a child; for we Indian people loved our gardens, just as a mother loves her children; and we thought that our growing corn liked to hear us sing, just as children like to hear their mother sing to them." Native Americans found this analogy compelling because (a) the kernels of corn were likened to the nurturing breasts of a mother, and (b) women brought forth living beings and were hence thought suited to bringing forth plant-beings too. And "most of the songs that were sung on the watchers' stage," she remembers, "were love songs, but not all" (Wilson, 1987: 33). Some songs were meant to tease. Young men would try to court the girls.

The Native Americans widened the notion of corn. What is corn? It is not only a plant and a food, but something that contains elements of a veritable collective imagination showing the outlines of a certain mental framework. Corn is also, and at the same time, a system of communication, a body of images, a protocol of usages, situations, and behavior. We have just seen in the stories above how corn is a protocol of situations and behavior. What about a body of images? Does corn convey the mental life of Native Americans or some aspect of it? Many of the myths and stories that make up their literature give explanations of things in terms of their origins or beginnings; in fact, some scholars classify the stories this way (see Macfarlan, 1968, for example). Corn is no exception; here is one titled "The Origin of Corn and Tobacco" from the Penobscot, a Maine tribe of the Abnaki confederation.

> A famine came upon the people and the streams and lakes dried up. No one knew what to do to make it different. At length a maid of great beauty appeared and one of the young men married her. But she soon became sad and retiring and spent much time in a secret place. Her husband followed her one day and discovered that she went to the forest and met a snake, her lover. He was sad, but he did not accuse her; he loved her so much he did not wish to hurt her feelings. He followed her, however, and she wept when she was discovered. Clinging to her ankle was a long green blade of a plant resembling grass. She then declared that she had a mission to perform and that he must promise to follow her instructions; if so, he would obtain a blessing that would comfort his mind in sorrow and nourish his body in want, and bless the people in time to come. She told him to kill her with a stone axe, and to drag her body seven times among the stumps of a clearing in the forest until the flesh was stripped from the bones and finally to bury the bones in the center of the clearing. He was told to return to his wigwam and wait seven days before going again to the spot. During this period she promised to visit him in a dream and instruct him what to do afterward. He obeyed her. In his dream she told him that she was the mother of corn and tobacco and gave him instructions how to prepare these plants to be eaten and smoked. After seven days he went to the clearing and found the corn plant rising above the ground and the leaves of the tobacco plant coming forth. When the corn had born fruit and the silk of the corn ear had turned yellow he recognized in it the resemblance to his wife. Thus originated the cultivation of corn and tobacco. The plants have nourished the bodies of the Indians ever since and comforted their minds in trouble. (Turner, 1977: 25-26)

There are several things to notice about this myth. The beautiful maiden is the mother of corn. The idea that the silks of the plant are the female element of the plant is a good genetic guess. So the story yields botanical information. The Indians knew that corn (plants) had a sex life! In a chapter entitled "Corn: Our Mother, Our Life," Margaret Visser (1986: 25) discusses how the corn plant works:

The Indians observed that different types of corn could cross and produce offspring with characteristics derived from both parents. They believed that the plants' roots mingled underground to produce this effect, and this theory was not proved wrong until 1724, when Judge Paul Dudley of Massachusetts noticed that changes took place in corn when different types were separated by a river, but not when they were separated by a high fence. The "crossing" must therefore take place in the air and not underground. In 1694 the German botanist Camerarius had first startled the world with the news that plants have a sex life. But James Logan, who worked as an administrator for the Province of Pennsylvania under William Penn, presented in 1727 the first theories about how sex worked in the corn plant. The silks, which hang like bunches of hair from the cobs, are the female element. The male maize flowers are borne on the tassel, and they produce the pollen, 25 million grains per tassel. When the pollen is ripe it is shed and drifts in the wind over the cornfield.

"A long green blade of a plant resembling grass" is another good genetic guess, because maize is a giant grass by botanical family (see Coe, 1994: 11, and Pope et al, 2001). All of this appeared in a dream which was thought to be a superior, trustworthy way of knowing. (Knowledge was not limited to the senses and reason.)

A variation of the Penobscot story appears in "*Mon-daw-min*, or the Origin of Indian Corn" (Ojibwa), (Macfarlan, 1968: 340-344), where an eldest son Wunzh asks the Great Spirit in his dreams why he did not make it easier for them to get their food other than by hunting and fishing. In order to answer, the Great Spirit became a celestial visitor and came dressed in a variety of green and yellow colored garments with a plume of waving feathers on his head. Wunzh is to wrestle and overcome him in order for his dreams or visions to be answered. The sky visitor lost the trial of strength for the fourth time in a row and was killed by Wunzh. He buried the corpse in the forest and it grew into a plant as tall as a man. Wunzh takes his father out to the burial plot and there stood a tall, graceful green plant, with bright colored silken hair and stately leaves with golden clusters on all sides. The legend ends thusly:

> "It is my friend," shouted the lad; "it is the friend of all mankind. It is *Mon-daw-min*. We need no longer rely on hunting alone; for as long as this gift of corn is cherished and taken care of, the ground itself will give us a living." He then pulled an ear. "See, my father," said he, "this is what I fasted for. The Great Spirit has listened to my voice, and sent us something new, and henceforth our people will not alone depend upon the chase or upon the waters."
>
> He then told his father the instructions given him by the stranger. He told him that the broad husks must be torn away, as he had pulled off the garments in his wrestling. And having done this, directed him how the

ear must be held before the fire till the outer skin became brown, while all the milk was retained in the grain. The whole family then united in a feast on the newly grown ears, expressing gratitude to the Merciful Spirit who gave it. So corn came into the world.

This myth gives us an account of the Ojibwas' transition from a hunting-fishing, nomadic way of life to an agrarian one, complete with cooking instructions. Here we find a justification of agricultural practices. Notice this wisdom comes from a youth and not from the elders. Wunzh had to teach his father, who knew only of hunting and fishing, the ways of farming. This is no longer "women's work." Also observe that the angelic figures in the two myths are both genders. The last myth further reflects the botany of the plant. Both myths taken together address the cultural or social divisions of most of the tribes and that there is some ambiguity as to roles pertaining to corn—but more on these implications below. "It will be noted," Will and Hyde (1917: 235) observe, "that in these eastern and central Algonquian tales the corn is male and is presented as a young man [as in the Ojibwa legend above]; while in the Upper Missouri area the corn is invariably referred to as female and is personified as a woman" [as in the Penobscot tale], but there were none who considered maize to be both genders at the same time. Accordingly, corn reflects an interesting cultural diversity among the tribes as well as biodiversity. Also, these two myths portray a time before there was corn—that corn was brought into being rather than something that always existed.

Another origin legend dealing with corn, "The Origin of the Buffalo and of Corn," (Macfarlan, 1968: 352-354), comes from the Cheyenne whose people were hungry. Two men came to a large cave where an old woman sat cooking corn and buffalo in separate earthen pots. They ate and then the old woman told them, "Take in your robes this uncooked corn. Every springtime plant it in low, moist ground, where it will grow. After it matures you will feed upon it. Take also this meat and corn which I have cooked, and when you have returned to your people, ask them all to sit down in the following order, to eat out of these two pots: first, all males, from the youngest to the oldest, with the exception of one orphan boy; second, all females, from the oldest to the youngest, with the exception of one orphan girl. When all are through eating, the contents of the pots are to be eaten by the orphan boy and the orphan girl." The tale concludes with an event of their corn being stolen by a neighboring tribe, "but [they] could not trace the thieves, nor could they learn anything regarding the stolen corn." I suspect that the moral of this ending is that corn is precious and is to be carefully monitored. The Iroquois, like the Cheyenne, had the custom of genders eating separately, and it was only after the disappearance of the Long House, when the families began to live in separate abodes, that this tradition gave way. Further agricultural information, where to grow corn and how to cook it, is also given in the tale.

Corn is associated with wisdom in the Cherokee tale, "The Hunter and

Selu,"[4] where the spirit Selu, the wife of Kanati, took the form of a single green stalk of corn and talked to the hunter, "teaching him hunting secrets and telling him always to be generous with the game he took, until it was noon and the sun was high, when it suddenly took the form of a woman and rose gracefully into the air and was gone from sight, leaving the hunter alone in the woods." The tale concludes with this moral: "He did as the spirit had directed, and from that time was noted as the most successful of all the hunters in the settlement." Selu is not only the corn mother but the hunting mother; she is all knowing.

Corn takes on cosmic, sometimes tragic, dimensions, and more importantly, it is portrayed in this section as a blessing and as a gift. It is something usually given to the people by a female—in these past few myths in a different sense than by Buffalo Bird Woman. Corn is a blessing, and cornmeal is accordingly sacred. The latter is sprinkled in a ceramic pit before the potter begins shaping her clay pot; Zuni warriors sprinkled sacred cornmeal in a line and warned the Spaniards not to cross (1540s).[5] Such a strategy was obviously pathetic—the Europeans were peoples who had no respect for maize (see Visser, 1986: 36). Several practices were or are still today involved with corn and cornmeal. The Iroquois had a corn planting ceremony or festival in which "certain women banded themselves together in a society," Arthur C. Parker (1968: 27) describes, in order to propitiate "the spirits of the three sisters [corn, beans, squash] by certain ceremonies." "In their ceremonial march," Parker (1968: 27) continues, "the leader holding an armful of corn and a cake of corn bread leads her band in a measured march about a kettle of corn soup. . . . Each year at planting time each community observed a planting festival in which the Creator was implored to continue his bounty and his accustomed ways. Sacrifices of tobacco and wampum were made to the spirits . . . and a general thanksgiving for past blessings was given." Such festivities usually involved a corn dance (e.g., Zuni) in which women would shake their long black hair to encourage the magically similar corn silks to flourish (Visser, 1986: 31). In northern New Mexico today, one can witness the Green Corn Dance of the Pueblo performing these ancient customs. And in the southeastern United States, we find the Green Corn Ceremonies of the Cherokees and Seminoles that are still important annual ceremonies, as they encompass repairing broken relationships, reinforcing communal bonds and family unity, etc. In the Southeast the Green Corn Ceremony has always been an important vehicle in the Native North American's quest for purity, i.e., "a means of purifying their social order" (Hudson, 1976: 367). In other words, these ceremonies or dances should not be thought of as entertainment or art, but as medical or therapeutic and religious in nature (see Hudson, 1976: 365-375). One lengthy story that warrants special attention comes from the desert of the Southwest—from the *Diné* or Navaho tribe, which introduces ideas and stories of gender change as exemplifying a valuing of diversity.

III

Another myth where corn comes from a spiritual people can be found in the Navaho creation story as told by chief Old Man Buffalo Grass (1928):

> So far all the people [this includes all the animals] were similar. They had no definite form, but they had been given different names because of different characteristics.
>
> Now the plan was to plant.
>
> First Man called the people together. He brought forth the white corn which had been formed with him. First Woman brought the yellow corn. They laid the perfect ears side by side; then they asked one person from among the many to come and help them. The Turkey stepped forward. . . . He danced back and forth four times, then he shook his feather coat and there dropped from his clothing four kernels of corn, one gray, one blue, one black, and one red. . . . They planted the seeds, and their harvest was great. (Turner, 1977: 181-182)

Soon afterwards, the myth continues, men and women were separated by a huge river. The men were happy since they hunted, planted their seeds, had a good harvest, and had the Turquoise Hermaphrodite or *Nadle* (which literally means *that which changes*, i.e., the first man to change into, or become, a woman) grind the corn and cook the food. (Later the Turquoise Hermaphrodite became masculine again and was known as the Sun Bearer, *Jo honaái*, Turner, 1977: 180n.) "Four seasons passed" (Turner, 1977: 183). As time passed, "the women became lazy, and only weeds grew on their land. The women wanted fresh meat. Some of them tried to join the men and were drowned in the river" (Turner, 1977: 183). One of the chiefs asked First Man why they should not bring the women across the river and all live together again. First Man's response and what follows are most interesting from the standpoint of social relations.

> "Now we can see for ourselves what comes from our wrong doing" [killing the females of mountain sheep, lion, and antelope], he said. "We will know how to act in the future." The three other chiefs of the animals agreed with him, so First Man told them to go and bring the women.
>
> After the women had been brought over the river First Man spoke: "We must be purified," he said. "Everyone must bathe. The men must dry themselves with white corn meal, and the women, with yellow."
>
> This they did, living apart for four days. After the fourth day First Woman came and threw her right arm around her husband. She spoke to the others and said that she could see her mistakes, but with her husband's help she would henceforth lead a good life. Then all the male and female beings came and lived with each other again. (Turner, 1977: 184)

We see another use of sacred cornmeal—to cleanse or "purify" men and women. Men's "wrong doing" I take to be the mistreatment of women in the myth—killing the females of mountain sheep, lion, and antelope. After all, they, too, are people in the story and its moral is the valuing of biodiversity. One of the basic tenets of environmental ethics is that all organisms are to be treated equally or the same. The Native North American accomplished this by calling animals "persons." When First Man and First Woman built their home, she ground white corn into meal and they sprinkled it inside the dwelling, and he said: "May my home be sacred and beautiful, and may the days be beautiful and plenty" (Turner, 1977: 190).[6]

Gender relations are complicated by the concept of *Nadle* (*Ashon nutli'*). It is curious that the Navaho saw the change in only one direction, i.e., man becoming woman, rather than the change occurring either way. Why not *Nadle* from woman to man? Two possible answers: Maybe women are the more complete beings and that is why they don't need to *Nadle*. (The story, I think, discounts this interpretation.) Or, maybe women do not have the capacity to *Nadle*, so they are less than complete beings. Be that as it may, both sexes need *Nadle* because if there was a quarrel (as in the story), then *Nadle* exercised the authority to resolve it, since s/he is in between and reflects neither's interests (Paul Zolbrod, 1984: 53, 354). Standing against the first interpretation is the report in the legend that women had grown lazy and wanted fresh meat, so I assume they cannot hunt. (One of man's functions is to hunt.) Nevertheless, the *Nadle* in the story is *tested* by First Man. He asked *Nadle* if he could cook and prepare food like a woman. "And when he had assured First Man that he could do all manner of woman's work, First Man said: 'Go and prepare food and bring it to me.' After he had eaten, First Man told the four chiefs what he had seen [i.e., discerned] . . ."(Turner, 1977: 183). It was on the basis of this decision that men and women were separated by the river. First Man wanted to be sure that men could both provide food and cook, as women (who gathered and cultivated) already did. In other words, man existing alone was problematic due to his traditional activities of hunting, ceremonies, and councils. Consequently, only when women's work was demonstrated by *Nadle* did The-Great-Coyote-Who-Was-Formed-in-the-Water appear to First Man and tell him to cross the river.

This particular story, like previous ones, reflects an understanding of corn genetics. We have thus far seen that Native peoples lived with the corn plant in all its life stages in a most intimate way, and that they experienced this life of corn as a physical and trans-physical set of phenomena that was portrayed as a set of mythical images. Since corn has both male flowers (its tassel) and female flowers (its silk), it is in a sense a hermaphrodite. In the process of domestication, corn was biologically "transmuted"[7] from a more male-dominated plant into a more female plant. This came about by the formation of the cob out of a male tassel. Visser (1986: 25-26) briefly describes the process:

> Each time a pollen grain falls on the sticky thread of a corn silk, either on its own plant or on another a kernel is conceived. The silk develops a tube, and the pollen travels through the tube to the embryo at the root

of the silk in the cob. There the baby corn kernel takes shape, tightly anchored by a short stem to its place amongst its rows of siblings. Every pollen grain contains two nuclei—one for the oil-germ and one for the starch-endosperm in the kernel. The corn plant adjusts the length of its own cobs according to the likelihood of the amount of grain it will be called upon to house. The factors which the plant mysteriously takes into account include the density of the plant population in a field, weed competition, moisture, the amount of nutrients it is getting, and the availability of light.

All of this is perfectly obvious to anyone who grows corn because it demonstrates many of the steps of this transmutation in the field in the form of maize "monsters," which are the tassels in varying degrees of feminization. The Native Americans were careful observers of nature and her processes. This dimension is touched on in the Navaho creation story where you have first the male, then the changeling, then the female and the male being united across the waters by which they were separated. The upshot of this discussion is that for Native Americans, gender and social relations have their basis, or at least an analogue, in corn genetics. The former may be artificial (i.e., conventional) relations, but they seem to be premised on natural relations. There appears to be no distinction here between different kinds of relations. Again, biodiversity is suggestive of cultural (sexual) diversity. If certain activities are found in nature, the Native North American would tolerate and be open-minded about behavior out of the ordinary. In fact, the extraordinary was prized and revealed more than the ordinary.

Socially and politically speaking, when men narrate the myths, the stories generally tell a different tale from women like Buffalo Bird Woman. But the Navaho story is not like these stories. As Zolbrod (1984: 416) interprets it: "It is that sort of equality [the solidly egalitarian relationship among the Navaho clans to be an extension of the egalitarian relationship which Changing Woman demands in her confrontation with Sun (Zolbrod, 1984: 272-275)] that neither First Man or First Woman could envision between them early in the story. Overall the narrative moves steadily toward a fully apprehended awareness of such equality." Women were generally born into a position of cultural subservience; however, there were exceptions. The Navaho story is a notable one. But history provides us with some other exceptions.

Within Plains Indian culture, for example, there was at least one nineteenth-century woman who took on a traditionally male role. She was known only as the Woman Chief of the Crow Indians of the upper Missouri. As a young girl, she was a member of another tribe, the Gros Ventres, but was taken prisoner by the Crow at age ten and adopted by a Crow warrior. Edwin T. Denig, a white frontiersman who lived with the Crow and knew her for twelve years, describes how as a young girl she desired to acquire "manly accomplishments." Her Crow foster father encouraged her in this—permitting her to guard the horses, presenting her with bow and arrows, and teaching her to ride fearlessly. She later learned to shoot, carried a gun, and was the equal—if not superior—to any men in hunting. As Jonathan Ned Katz (1976: 310) describes it: "Long before she had ventured on the warpath, she could rival any of the young men in all amusements and occupations, was a capital shot with a rifle, and would spend most of the time killing deer and bighorn [sheep], which she butchered and carried home on her back when hunting on foot." She never wore men's clothing, however, except for her hunting costume. After the death of her foster father, she assumed responsibility for his lodge and family. When the Blackfeet made a charge on the Crow lodges, she single-handedly led a counterattack against them—killing one with a gun and shooting arrows into two more. This act made her a hero to the entire Crow Nation. The following year, she led a number of young men on their first excursion against the Blackfeet, returning with seventy horses and two scalps. Soon after, she married a woman, and later added three more wives. Before taking a young woman in marriage, she always went through the expected procedure of giving horses to the family of her intended. For twenty years Woman Chief seems to have "conducted herself well in all things appertaining to war and a hunter's life," as Katz (1976: 311) narrates. Then, in the summer of 1854, she was killed while on a peacemaking expedition to the Gros Ventre tribe. Hence, here is a historical case that demonstrates that *Nadling* was symmetrical after all.[8] Incidently, *Nadle* was not a derogatory term, at least not in the Navaho story. *Nadle* has status in the Navaho creation cycle (i.e., they create pottery, wicker water-bottles, grinding stones, and other domestic utensils and procedures), and they seem to have no particular stigma to overcome.[9]

What about the word "woman?" "From the Iroquois in the East to the tribes of the Northwest one of the worst insults that could pass from one man to another," Turner (1977: 376) reports, "was 'You are a woman.'" But this was not universally true; for instance, the Delawares generically referred to themselves as "women," regarding it as a great compliment. Some women were equal counterparts to men: The Narragansett had female chiefs, the last of whom—Magnus—was executed by the English along with other members of her government (Allen, 1986: 33f.). Within the Haudenosaunee or the Iroquois, the clan mothers selected, and had the right to depose male council members (Morgan, 1995: Book One, ch. V). The Women's Council of the Cherokee decided on the fate of captives, and the clan mothers had the right to wage war and to depose leaders (Jahoda, 1975: 112). So the role of women in terms of freedom and political power varied from tribe to tribe. In other words, it is difficult to generalize about gender relations among the Native Americans. As in so many other societies and cultures, gender roles are ambiguous, with no one clear interpretation that can be given to them.

Gender relations among Native Americans demonstrate that the second category (self: person, clan, tribe, nation) has significant consequences that have a place in the story of corn. That place varies whether one is born male or female. From a female perspective, *Buffalo Bird Woman's Garden* gives us insight into how a sense of community was achieved in an agrarian society and into the importance of women in that society. Men had a role, too, in clearing the land of trees, stumps, brush, and rock (Parker, 1968: 21). Later, men assumed more and more of the agricultural tasks like planting and harvesting. With a mixed metaphor, the Zuni poem "Offering" begins with these lines: "That our earth mother may wrap herself /In a fourfold robe of white meal" (Turner, 1977: 240). The ideas and stories of gender change also exemplify a valuing of diversity. In many societies, the *berdache* or transsexual would be chief of the tribe. Changing roles within the culture are tied to the Vision Quest and the idea that a person who is vastly different from others within the tribe has a new vision for what it means to be male, or female, or just human that expands everyone's possibilities. That is why the *berdache* or the schizophrenic might wind up as leader of the tribe. Consequently, we have seen that the Navaho story of corn has an account of gender relations which reflects individual diversity in a way not seen in the other Native North American stories of corn.

IV

The central question of metaphysics is "Are the many one or the one many?" Interestingly, such an issue is manifest in the story of corn. As Visser (1986: 35) succinctly puts it:

> Corn for the Indian was both One and Various. Its many colours—orange, white, blue, black, and the rest—seemed to him the many-faceted manifestation of the single and divine sap of *mays*. There was a deep obligation to preserve its variety. The Hopi Indians allotted to each family in a village one type of corn, and it was that family's responsibility to maintain the purity of that corn type through the generations. In other words, hybridization, the core of the modern development of corn, would have been anathema to the Indians: hybridization confuses categories, refuses priorities, and denies the aspect of Many to what was One.

The Many were five subspecies: (1) soft corn or dent which came in white, purple, and red; (2) flint corn from which they made hominy and which was either yellow or calico in color; (3) sweet corn which was puckered (wrinkled), and some of which was black; (4) pod or pop corn which was either red or white; (5) flour or sacred corn which was the original corn. (Parker, 1968: 43ff., and Coe,1994: 14, have discussions of these in terms of their uses and their differences in growth requirements.) Keeping these five subspecies and even their respective colors apart was designated to particular families (see, for instance, Will and Hyde, 1917). Consequently, here is an excellent example of cultural diversity preserving biodiversity. In a sense (by "decree"), the entire community is involved in preserving diversity.

Most of the tribes of the upper Missouri and the southwest knew that "corn travels" (Betty Fussell, 1992: 65) and they laid out their gardens appropriately. In their classic work, *Corn among the Indians of the Upper Missouri*, George F. Will and George E. Hyde (1917: 291) mention that "the older women say that sixty to one hundred yards apart was sufficient in the sheltered bottom lands to prevent any but a very slight mixing, and thus two varieties might be grown at opposite ends of the same garden." Some Native North American varieties, nevertheless, were badly mixed by some of the tribes, e.g., Omahas, but most tribes attempted to keep the varieties pure "by planting in patches at some distance from each other, and you can see that it was necessary to keep the varieties pure for ceremonial reasons, because for instance, if red corn (which was tabu [taboo to eat]) became generally mixed among their corn it would be impossible" (Will and Hyde, 1917: 296) to tell them apart. Pawnee men grew the red corn (plus three other varieties of sacred corn: white, black, and yellow) for ceremonial purposes along with tobacco in their gardens, and women grew the other varieties of corn in theirs (Will and Hyde, 1917: 278/248f.). Each of the varieties of sacred corn had a meaning associated with it and represented specific stars in the heavens. Is such gardening or "farming" encouraged today? Nabhan (1989: 63) has this to say:

> Fortunately, tribal governments no longer believe fatalistically that this [the USDA policy, which is "a policy of neglect"] must be their policy as well. Among the Iroquois, the Sioux, the Mississippi band of the Anishanabey, San Juan Pueblo, the Winnebago, the Tohono O'odham, the Navajo, and other tribes, there have emerged community or tribal projects to conserve and revive native crops as cottage industries for their rural-based members. On both reservations where the Pima live, they have initiated tribally supported farm efforts to increase the supplies of traditional crop plants.

The southwestern tribes developed drought-resistant flour corn and had their own irrigation system. The tribes of the upper Missouri developed cold-resistant corn varieties and irrigated from the river in unusual ways. "Some native farmers," Nabhan (1989: 96) reports, "don't necessarily plant the same kind of corn every season, but vary their selection depending upon the weather." For example, Mexico's Mountain Pima, relatives of the Pima and Tohono O'odham of Arizona, keep several varieties of maize on hand, "including a quick-maturing corn in case spring drought should delay planting, thus shortening the growing season" (*ibid.*). In addition to planting different varieties of corn depending upon weather conditions, "many Native American farming traditions," Nabhan (1989: 194) continues, "integrate . . . wild species within their cultivated fields . . . [so as to produce] a dynamic balance of *wildness* with *culture.* This is what modern farmers lose when they cultivate their fields from edge to edge, leaving no hedges, no weeds, no wildlife habitat. The trend in industrial farming is, in fact, a repudiation of wildness. And yet, a certain wildness may be exactly what our ailing agricultural system needs." Why? Because the wildness provides a habitat for the pollinators. The Native North American didn't understand the pollination process, but did appreciate the codependency of wildness with culture. Besides an understanding of agriculture, the Native North American understood the nutritional aspect of corn.

V

What can be said about corn as a food product or staple? "One grain of modern domesticated maize," Coe (1994: 4-5) answers, "contains more nourishment than the entire cigarette-butt-sized ear of the earliest domesticated maize." She reminds us that the husk of the modern ear is an effective guardian of the calories it contains (Coe, 1994: 6). However, corn has to be processed in order for it to have appreciable protein value. Processing by fire or cooking makes corn a major part of the Native American diet. This aspect of corn leads us to another happy guess or discovery—nixtamalization. This chemical process is one of releasing the vitamin niacin. Nixtamalization starts with soaking the ground kernels or grains and then cooking them with lime or wood ashes in the water or directly in contact with the coals. In the sixteenth century, when the Europeans took dried corn kernels back to their countries, they treated the corn like wheat and skipped this chemical process. The result was disastrous in those for whom corn was a major part of the diet—they suffered from dietary deficiencies like pellagra and kwashiorkor (Coe, 1994: 15, and Fussell, 1992: 202f.), or severe malnutrition in infants and children that is characterized by "failure to grow and develop, changes in the pigmentation of the skin and hair, edema, fatty degeneration of the liver, anemia, and apathy, and that is caused by a diet excessively high in carbohydrate and extremely low in protein" (Merriam-Webster). Nixtamalization corrects dietary deficiencies like this.

Let me briefly discuss "seed corn," in order to complete our discussion of the agricultural and nutritional aspects of corn. In discussing the Hidatsas, Will and Hyde (1917: 127) report that "whenever an exceptionally good ear, ripe, and hard, long, straight-rowed, and of good color, came to hand it was stuck into a bag reserved for the seed corn, which was later plaited into separate braids." However, the above desirable traits were not the only traits selected and grown generation after generation, producing bigger, better corn. Nabhan (1989: 76) tells of an interesting encounter with a Hopi woman:

On one occasion, I asked a Hopi woman at Moenkopi about seed selection of "trueness to type." I had heard that other people discard any unrepresentative seeds in order to maintain a semblance of purity within each seed stock. I wondered if she regularly selected only the biggest kernels, or ones from one end of the cob, or those consistently of the same hue. The elderly woman listened to my loaded questions, then snapped back at me, "It is not a good habit to be too picky. . . . We have been given this corn, small seeds, fat seeds, misshapen seeds, all of them. It would show that we are not thankful for what we have received if we plant certain of our seeds and not others." Her acceptance of heterogeneity contrasts markedly with the prevailing preoccupations of modern agriculture: uniform seed, for standardized field conditions.

Mixing various crop strains in the same area was practiced by the Hopi and other Native North American tribes. Uniformity of genetic traits of seeds has a vulnerability if something like a pest or disease devastates areas of a single crop genotype. Ensuring diversity of genetic material within different species of a plant like corn can help defend against some of the pathogens that may attack a plant.

The myths and stories we have thus far examined have suggested several themes—sexual and gender relations, genetics, nutrition, and social customs. Another theme assigns a function to corn that is, in some sense, commemorative: corn permits a person to partake each day in the national or tribal past. (Commemoration is a ritual that reflects the role of cultural diversity in preserving biodiversity.) In this case, the historical quality is obviously linked to culinary techniques: growing, preparing, and cooking. These activities have long roots, reaching into the depths of the Native American past. They are, we are told, the repository of a whole experience—of the accumulated wisdom—of their or our ancestors. For example, succotash is an Indian invention; we find references to it throughout the literature. In the *Captivity and Restoration of Mary Rowlandson* (1675), she mentions going into a wigwam "where they were boyling [boiling] Corn and Beans, which was a lovely sight to see, but I could not get a taste thereof" (Turner, 1977: 342). In a dietary sense, corn and beans complement each other. "Corn supplies some of the protein which is essential for good nutrition," Hudson (1976: 294) reports, "but it lacks the amino acid lysine, which, as it turns out, is relatively abundant in beans. Thus when eaten together corn and beans are a relatively good source of vegetable protein."

In *American Cooking*, Dale Brown (1968: 43) has this to say about the Native American dish:

The early settlers learned about succotash from the Indians, who not only grew corn and beans together in the same garden patch, but often cooked them in the same pot. The Indians made this dish from dried corn and beans in winter, and from fresh vegetables in summer. The best succotash, to most tastes, is the summer variety, made from fresh whole-kernel corn and freshly shelled baby lima or kidney beans, or a combination of green beans and shelled beans. The best out-of-season substitutes are frozen corn and beans. Cook with salt pork or bacon, and season the succotash with salt, pepper, a little sugar and butter. (The corn should not be added until the beans are almost done and should be cooked not longer than 10 minutes.)[10]

My Indian (Cherokee) maternal grandmother taught me to sauté fresh corn (cut from the cob) in some bacon drippings with chopped yellow onion and red bell pepper—the latter for looks or presentation. Sometimes toward the end of the preparation she would add a little milk or cream, season with salt and pepper to taste, mix the ingredients together with the beans which were cooked separately with a smoked ham hock, and serve. I still make this dish, and when I do I fondly think of her and the times we had together conversing in the kitchen.[11] Through their food Native Americans experience a certain national or tribal continuity. I am reminded of a conversation about a dark onion soup with croutons in *Death Comes for the Archbishop* by Willa Cather (1926: 38):

> "Think of it, *Blanchet*; in all this vast country between the Mississippi and the Pacific Ocean, there is probably not another human being who could make a soup like this."
>
> "Not unless he is a Frenchman," said Father Joseph. He had tucked a napkin over the front of his cassock and was losing no time in reflection.
>
> "I am not depreciating your individual talent, Joseph," the Bishop [Latour] continued, "but, when one thinks of it, a soup like this is not the work of one man. It is the result of a constantly refined tradition. There are nearly a thousand years of history in this soup."

The same can be said of Native North American cuisine. Food, especially maize products, in addition to succotash, consisted of parched corn or popcorn; dried green corn that was boiled when ready to eat after the season ended for fresh corn, which was usually served as corn on the cob; smoked corn; mush (a coarse meal); roasted maize buttered with fat or marrow, sometimes seasoned with salt (and in the southwest it was seasoned with red chili pepper); breads, cakes, corn balls made of sugar corn and grease sometimes mixed with ground sunflower seeds and boiled beans; hominy (called posole in the southwest); piki (the original cornflakes); boiled dumplings; pancakes; fried grits; wafers; and tortillas; see Will and Hyde (1917: ch. IV) and Fussell (1992: ch. 4).[12] These foods permitted tribes to interject themselves daily into their own past and to believe in a certain culinary "being" of Native America. Corn puts you back in touch with the earth, with Mother Nature, with your people. One amendment should be made to Brown's account. Today's Native Americans who adhere to the culinary traditions would not use frozen corn. They would perceive its use as very "un-Indian." In some families, the worst thing you can say about someone is that they served their families or guests frozen corn. Birds Eye would not handle its corn in a reverential manner. But that being said, if the Native Americans could have figured out a way to freeze it, they probably would have, just as drying it was their alternative to fresh corn. In northern New Mexico, there were ice caves that were used year-round as refrigerators by local tribes to preserve their food.

One contemporary food writer, Michael Frank (1993: 56), echoes this intimate relationship between food and time:

> Food can be counted on to produce a sensation in time present that will duplicate a sensation from time past. With its myriad connections to the nurturing and sustenance of mothers and grandmothers, nannies and governesses, food is an uncanny defogger of early memory. But not only of early memory: its habits and associations, the ritual of its acquisition and preparation, the quarrels it can provoke and the solace it can provide have a way, I think, of recovering and linking a good deal of lost history.

The power of corn is seen in the thoughts and emotions that it evokes. To generations of Native American people, the taste of succotash evoked memories of shaded outdoor spaces and hot summer afternoons, or in winter the warmth and coziness of a wigwam.

Corn, and the food derived from it, is something thought out not by specialists or professionals, but by the entire tribe and its ancestors (see above, the myths and stories), even if this thinking is done within what we might consider a framework of highly mythical notions. As in so many decisions made by tribal members, a council was probably called and they debated what to do with corn. Corn has a central role to play in the Navaho creation story in a way other than what we have seen so far: "The first Earth Surface People are generally said to have been made from corn and jewels such as turquoise and white shell, or, from many different elements including soil, lightning, and water"; and so "whatever the elements used, they were, by various accounts, given life by means and processes similar to those used in giving life to the inner forms of natural phenomena and to other Holy People: Wind gave the corn 'the breath of life'" (McNeley, 1981: 25-26). In the course of this chapter we have seen several situations and behaviors, especially celebration, expressed through corn for the Native American. Why? Because food has a constant tendency to transform itself into situation. As we speak of Asia as rice cultures (Dogen), we can talk of the Americas as corn cultures.[13]

VI

Paul Zolbrod (1995: 2) hypothesizes that "the verbalized world view of a culture has roots in a shared sacred vision of the universe." I would argue that corn is central to the Native American sacred vision and world view respectively. Corn is a revelatory and interactive metaphor for the Native American understanding of myth, genetics, plants, animals, Nature, person, gender, society, agricultural and cultural practices (including culinary skills), and life in general. In a kernel, to understand corn is to understand the Native American.

All of these phenomena interact in the Native American imagination. Out of all this I have developed above "an ontology of corn," or "a maize metaphysics." This could very well serve as a model for organizing cultures today and as a model for cultural diversity and biodiversity. Does such modeling sound feasible? Wendell Berry thinks so. In the conclusion of "Conserving Forest Communities," Berry (1995: 41-44) takes his cue from the Menominee Indians: "To assure myself that what I have described as a good forest economy is a real possibility, I went to visit the tribal forest of the Menominee Indians in northern Wisconsin." While there, Berry saw that they understood that if they were to survive as a people, they would have to preserve the forest while they lived from it. The Menominee forest management has remained essentially the same over the centuries: "It is still rooted in cultural tradition, and its goal has remained exactly the same: to preserve the identification of the human community with the forest, and to give an absolute priority to the forest's ecological integrity." Their practices of forest management, Berry believes, are practices that we have much to learn from. We, likewise, have much to learn from the Native North American practices of maize management.

The first lessons learned from the above stories pertain to biodiversity. Seed corn was selective of the best stock to continue the variety, but in some cases it was not selective but representative of the variety. Most Native North Americans planted two varieties per season: an early maturing corn ("green corn") and a late harvest corn. They learned about growing conditions from what area of the country they settled. They also learned about different varietals growing under different climatic conditions. And the preservation of different varietals was in part motivated by religious practices, such as the use of corn in ceremonies. This corn was grown apart from the food or staple corn, which again demonstrated an understanding of cross-pollination that could "pollute" the corn.

So through cultural diversity (in many forms) we find that preservation of biodiversity is important for several reasons among the Native North Americans: among them are that it increases productivity, enhances the ability to recover from natural disasters, and ensures that a larger variety of plants and animals are available to help sustain Mother Nature. The stories of corn testify that the Native North Americans understood these reasons for preserving biodiversity. They did it through cultural diversity rather than with science, but they accomplished the same end or purpose: the preservation of biodiversity.[14]

Notes

1. There is current debate about the existence of wild maize. Nabhan (1989: 34-35) claims "the wild maize of Nabogame [Mexico] has become distinct in terms of a number of genetic criteria. Its chromosome knobs, its enzyme 'fingerprints,' and its mitochondrial DNA all exhibit minor differences from other annual and perennial teosintes." The major skeptic is Hugh H. Iltis (1983) and (1987) who argues that there was not any wild maize to become extinct. He suggests a catastrophic sexual transmutation theory (CSTT) that claims the maize ear is the transformed, feminized, and condensed central spike of the teosinte lateral branches and that this morphological revolution was nearly instantaneous. Fussell (1992: 76ff.) labels this debate as "The Corn War." Whatever the origins of maize, its evolution can be traced from the early domesticated forms.

2. Wilson (1987), excerpt in Curtin and Heldke (1992: 270-279). In *America's First Cuisine*, Sophie D. Coe (1994: 10) has this to say: "Why not call maize, the bread of the Indies, corn? Because corn is a generic term for a staple grain that has been used for different plants in different countries at different times. Maize is a New World name, derived from a word that the Europeans picked up in the Antilles and then, after an acquaintance of some thirty years, imposed upon the Mexicans, who had domesticated the plant and then lived with it, and depended on it, for millennia. Maize is an indigenous name for this one particular plant, *Zea mays*, and nothing else. Admittedly popped maize sounds ridiculous to the American ear, but we will have to put up with this for the sake of precision." That being said, I have used the terms interchangeably, but I mean *maize* when I or the other below write "corn," or I will put quotation marks around the word to signify the generic sense.

3. May, too, in the Navaho year (the eighth month) is the time to plant: "The flowers come forth and plants open their leaves. It is the time to plant. The early part of this month is called the planting time" (Turner, 1977: 195). There was early corn and late corn which were planted and harvested at different times, so the Native Americans had fresh corn over a longer period of time than if they had only one planting (see, for instance, Hudson, 1976: 293). Not all Native American calendars were organized around the planting and harvesting of corn; the Inuit of the Arctic obviously did not raise corn, and after the advent of horse culture some Plains peoples organized their calendars by other relevant changes in nature.

4. "The Hunter and Selu" (Cherokee), in Macfarlan (1968: 338-340). This tale has inspired a book, *Selu: Seeking the Corn-Mother's Wisdom*, by Marilou Awiakta (1993).

5. *The World of the American Indian*, Billard (1974: 177, 162). For a historical study of the Pueblo Indian world and the Spanish conquest of New Mexico, see Gutierrez (1991), *When Jesus Came, the Corn Mothers Went Away: Marriage, Sexuality, and Power in New Mexico, 1500-1846*.

6. For the centrality of beauty in the scheme of things, see Witherspoon (1996).

7. Iltis (1983) and (1987) of the University of Wisconsin-Madison has done research on this unique process.

8. That is, that women became men; three lengthy studies have appeared recently that substantiate this symmetry, *Women and Power in Native North America*, edited by Laura F. Klein and Lillian A. Ackerman (1995), Sabine Lang (1998), *Men as Women, Women as Men: Changing Gender in Native American Cultures*, and Will Roscoe (1998), *Changing Ones: Third and Fourth Genders in Native North America*. As early as Hudson (1976: 201), Cherokee women, it was observed, have always had as much sexual freedom as the men, and this is consistent with Indian women's own accounts of sexual and economic freedom. Accounts of sex among Native North Americans will vary according to what regions and tribes one discusses, so generalizations are dangerous in this sensitive area.

9. Some answers to the questions I have raised here concerning the nature of *Nadle* may be found in the research on the *Berdache* tradition. This is beyond the scope of the present chapter. Consult Callender and Kochems (1983); Roscoe (1988) and (1991); Fulton and Anderson (1992); Williams (1986), and the four studies mentioned in the preceding note.

10. Parker (1968: 68) writes about succotash (in Mohawk, *O'gaserho'da*): "Iroquois succotash was prepared much as is the modern form made by white people. The green corn cut or scraped from the cob was thrown in a pot of beans which had nearly been cooked and the mass cooked together until both ingredients were done. A sufficient quantity of salt and grease or oil was added for seasoning and flavor. The favorite corn for this dish was Tuscarora or sweet corn."

11. In *Land of the Spotted Eagle*, Luther Standing Bear (1978: 5) recalls: "Grandmothers became skilled in preparing food for children, and most of them had a host of little ones running after them all the time. When children became hungry, they nearly always ran to grandmother first for food and she was never found lacking in a supply. Nor were children ever refused in their request for food." We—my grandmother and I—clearly fit this filial description.

12. The specific varieties of maize were used for certain foods, e.g., flint corn for flour, green or sweet corn for boiling, hard or ripe corn for hominy or meal, sugar or sweet corn for corn balls, pop corn for popcorn. Furthermore, "We know that different Indian tribes," Fussell (1992: 174) comments, "grew many different varieties of corn and varied their cooking methods according to type." Biodiversity dictating cultural diversity. For those interested in Native North American cuisine; consult Cushing (1920), Kimball and Anderson (1965), Hesse (1973), Niethammer (1974), Hughes (1977), Kavena (1987), Keegan (1987), and Edaakie (1999). These books dispel the myth that Indian food is unappealing if not downright awful and disgusting. If the Native North American had the time and resources for her meals, they were delicious and appealing.

13. For other myths and legends pertaining to corn which I have not dealt with, but that are just as rewarding as those which I have discussed, see "The Origin of Corn" (Abanaki), in Thompson (1995: 51-52); "The Buffalo Woman" (Left Heron; Hokacatka or Makula), in Walker (1983:109-118); "The Song of the Maize" (Osage), "The Corn Spirit" (Skidi Pawnee), and "The Growth of the Corn" (Zuni) [also called "Offering" in Turner, 1977: 240, but abbreviated] in Astrov (1962: 100, 106-108, 233-234); "Turkey Makes the Corn and Coyote Plants It" (White Mountain Apache), and "Deer Hunter and White Corn Maiden" (Tewa), in Erdoes and Ortiz (1984: 352-354, 173-175; Courlander, (1970, e.g., 15ff.); Bahr, et al, (1994: Part 3, "New Creation and Corn," 75-110); "corn" is a common proper name in some of the stories, for instance, "The Hopi Legend of the Snake Order of the Moquis, as Told by Outsiders" (Stephen,1888) is about seven brothers, Red-Corn, Blue-Corn, Yellow-Corn, White-Corn, Green-Corn, Spotted-Corn, and Black-Corn, and the youngest—Black-Corn—marrying a beautiful girl who emerged from a snake ritual and gave birth to snakes (Turner, 1977: 206-212); for a recent study centered around a captivity narrative, consult Karen Oakes (1995: 45-52); the text Oakes refers to is by James E. Seaver (1992).

14. This chapter has had several different audiences: it was first presented at the Conference on Native American Philosophy held at New Mexico Highlands University in Las Vegas, New Mexico, on July 19, 1996, in the Opening Session on Approaches to Studying Native American Philosophy. This philosophical conference ended like no other–with song and dance to celebrate what we had done (started). Everyone left with a sense of elation. Also, an abbreviated version of the chapter was presented at the annual meeting of the Rocky Mountain Division of the American Society for Aesthetics held in Santa Fe, New Mexico, on July 15, 2001, at one of the concurrent panels on Native American Perspectives. The most recent (present) version of the chapter was read and discussed at a food and philosophy conference, entitled "Know Thyself: Food and the Human Condition," held at Mississippi State University in Starkville on April 5-6, 2002. Several people have read and commented on ancestors of this chapter and I want to thank them, especially an anonymous reviewer for the *Journal of Agricultural and Environmental Ethics*, its Editor-in-Chief, Richard Haynes, and its Associate Editor, Jan Elliott, for their perceptive suggestions. I dedicate this study to the memory of my maternal grandmother, Elizabeth Kiefer Tressler, whom we (the enlarged family) affectionately called "Tressie." For additional discussion of the Native American conception of food, see chapter 1.

References

Allen, Paula Gunn, *The Sacred Hoop: Recovering the Feminine in American Indian Traditions*, Boston: Beacon Press, 1986.

Associated Press (AP) releases, summer and fall 2000.

Astrov, Margot (ed.), *American Indian Prose and Poetry [The Winged Serpent]: An Anthology*, New York: Capricorn Books, 1962. Originally published in 1946.

Awiaka, Marilou, *Selu: Seeking the Corn-Mother's Wisdom*, Golden, Colorado: Fulcrum Publishing, 1993.

Bahr, Donald, Juan Smith, William Smith Allison, and Julian Hayden, *The Short Swift Time of Gods on Earth: The Hohokam Chronicles*, Berkeley: University of California Press, 1994.

Berry, Wendell, *Another Turn of the Crank*, Washington, DC: Counterpoint, 1995.

Billard, Jules B. (ed.), *The World of the American Indian*, Washington, DC: National Geographic Society, 1974.

Brown, Dale, *American Cooking*, Foods of the World series; New York: Time-Life Books, 1968.

Buchmann, Stephen L., and Gary Paul Nabhan, *The Forgotten Pollinators*, Washington, DC: Island Press, 1996.

Callender, Charles, and Lee M. Kochens, "The North American Berdache," *Current Anthropology* 24 (4) (1983), 443-456, with comments, 456-464, with reply, 464-470.

Cather, Willa, *Death Comes for the Archbishop*, New York: Alfred A. Knopf, 1926.

Coe, Sophie D., *America's First Cuisine*. Austin: University of Texas Press,1994.

Courlander, Harold, *People of the Short Blue Corn: Tales and Legends of the Hopi Indians*, New York: Henry Holt and Company, 1970.

Curtin, Deane W., and Lisa M. Heldke (eds.), *Cooking, Eating, Thinking: Transformative Philosophies of Food*, Bloomington: Indiana University Press, 1992.

Cushing, F. H., *Zuni Breadstuff*, New York: Museum of the American Indian, Heye Foundation, 1920.

Dogen, Japanese Zen Master (thirteenth century CE), *Fushuku-Hampo (Meal-Time Regulations)* and *Tenzo Kyokun (Instruction for the Tenzo[mindful temple chef])*, in Curtin and Heldke (1992:153-163, 280-285; see also Curtin's "Recipes for Values,") 126-129.

Edaakie, Rita, *Idonapshe/Let's Eat: Traditional Zuni Foods*, Albuquerque: The University of New Mexico Press. A:shiwi A:wan Museum and Heritage Center, 1999.

Erdoes, Richard, and Alfonso Ortiz (eds.), *American Indian Myths and Legends*, New York: Pantheon Books, 1984.

Frank, Michael, "The Underside of Bread: A Memoir with Food," in Daniel Halpern (ed.), *Not for Bread Alone: Writers on Food, Wine, and the Art of Eating*, Hopewell, New Jersey: The Ecco Press, 1993.

Fulton, Robert, and Steven W. Anderson, "The Amerindian 'Man-Woman': Gender, Liminality, and Cultural Continuity," *Current Anthropology* 33 (5) (1992), 603-610.

Fussell, Betty, *The Story of Corn*. New York: North Point Press of Farrar, Straus and Giroux, 1992.

Gutierrez, Ramon A., *When Jesus Came, the Corn Mothers Went Away: Marriage, Sexuality, and Power in New Mexico, 1500-1846*, Stanford, California: Stanford University Press, 1991.

Hesse, Z. G., *Southwestern Indian Recipe Book*, Palmer Lake, Colorado: Filter Press, 1973.

Hudson, Charles M. *The Southeastern Indians*, Knoxville: University of Tennessee Press, 1976.

Hughes, Phyllis (ed.), *Pueblo Indian Cookbook*, Second, Revised Edition; Santa Fe: Museum of New Mexico Press, 1977.

Iltis, Hugh H., "Maize Evolution and Agricultural Origins," in *Grass Systematics and Evolution*, edited by Thomas R. Soderstrom, et al, Washington, DC: Smithsonian Institution Press, 1987.

Iltis, Hugh H., "From Teosinte to Maize: The Catastrophic Sexual Transmutation," *Science* 222 (4626) (1983), 886-894.

Jahoda, Gloria, *The Trail of Tears*, New York: Wings Books, 1975.

Katz, Jonathan Ned, *Gay American History*, New York: Thomas Y. Crowell Company, 1976.

Kavena, J. T., *Hopi Cookery*, Tucson: The University of Arizona Press, 1987.

Keegan, Marcia, *Southwest Indian Cookbook*, Santa Fe, New Mexico: Clear Light Publishers, 1987.

Kimball, K., and J. Anderson, *The Art of American Indian Cooking*, Garden City, New York: Doubleday & Company, 1965.

Klein, Laura F., and Lillian A. Ackerman (eds.), *Women and Power in Native North America*, Norman: University of Oklahoma Press, 1995.

Kopper, Philip, *The Smithsonian Book of North American Indians Before the Coming of the Europeans*, Washington, DC: Smithsonian Books, 1986.

Lang, Sabine, *Men as Women, Women as Men: Changing Gender in Native American Cultures*, translated from the German by John L. Vantine, Austin: University of Texas Press, 1998.

Lappé, Marc, "Tasting Technology: The Agricultural Revolution in Genetically Engineered Plants," *Gastronomica* 1 (1) (2001), 25-30.

Macfarlan, Allan A. (ed.), *American Indian Legends*, Los Angeles, California: The Ward Ritchie Press, 1968.

McHughen, Alan, *Pandora's Picnic Basket: The Potential and Hazards of Genetically Modified Foods*, Oxford: Oxford University Press, 2000.

McNeley, James Kale, *Holy Wind in Navajo Philosophy*, Tucson: University of Arizona Press, 1981.

Minnis, Paul E., and Wayne J. Elisens (eds.), *Biodiversity and Native America*, Norman: University of Oklahoma Press, 2000.

Morgan, Lewis H., *League of the Ho-de'-no-sau-nee or Iroquois*, North Doghton, Mass.: JG Press, 1995. Originally published in 1851.

Nabhan, Gary Paul, *Cultures of Habitat: On Nature, Culture, and Story*, Washington, DC: Counterpoint, 1997.

Nabhan, Gary Paul, *Enduring Seeds: Native American Agriculture and Wild Plant Conservation*, San Francisco, California: North Point Press, 1989.

Nazarea, Virginia D., *Cultural Memory and Biodiversity*, Tucson: University of Arizona Press, 1999.

Nazarea, Virginia D. (ed.), *Ethnoecology: Situated Knowledge/Located Lives*, Tucson: University of Arizona Press, 1998.

Niethammer, C., *American Indian Food and Lore*, New York: Collier Macmillan Publishers, 1974.

Oakes, Karen, "We planted, tended and harvested our corn: gender, ethnicity, and transculturation in 'A Narrative of the Life of Mrs. Mary Jemison,'" *Women and Language* 18 (1) (1995), 45-52.

Parker, Arthur C., "Iroquois Uses of Maize and Other Food Plants," in *Parker on the Iroquois*, edited by William N. Fenton, Syracuse: Syracuse University Press, 1968, Book One, 1-119. Originally published in 1910.

Pope, Kevin O., Mary E. D. Pohl, John G. Jones, David L. Lentz, Christopher von Nagy, Francisco J. Vega, and Irvy R. Quitmyer, "Origin and Environmental Setting of Ancient Agriculture in the Lowlands of Mesoamerica," *Science* 292 (5520) (2001), 1370–1373.

Posey, Darrell Addison (ed.), *Cultural and Spiritual Values of Biodiversity*, London: Intermediate Technology Publications, and Nairobi: United Nations Environment Programme, 1999.

Roscoe, Will, *Changing Ones: Third and Fourth Genders in Native North America*, New York: St. Martin's Griffin, 1998.

Roscoe, Will, *The Zuni Man-Woman*, Albuquerque: University of New Mexico Press, 1991.

Roscoe, Will, "We'wha and Klah: The American Indian Berdache as Artist and Priest," *American Indian Quarterly* 12 (2) (1988), 127-150.

Seaver, James E., *A Narrative of the Life of Mrs. Mary Jemison*, edited by June Namias, Norman: University of Oklahoma Press, 1992. Originally published in 1824.

Standing Bear, Luther, *Land of the Spotted Eagle*, Lincoln: University of Nebraska Press, 1978. Originally published in 1933.

Stephen, A. M., "The Hopi Legend of the Snake Order of the Moquis, as Told by Outsiders," in Turner (1977: 206-212).

Thompson, Stith (ed.), *Folk Tales of the American Indians*, North Dighton, Mass.: JG Press, 1995.

Turner III, Frederick W. (ed.), *The Portable North American Indian Reader*, New York: Penquin Books, 1977.

Visser, Margaret, *Much Depends on Dinner: The Extraordinary History and Mythology, Allure and Obsessions, Perils and Taboos of an Ordinary Meal*, New York: Macmillan, 1986.

Walker, James R., *Lakota Myth*, edited by Elaine A. Jahner, Lincoln: University of Nebraska Press, 1983.

Will, George F., and George Hyde, *Corn Among the Indians of the Upper Missouri*, St. Louis: William Harvey Miner, 1917, and Lincoln: University of Nebraska Press, 1964. Little Histories of the North American Indians, No. 5.

Williams, Walter L., *The Spirit and the Flesh: Sexual Diversity in American Indian Culture*, Boston: Beacon Press, 1986.

Wilson, Gilbert L. (ed.), *Buffalo Bird Woman's Garden: Agriculture of the Hidatsa Indians*, Reprinted edition; St. Paul: Minnesota Historical Society Press, 1987. Originally published in 1917, and excerpted in Curtin and Heldke (1992: 270-279).

Witherspoon, Gary, "Navajo Aesthetics: Beautifying the World through Art," in *Aesthetics in Perspective*, edited by Kathleen M. Higgins, New York: Harcourt Brace College Publishers, 1996, 736-743. Reprinted from his *Language and Art in the Navajo Universe*, Ann Arbor: University of Michigan Press, 1977, 151-178.

Zolbrod, Paul, *Reading the Voice: Native American Oral Poetry on the Written Page*, Salt Lake City: University of Utah Press, 1995.

Zolbrod, Paul, *Diné Bahane': The Navajo Creation Story*, Albuquerque: University of New Mexico Press, 1984. This is a substantial improvement over the translation by Aileen O'Bryan (1956) in Turner (1977:175-205).

10

Are Genetically Modified Foods Good for You? A Pragmatic Answer

* * *

1. Introduction

One of the central issues in food ethics is the safety of genetically modified foods (GMFs). There are several arguments that both advocates and opponents have put forth recently, which I shall review here. Then I will make a recommendation as to how we can get past the rhetorically-charged debate. In his "Introduction: The Meaning and Ethics of Food," Gregory E. Pence announces:

> Food makes philosophers of us all. Death does the same, but most of us try to avoid thinking about death. Of course death comes only once, so we can postpone thinking about it, but choices about food come many times a day, every day. Like sex, food is an essential aspect of human experience. Like sex, the decisions we make about food define who we have been, who we are now, and who we want to become. How we make those choices says much about our values, our relationships to those who produced our food, and the kind of world we want.[1]

Some of these dietary decisions or choices involve GMFs (or foods modified by genetically modified organisms, popularly known as GMOs). Since over 60 percent of the produce in your local supermarket is unlabeled GMFs (105), you are most likely unwittingly consuming them.[2] For example, Texas A&M agricultural extension service has created the maroon carrot (obviously so the Aggies are not reminded of UT when they eat regular carrots) and the no-heat, totally mild jalapeno. Also, there is that strange veggie that is half cauliflower and half broccoli (called "broccoflower") which tastes like neither![3]

Federal laws governing food labeling are rapidly changing this very moment, so it is hard to keep up with them. The intent of these laws is to provide the consumer with the relevant information to decide whether to purchase the produce or not. But first things first: some definitions to guide our discussion. "GMFs" refers "to the use of transgenic crops, i.e., those grown from seeds that contain the genes of different species"(76). "One-hundred percent Organic Products" are made from entirely organic ingredients. "Organic" means products that contain 95 percent organic ingredients (these two definitions come from the USDA). In both definitions of "organic," the term means without conventional pesticides or petroleum-based fertilizers, and the animal products are free of antibiotics and growth hormones. USDA-accredited certifiers determine whether a product is organic. Now, on to the arguments.

2. Arguments for GMFs

The principals are: Norman Borlaug (74-79), Henry I. Miller (96-99), Ronald Bailey (100-115), Gregory E. Pence (116-122), Anthony J. Trewavas (148-155; 168-178), and C. Ford Runge and Benjamin Senauer (180-190). Norman Borlaug is the 1970 Nobel Peace Prize laureate, who engineered dwarf wheat that diverted energy from the stalk into the grain, which increased the grain yields. Borlaug also carried the Green Revolution to Asian nations and argues "from a global perspective, without the very large U.S. food surpluses, it is likely that millions would go hungry and even be threatened by starvation" (75). For some, like Garrett Hardin (54-70), this situation would be acceptable, since by trying to feed all, we all perish, i.e., his lifeboat metaphor for his ethical stance: if everybody tries to get on board, the boat will sink and we all drown. Be that as it may, these surpluses are due to genetic engineering of crops like corn that produce huge yields, so they are a good thing because they alleviate pain and suffering. (A good old utilitarian reason offered here.) But critics or opponents think that GMFs are unnatural and unsafe. Borlaug believes this is an appeal to ignorance:

> The facts are that genetic modification started long before humankind started breeding. Mother Nature did it, and often in a big way. For example, the wheat crops we rely on for much of our food supply are the result of unusual (but natural) crosses between different species of grasses. Today's bread wheat is the result of the hybridization of three different plant genomes, each containing a set of seven chromosomes, and thus could easily be classified as "transgenic." Maize is another crop that is the product of transgenic hybridization. Indeed, it is hard to see how the modern maize plant evolved from Teosinte and Tripsacum—reputed to be its putative (ancient) parents.[4]

So Borlaug thinks of genetic engineering not as something *foreign* which is introduced into natural processes, "but rather a complementary 'research tool' to identify desirable genes (traits) from remotely related taxonomic groups and transfer them more quickly and precisely into high-yielding, high-quality crop species"(77). If people had received better information about genetic diversity and variation, he conjectures, there wouldn't have been the confrontation of consumers against the use of transgenic crop technology in Europe and elsewhere. The science is safe and should be used to feed the ever-expanding world community. (This is definitely a utilitarian argument: the greatest good for the greatest number.)

Like Borlaug, Miller stresses the compatibility of genetic engineering with conventional breeding techniques. "The agency's approach" (the FDA's 1992 policy on products from "new plant varieties"), Miller concludes, "was consistent with a widely held scientific consensus that 'conventional' and new biotechnology are *essentially equivalent*, and that the highly precise gene-splicing techniques, in fact, yield a better characterized and more predictable product"(97; emphasis added). He also worries about new legislation because "the overregulation of gene-spliced foods will prevent its wide application to food production, deprive farmers of important tools for raising technology, and deny to food manufacturers and consumers greater choice among improved, innovative products"(99).

Our next advocate is Ronald Bailey, who answers some of the objections made by opponents of GMF. He declares:

> If anti-biotech activists really are concerned about gene flow, they should welcome such technologies. The pollen from crop plants [like corn] incorporating TPS [Technology Protection System] would create sterile seeds in any weed that it happened to cross-breed with, so that genes for traits such as herbicide resistance or drought tolerance couldn't be passed on. (111)

The activists' objections are not really to the science or technology, but to the ideology behind the science: capitalism, international markets, and the slow pace of democratic change (100).

Gregory Pence takes a different approach by arguing that GMFs are actually safer than (some) organic foods, because "organic food is usually grown in soil with manure"(117), and manure can be contaminated with *E.coli*, especially the strain 0157:H7 that has sickened and killed many people, particularly children. (For the gruesome details, see Nicols Fox, "The Hamburger Bacteria," 215-266.) This is not true of GM veggies (119). "We take our system of producing meat as normal and safe," Pence says, "yet it may be far more dangerous than any GM foods" (119). He concludes:

Overall, our present system for testing food is more than a bit hypocritical about the safety of traditional food and more than a bit hysterical about genetically modified veggies. As always, people fear the new kid on the block, especially if his name is "Gene." (122)

The Scotsman Anthony Trewavas echoes the same complaint but from the utilitarian standpoint: "When Greenpeace tells us to 'go organic' I ask myself which three billion will live and which three billion will die"(150). Golden Rice, a genetically improved rice that provides vitamin A in its chemical makeup, was developed to help solve this dilemma. It was given to the population of the Philippines to ameliorate vitamin A deficiency in children and to feed the hungry. Quite recently, in 2013, the debate has resurfaced because of the Golden Rice Project and its promise for feeding the hungry in underdeveloped countries. With this in mind, Trewavas warns us about global warming:

Even if the climate is only wetter and warmer, new crop pests and rampant disease will be the consequence. GM technology can enable new crops to be constructed in months and to be in the fields within a few years. This is the unique benefit GM offers. The UK populace needs to be much more positive about GM or we may pay a very heavy price. (151)

This line of reasoning suggested to Trewavas that the utilitarian argument could be replaced with an environmental one; i.e., a move away from the good for the majority of people to the good for the environment, or as he puts it, "conserving forests, habitats, and biodiversity by increasing the efficiency and productivity of land utilization" (172). This means agricultural production through biotechnology. "However, the consequence of less-efficient agriculture [like sustainable development]," Trewavas predicts, "will be the elimination of wilderness that by any measure of biodiversity far exceeds that of any kind of farming system"(173). So, according to Trewavas, the saving of the wilderness depends upon biotechnological developments. GM technology, Trewavas concludes (178), offers some good solutions to environmental problems in addition to the utilitarian argument for feeding the hungry. These are the two main arguments offered by the advocates of GMF.

Our last advocates, Ford Runge and Benjamin Senauer, assert that GMF trade agreements must be part of a larger set of agreements among nations that increase trade for all and will protect the environment and ensure food safety (180). What is called for is:

A larger and more comprehensive multilateral vision, which recognizes a legitimate and growing role for developing countries—and food security in particular—would ultimately benefit the United States. Realizing this vision will require more and better international institutions, not fewer and worse ones. (190)

So far the political climate, especially in the United States, is not conducive to such an enlightened vision. Consequently, it remains just that—a vision.

3. Arguments Against GMFs

The principals are: Greenpeace International (71-73), Mae-Wan Ho (80-94), Tanya Maxted-Frost (123-127), Vandana Shiva (130-146), Marc Lappé and Britt Bailey (156-166), and Helena Norberg-Hodge, Peter Goering, and John Page (191-212).

The first counterargument is from a press release, entitled "Golden Rice Is Fool's Gold" by Greenpeace International, that claims "genetically engineered 'Golden Rice' containing provitamin A will not solve the problem of malnutrition in developing countries" (71). The reason is that "an adult would have to eat at least twelve times the normal intake of 300 grams to get the daily recommended amount of provitamin A" (72). This would amount to nine kilos or over 20 pounds of cooked rice per day for an adult, and twice that amount for a breast-feeding woman (72)! But this quantitative account is misleading, because rice is only a part of the Philippino diet, and provitamin A comes from other food products that make up that diet. However, Golden Rice doesn't look as promising as it was initially touted to be.

The same holds true of the world's first genetically engineered whole food—the Flavr Savr tomato.[5] This vegetable cost millions of dollars to develop and was promised to have an unusually long shelf life which, as it turned out, it did not have. The Flavr Savr tomato was a disaster both biotechnically and economically to the company (Calgene) that developed it. (This occurred in the late 1980s and early 1990s.)

A critic from the scientific community is Mae-Wan Ho, who reports unexpected effects of genetic engineering that impact agriculture and biodiversity. "The technology will contribute to an increase in the frequency of horizontal gene transfer [the transfer of genes to unrelated species]," Ho says, "of those genes that are responsible for virulence and antibiotic resistance, and allow them to recombine to generate new pathogens"(91).

Another unexpected effect was cross-pollination that occurred from GM food production to organic food production (125). For example, in the Midwest, a woman's organic corn crop was recently contaminated by GM corn grown in a nearby field, and consequently she was unable to sell her produce as organic. As a result, she took a large loss on the sale of her crops (AP release, summer 2003). For the opponents of genetic engineering, the unexpected or unintended effects of genetic engineering are either out of our control or we do not have the means to deal with them. Advocates like Trewavas, on the other hand, reflect the typical scientific attitude:

> All technologies have problems because perfection is not in the human condition. The answer is to improve technology once difficulties appear; not, as some would wish, discard technology altogether. Remove the problems but retain the benefits! The benefits of modern agricultural technology are well understood; now is the time to reduce the undoubted side effects from pesticides, soil erosion, nitrogen waste, and salination. GM technology certainly offers some good solutions. (178)

The question is whether we can remove the problems that develop from genetic engineering. The opponents argue that the problems we face are not like any we have faced before, and consequently we cannot really solve them before they get out of control. One cannot reverse genetic manipulation in techniques like horizontal gene transfer. However, the advocates don't see any danger of the magnitude that the opponents see.

Another opponent of GMFs is Vandana Shiva, a native of India, who argues that it is large Western corporations like Monsanto who benefit from GMFs because they can patent the genetic changes. Monsanto developed crops like soybeans and cotton that resisted their Roundup herbicide, so that farmers who used herbicides for weeds, besides paying for the special seeds, had to buy their herbicide too. "Dairy cows that consume Roundup Ready soybeans," Shiva notes, "produce milk with higher fat levels than cows that eat regular soybeans" (137). She concludes:

> The Green Revolution narrowed the basis of food security by displacing diverse nutritious food grains and spreading monocultures of rice, wheat, and maize. However, the Green Revolution focused on staple foods and their yields. The genetic engineering revolution is undoing the narrow gains of the Green Revolution both by neglecting the diversity of staples and by focusing on herbicide resistance, not higher yields. (137)

She sees biodiversity as the solution to many of the problematic consequences of genetic engineering brought about by the biotech monocultures, and as the key to a necessary shift from an engineering paradigm to an ecological one (146). In other words, conserving biodiversity will meet our needs for food and nutrition and will avoid the dangers of genetic pollution. So biodiversity is appealed to by both opponents (Shiva) and advocates (Trewavas), but obviously for different reasons: Shiva for discounting agricultural monocultures and Trewavas for saving what wilderness is left.

4. Conclusion

The advocates make it sound like "the scientific community" agree on the facts behind transgene technology and that it is safe—that is, there is a consensus among scientists on this issue. The opponents, who themselves are for the most part scientists, disagree on these facts. Consequently, we have no consensus. The dispute here is mainly factual, but not entirely. Values play a part here as well. Vandana Shiva (146) anticipated this when she spoke of a shifting from an engineering paradigm to an ecological one. These two perspectives are value laden and focus on different activities or processes. We think about problems or processes differently from within different paradigms.

The major philosophical difference between the two camps boils down to this: the advocates conceive of genetic engineering as *equivalent* to conventional breeding; the opponents do not, because with genetic engineering, genes are moving across phyla (kingdoms) and not just species. In other words, we have plant genes inserted into animal DNA and the converse.[6] Shiva calls this "gene pollution." When a human being ingests some GMFs, genetic or DNA material is left in the gut and can penetrate the lining of organs and make its way into the rest of the body. So far, no (short-term) effects have been observed from eating GMFs. But what about long-term effects? Perhaps GMFs have effects that have gone unnoticed in that we don't really know what to look for, since we are talking about gene-altering conditions of the likes we have never seen before. For example, after genetic material has been inserted into an organism, one doesn't know where it will end up on the DNA ladder, in that it can move up or down. We have no control over its direction, so we are not sure of the outcome. As Lappé and Bailey state: "Even as more and more crop releases are planned, we remain uncertain of the long-term consequences of the wholesale shift to herbicide-tolerant or *Bt* containing food crops"(157). They conclude by raising these rhetorical questions:

> We are thus left with disturbing questions as transgenic crops go into mass production. How much are we willing to jeopardize the evolutionary future of our food crops? How much uncertainty is generated by transgenic creation of new plants? And are we really ready to let large corporations play God in the critical area of food biotechnology? (166)

Because of circumstances like these, it is perhaps prudent that the public be made aware of the uncertainties involved in GMFs. Furthermore, labeling of GMFs should be enforced so that the public can make their own decisions as to what they should eat. Not only should GMFs be labeled— non-GMFs should be labeled also, for the reasons that Pence gave.[7] Indeed, consumers are the ones who should make the final decision regarding whether or not to consume GMFs. They should not be left in the dark (see note 2). Alan McHughen leaves us with the best advice:

> Our best course of action is to learn the facts behind GM technology and *each* GM product, as well as their conventional alternatives. Then we can ignore both the scaremongers and the soothsayers, and consider the risks and benefits of genetic technology from different perspectives and in proper context. The only way to keep from being overwhelmed is by using your tools [research] to learn the facts and decide for yourself.[8]

So we need to proceed on a case-by-case basis. For example, Olathe Sweet Corn,[9] like all the genetically engineered sugar-enhanced or super-sweet corn varieties, is bred for sweetness: its sugar has more staying power than older sweet-corn varieties, changing to starch less quickly after the corn is picked, so it travels better and stays fresh longer. Olathe Sweet Corn is produced by a "safe" GM technology that has no potentially bad side-effects, i.e., no horizontal transgenic transfer with unintended consequences. Plant species respond differently to transgenic transfer.[10] Olathe corn tastes better than its competitors and comes available at a time of year when conventional corns are on the wane. Consequently, if taste is one of your criteria for selection of food products, this is one GMF that you might choose. As other products appear on the market shelves, we will have to examine them and evaluate them on their own individual merits or drawbacks.

Finally, here is our pragmatic solution. Our initial question, "Are genetically modified foods good for you?" cannot be answered except in a piecemeal fashion—by proceeding case by case. The answer is yes in the case of Olathe corn, but the answer is no in the case of the Flavr Savr tomato. We cannot answer our question categorically, because GMFs are produced by different technologies. If they were produced by the same technology, then our answer could be categorical. But, alas, they are not. These biotechnologies are changing dramatically. Let me give an example.

Until recently, non-GMFs were confined to conventionally bred plants or organically grown plants. Now, "super organics," a new generation of food, has appeared on the market without the negative rhetoric that GMFs had received. "Smart breeding" is now possible without the assistance of transgenics. What smart breeding consists of is understanding the gene banks and the DNA markers of plants. These markers are inserted in a plant and crossbred with regional versions. Then food scientists analyze, test, and repeat the process until they reach the end result, which is a plant with the desirable inserted trait that will thrive in local conditions.[11] Smart breeding, in short, is possible because food scientists now understand, i.e., can create, a gene map of a plant genome. This situation has opened up agriculture through methods that are largely uncontroversial and also un-patentable.[12] Consequently, Monsanto is losing its monopoly and its patents. "We are on the verge of something enormous," Manning concludes, because

> Plant genomes carry age-old records that reveal the complex man-ner by which nature manages itself. Researchers around the world—McCouch, Goldman, and Jefferson are a few examples—are learning to not only read those records but re-create them. (215)

So super organics will produce new foods that change what we eat, but also the way we relate to the planet.[13] GMFs will still be available. Some, like Olathe Sweet Corn, will remain a welcome addition to the market-place, but I suspect that they will play a smaller role in the years to come and will eventually be replaced by super organics in the marketplace. Nev-ertheless, as McHughen reminds us, we must learn the facts behind GM technologies, biotechnologies, and each new product, and that is our best course of action.

The GMO (or GMC—Genetically Modified Crops) debate has shift-ed to Hawaii with the Rainbow papaya, which is genetically modified to resist a virus (the Ringspot virus) that devastated other papaya varieties on the big island.[14] There is serious disagreement among local university scientists and the local farmers concerning the GMC Rainbow papaya. The debate breaks down in a way that is similar to the arguments for and against GMCs. There are, however, some novel objections to their use. First of all are the results of tests on rats. A French researcher found that rats that ate Monsanto corn developed more tumors and died earlier than those in the control group. So are humans next if we permit GMCs? asked the opponents who wish to ban them. Other unintended consequences can affect plants. GMCs that were modified with a gene from a bacteria can tolerate herbicides, but unwanted plants can develop the toleration and are known as "superweeds," which farmers cannot control by conven-tional agricultural methods. Other unwanted consequences allegedly are the disappearance of bees and butterflies, an increase in allergies among children, and genetic contamination. The novice politician Greggor Ilagan and other local council members declined to form a task force to look into the matter and sought answers on their own. But they had difficulty find-ing out what the true facts were concerning GMCs, because the debaters discredited each other's arguments. After much debate, the ban on GMCs was voted on and approved, and the mayor signed the bill into law. Mr.

Ilagan was stunned, but it was time to move on to other political matters, like funding and building a long-awaited community park. Once again, politics trumps health and food issues. But the debate continues. Vermont has passed a bill to label genetically altered foods,[15] but big ag companies fear that labeling will mean consumers will not buy the foods. For the most part, it appears that the foods are safe. What is needed is to educate the public and to label foods so that consumers may have an informed choice among products.

Another advancement in plant science that has advantages over GMOs is marker-assisted or molecular breeding that speeds development of crops and new plants through DNA screening.[16] This won't replace GMOs, because that technology can achieve highly specific tasks that marker-assisted breeding cannot presently do. One advantage that marker-assisted breeding has is in bringing heirloom flavors back to tomatoes, which were lost when they were genetically modified in order to gain shelf life. Also marker-assisted breeding is spared public opposition because it lays bare the inherent genetic potential of an individual plant through DNA screening. "This technology is far removed from the better-known and more controversial field of genetic engineering, in which a plant or animal can receive genes from a *different* organism" (Higgins, A-4; emphasis added). So the desired traits can be developed within a couple of growing seasons instead of decades, and consequently we can perhaps sustainably feed an expanding population while coping with extremes of climate change.

Notes

1. Gregory E. Pence, "Introduction: The Meaning and Ethics of Food," in his *The Ethics of Food: A Reader for the 21ˢᵗ Century* (New York: Rowman & Littlefield Publishers, Inc., 2002), vii. Further references are made parenthetically by page number. For convenience to the reader, most of my discussion comes from this anthology.
2. Progress has been made on labeling information on the little stickers on loose fruits and vegetables. In a letter to the readers of *Gourmet* LXIII # 10 (October 2003): 58, Dr. Heather Koshinsky tells us: "A label with four digits indicates conventionally grown food. Labels with five digits starting with an 8 indicate that food is genetically modified. Labels with five digits starting with a 9 indicate that the food is organically grown."
3. For a more complete inventory of GMFs, see Marc Lappé, "Tasting Technology: The Agricultural Revolution in Genetically Engineered Plants," *Gastronomica: The Journal of Food and Culture* I # 1 (Winter 2001): 25-30.
4. For further discussion of this point about maize, consult the previous chapter (9).
5. Belinda Martineau, "Food Fight: The Short, Unhappy Life of the Flavr Savr Tomato," *The Sciences* XLI # 2 (Spring 2001): 24-29.
6. For a more complete, detailed discussion of this point, see Helena Norberg-Hodge, Peter Goering, and John Page, "From Global to Local: Sowing the Seeds of Community," 191-212, esp. 202ff.: "This new technology [genetic engineering] manipulates organisms in a fundamentally different and hazardous new way, precisely because it allows us to transcend the reproductive limitations imposed by nature, and because its anticipated effects can never be completely certain." And more importantly, "Genetically engineered foods already on the market in the US include corn, soybeans, potatoes, squash, tomatoes, chicory, and papaya, as well as milk and other dairy products from cows treated with a genetically engineered growth hormone (rBST). BST (also known as rBGH–recombinant bovine growth hormone) is a genetically engineered

hormone injected into one-third of dairy cows in the US to increase milk production. It is currently banned in Europe. There is a real possibility that the US Government and Monsanto, the manufacturer of BST, will use the WTO [World Trade Organization] to force the product into the EU [European Union]. The BST hormone causes a five-fold increase in the protein IGF-1, which passes into the milk. An EU Scientific Committee report links IGF-1 to breast and prostate cancer." Their prediction came true in June 2003 when the EU lifted the ban.

7. For an argument along this line of reasoning, see Kirsten Hansen, "Does Autonomy Count in Favor of Labeling Genetically Modified Food?" *Journal of Agricultural and Environmental Ethics* XVII # 1 (2004): 67-76.

8. Alan McHughen, *Pandora's Picnic Basket: The Potential and Hazards of Genetically Modified Foods* (Oxford: Oxford University Press, 2000), 263; emphasis added.

9. Olathe (pronounced "Oh-LAY-thuh") is a small town in the mountains of western Colorado in a high-desert area, where summers typically feature warm days and cool nights (the heat from the warm days is necessary for the corn to mature and the cool nights promote conversion of starches into sugar). This much-sought-after corn can be white, yellow, or bicolor: it is very fragile, so it requires picking by hand and cooling down in a slushy ice-water bath for immediate shipping. (My information about this delicious, late summer corn comes from Amy Culbertson, "Saluting Olathe Corn's Sweet Kernels," *Fort Worth Star-Telegram*, Wednesday, July 28, 2004, Food Section, E: 1 and 4.) Besides this corn, genetically modified Granny Smith and Golden Delicious varieties of apples have been engineered to suppress an enzyme that causes them to brown when sliced. (This was also done for the potato.) See Andrew Pollack (w. The New York Times), "Genetically altered apples approved," *Santa Fe New Mexican*, Sunday, February 13, 2015, A-2.

10. McHughen, *Pandora's Picnic Basket*, 49ff. There is a variety of ways that transgenic transfer can be accomplished. For *The Corn Growers' Guidebook*, see the web site: http://www.agry. purdue.edu/ext/corn/swt-corn-spec.html 11. Richard Manning, "Super Organics," *Wired* XII # 5 (May 2004): 176-180, 215. This issue is called "The Future of Food."

12. Manning, 178.

13. Manning, 215.

14. Amy Harmon, "On Hawaii, a Lonely Quest for Fact: Debate on Genetically Modified Crops Entangles a Novice Politician," *The New York Times*, vol. CLXIII, no. 56, 372 (Sunday, January 5, 2014): 1, 18, 19.

15. Dave Gram and Lisa Rathke (The Associated Press), "Vermont passes bill to label genetically altered foods," *Santa Fe New Mexican* (Friday, April 25, 2014): A-5. The state of Oregon has followed suit: see Jeff Barnard (The Associated Press), "Genetically modified food debate before Oregon voters: Small farmers want to stop cross-pollination of crops," *Santa Fe New Mexican* (Sunday, May 18, 2014): A-2.

16. Adrian Higgins (The Washington Post), "Molecular breeding speeds development of crops, new plants," *Santa Fe New Mexican* (Monday, April 21, 2014): A-4. Technology sometimes makes beneficial advances and we, as consumers, should be receptive to these improvements. We should look at these changes on a case-by-case basis. For a good argument for this position, see Julian Baggini, *The Virtues of the Table: How to Eat and Think* (London: Granta Publications, 2014), ch. 10, esp. 124. Food companies are hopeful that there will be changes in the public's attitude toward GMOs; see Mary Clare Jalonick, "Next-generation GMOs may have healthy benefits," *Santa Fe New Mexican* (Thursday, April 2, 2015): A-4; and "GMOs: Safe to eat, says science," *The Week*, vol. 16, issue 773 (June 3, 2016): 16. Also Danny Hakim (with the *New York Times*): "Doubts about promised bounty of genetically modified crops: Use of GMOs in U.S., Canada, has not accelerated yield increases or led to reduced pesticide use," *Santa Fe New Mexican* (Sunday, October 30, 2016): A-12. This research questions one of the (utilitarian) arguments for GMFs.

11

Is There a Pornography of Food?

* * *

There is some literature on food porn, and it is fairly recent. The most current, and most controversial, is a piece by Andrew Chan that appeared in *Gastronomica*.[1] But associating food with pornography is not a new idea: "It . . . [has] finally begun to dawn on the public that food of a country is [as] legitimate . . . a field of study as its politics or its philosophy," Sophie Coe writes, "and that the old school of food writing, which might be called gastro-pornography, is not the only way to approach a cuisine."[2] This kind of writing is encapsulated in advertising. Roland Barthes is probably the first to observe this phenomenon: "Visual advertising makes it possible to associate certain kinds of food with images connoting a sublimated sexuality. In a certain sense, advertising eroticizes food and thereby transforms our consciousness of it, bringing it into a new sphere of situations by means of a pseudo-causal relationship."[3] The most blatant TV advertisement employing food porn is the fast-food hamburger chain Carl's Jr. "Texas BBQ sauce burger" advertisement (August 2014), which shows a scantly dressed young woman (wearing a black bikini) washing a black truck while eating the burger with a seductive look and pose, and another female counterpart shows up to join the scene. (There is no doubt where the focus of attention is supposed to be.)[4] Cooking shows accomplish this kind of communication by visual association or connotation of meaning. How they do this is explained by Jean-François Revel: "To as great a degree as sexuality, food is inseparable from imagination."[5] Chan acknowledges this premise but lacks a sufficient argument to show how it works in the analogy between food and pornography.

From a philosophical point of view, there are serious flaws in Chan's argument. First of all, he thinks *all* cooking shows are pornography. Anyone who has watched a number of cooking shows knows that this is not the case. He claims that "contemporary TV cooking shows create a gap that separates the viewer from the reality of actual cookery." His reason for this claim is that "everything has been carefully planned and prepared beforehand to appear spontaneous and effortless on-camera."[6] Good home cooks do precisely this kind of planning and preparation of the ingredients of a recipe in order to save time and to be more efficient. The appearance of spontaneity and effortlessness on camera is mostly due to practice and time constraints. Chan's belief that the complete steps in cooking have been omitted for the same reasons is simply not true. If one watches Rachael Ray's *30 Minute Meals* or Ina Garten's *Barefoot Contessa* on the Food Network, he or she will see that all the steps in preparation are indeed there. These ladies are self-trained and didn't attend cooking school, so their approach is more that of the home cook than that of a professional chef. So the wide gap he perceives between a professional restaurant kitchen and the everyday domestic kitchen is greatly exaggerated. Consequently most of Chan's characterization of cooking shows (which I will review below) is off the mark.

The analogy between cooking shows and pornography is stretched beyond belief with remarks like "food preparation is a form of foreplay" and perfect presentations of food and vertical displays are comparable to "human sex-toy actors in porno films." His list of cooking shows is selective at best. First up is the BBC's *Gourmet Ireland* that centers around a married couple who are professional chefs and restaurateurs that travel around Ireland, and when the show cuts to the studio, "the viewer gets to watch the couple 'do it,' as it were." "We watch them banter and chuckle in a type of foreplay" as they cook "and tease each other over the preparation methods." I suspect that these remarks (and similar ones) are more about Chan's thesis than the couple cooking. As it is stated, Chan's analogy doesn't work. The analogy between cooking shows and pornography, however, is not without merit. My guess is that he hasn't thought through what pornography is in order to make the notion of food porn more convincing.

For the analogy to have more merit, we have to think of pornography in relation to food in a less explicit, sexual way than Chan has done. Pornography is thought of as objectionable because it treats women disrespectfully, as mere objects.[7] It is intended to stimulate erotic or sexual rather than aesthetic feelings. When it is highly offensive or morally repugnant, it becomes obscene. And for obscenity there are statutory definitions in both US and Canadian law, but not for pornography.[8] In addition to lack of respect for women, there is the lack of (proper) emotion in motivating sex. Food porn, analogously, is objectionable because it disrespects food.[9] How that disrespect is carried out is by exaggerating gastronomic features. In other words, disrespect is present when these features are intentionally manipulated or mistreated in food practices that have sexual suggestions running through them. Chan gives a good example of this with Jamie Oliver in his *The Naked Chef* series, where sexual scenarios become manifest with his gestures, as when he *pokes* at some meat he is preparing. Actions like poking need to be quite suggestive in order for labels like food porn to be legitimately applied to food practices; generalities like *food preparations are a kind of foreplay* do not hold because most food preparations are not like Oliver poking at meat. Poking at meat can be rather perverse and hence disrespectful of food items, in addition to telling us something about Oliver. You cannot find any episode in Ray or Garten cooking shows that even remotely suggest this. The Oliver incident indicates that food porn has two dimensions that need to be fleshed out. Pertaining to the object, the exaggerated gastronomical features could be size, shape, ingredients (especially unhealthy ingredients or portions), or cost. Pertaining to the subject or viewer, the object excites the appetite, overeating, overindulging, or desire for the object without regard to constraints or restrictions. Food porn creates lack of respect for food, especially the presentation and consumption. Hot dog and chicken wing eating contests are prime examples. Food porn encourages bad food habits. Nutrition and health concerns are minimized or marginalized.

There is a dark side to food production. Many vegans and vegetarians object to the slaughter and butchering of animals, and Carol Adams goes so far as to label this as *The Pornography of Meat*.[10] Chan concludes from this perspective that "by its nature, the cooking program is deceptive, because the primary nature of food is disguised or excised." Apparently Chan and I do not watch the same cooking shows. Some of these do show viewers how to cut up a chicken or to quarter a side of beef. Indeed some show the slaughter and butchering of animals; for instance, some of Anthony Bourdain's shows (*No Reservations* and *A Cook's Tour*) portray this dark side of the kitchen. In detail, Chan writes:

> This voyeurism seems almost kinky, as though Bourdain is living out our darkest desires and fantasies by dining off the carcass of some freshly slaughtered beast or sucking the flesh from deep-fried spiders in a market in Thailand or Vietnam (and that's only breakfast). It is visceral, covert television at times. Through the grainy, blurry footage, we see our intrepid chef on the move and in possible danger—venturing into parts unknown and meeting someone he doesn't know, every image caught in a steamy, pseudo-wildlife-documentary style.

This passage contradicts his earlier conclusion (see above) where he claims these events are either disguised or excised in culinary programs. Obviously Bourdain exploits these moments for the purposes that Chan gives.

The context and intent of most cooking shows are educational.[11] I cannot imagine Sara Moulton's *Sara's Secrets* making viewers feel "inadequate or unconfident in their own culinary prowess." Her shows are no-nonsense, with the focus on the food and not her. In contrast to Moulton is Nigella Lawson and her series *Nigella Bites* (and more recently on the Cooking Channel three shows have emerged: *Nigella Kitchen, Nigellissima,* and *Forever Summer with Nigella*) in which she "jokes about her inadequacies with a knife or her weakness for licking the bowl and then sensuously licking her fingers." Chan continues:

> As a naughty (and seemingly unfulfilled) housewife and self-declared amateur cook, her premise (and promise) is that at home—or at least in her TV home—we can and indeed should all get down and dirty. She assures the viewer that it's perfectly natural and not shameful to cook like she does, or at least to watch her cook—and like a spectator at a nudist camp, we buy into her libertine ways. . . . Nigella leads by example, exuding passion and emotion as she handles food, which she fondles and caresses before voraciously devouring it in front of our eyes. She flirts with her unseen audience as the camera plays up her physicality.

Chan is *interpreting* these shows from the actions that make up preparing, cooking, and presenting. Any of these actions could be interpreted differently, but with Nigella he is on the money.

Another British cooking series that Chan takes delight in discussing is *Two Fat Ladies,* which was not only very popular in England, but also here in the United States. Clarissa Dickson and Jennifer Paterson rode around on a three-wheel motorcycle to cook for groups of people—whether they were scouts, nuns, or preparatory students. TV viewers loved them because they were so irreverent in their culinary approach—using ingredients like butter that most chefs would avoid or use in moderation. These women took delight in breaking the culinary establishment rules even though they were classically trained chefs. This is the main reason why they were so much fun to watch—you never knew what they were going to do next. Was their show "food porn"? No. So it is interesting that he included them, since they appear to be a counterexample to his thesis.

Where Chan uses the analogy between pornography and TV cooking shows the most is in his discussion of Emeril Lagasse. He speaks of him as "a larger-than-life human phallus." In describing Emeril's style, Chan says "even the introduction of the ingredients is a performance in itself, with a loud exclamation of 'Bam!' every time Emeril adds a handful of spice to a dish, which acts like a laugh track to cue the studio audience and work it up into a frenzy."(Emeril explained recently that the reason why he shouts "Bam!" is to wake up the audience.) Furthermore, "each dish is an act that culminates in the meal, and every finished plate . . . in each course is like the 'money shot.'"[12] So the analogy carried to food is "the money shot as the signifier, as in Emeril's exclamatory 'Bam!,' prompts the audience in the studio (and presumably at home) to issue his/her own groan or sigh in a collective virtual orgasm with the chef presenter . . . the hook, presumably, to keep them 'coming' again. Sometimes the money shot comes when the chef tastes the meal or invites a member of the studio audience (as in *Emeril Live*) or 'real people' (as in *The Two Fat Ladies*) to taste along." So here we have it: the completed analogy between cooking shows and pornography for Chan. What are we to make of this? Not much. For any of Emeril's actions to be pornographic, he needs to be complicit with them, or for them to be carried out in a manner where he intends them to be erotic or sexual in meaning or connotation. I see no intentions of this sort displayed. So these actions are not pornographic.

Some of Chan's analogical remarks are *ad hominem,* or what is commonly referred to as the fallacy against the person or fallacy of abusiveness; for instance, referring to Emeril as "a larger-than-life human phallus." This also borders on the fallacy of false analogy, because the dissimilarities are greater than the similarities.[13] The greatest dissimilarity is that obviously pornography involves people, especially the degradation of women, and those who do the degrading (usually men) tacitly approve of it, whereas food shows (and only a few) show disrespect or abuse of food, and the cooks or chefs are conscious that what they are doing is abuse. The similarities are superficial: both pornography and TV cooking shows can be entertaining, and both can stimulate the appetites (this is probably the most important analogical feature—and it is superficial). Another significant similarity between food and pornography is touch or tactile sensations in food preparation. With food, it is handling it, cutting and tearing it up. With pornography the touch or tactile sensations are obviously parts of the human body. Given the remarks like those I have cited above of Emeril (and Jamie), it is no wonder that their agents refused to grant permission to use photographs of them within Chan's article.[14] So the editors of *Gastronomica* decided to go with empty picture frames (except for Canova's editorial, which appears in the first frame as a preface to Chan's piece)!

To reiterate, Chan's analogy as it stands is too strong to be credible. But the analogy is useful. It needs to be weakened, however, along the lines that I have suggested. The definition I propose is: *food porn* is objectionable because it disrespects food. How that disrespect is carried out is by exaggerating gastronomic features. In other words, disrespect is present in an action when these features are intentionally manipulated or mistreated in food practices that have sexual suggestions running through them. For instance, Nigella leaning over a pot of soup with her breasts partially exposed for the camera to capture for the viewer is suggestive, if not exactly pornographic. The aim of pornography is to entice the viewer to engage in sexual activity, whereas food porn distracts the viewer from thinking about the food to thinking about sex. Food becomes secondary. This extended definition I think captures those actions in some TV cooking shows that could be labeled as food porn. Most importantly, it leaves out those that wouldn't be labeled as such without strong interpretation.

Notes

1. Andrew Chan, " '*La grande bouffe*' Cooking Shows as Pornography," *Gastronomica—The Journal of Food and Culture* III no. 4 (Fall 2003): 47-53.
2. Sophie Coe, *America's First Cuisines* (Austin: The University of Texas Press, 1994), 250.
3. Roland Barthes, "Sugar and Other Systems," *The Journal of Gastronomy* III (Fall 1984): 88; first published in 1961.
4. This TV ad has caught the eye of women's groups; see Brady McCombs (w. The Associated Press), "Women target Carl's Jr. ads," *Santa Fe New Mexican*, Wednesday, September 3, 2014: B-3. Carl's Jr. has a newer ad (September 2014) minus the sexual overtones, so they may have pulled the previous ad because of the pressure from women's groups. The later ad just shows an unshaven guy, dressed in black, eating the Texas BBQ thick burger. Another ad shows a woman dressed as a stewardess getting ready to take a big bite out of a Mile High Burger (September 2014), but by the November 2014 ad, a sexy stewardess is removing clothing while eating the burger. The list goes on.
5. Jean-François Revel, *Culture and Cuisine: A Journey through the History of Food*, trans. by Helen R. Lane, (Garden City, New York: Doubleday & Co., 1979/1982), 8. For an analysis of Revel's conception of cuisine, see chapter 7.
6. Early on in TV cooking shows, things did not always run smoothly. On *The French Chef* series, Julia Child in the early sixties started taping the shows. In one of them she picks up a chicken she was washing and drops it on the floor. She promptly picks it up and continues her prep work with it. All this was caught on camera and was not edited out in the showing of that session. Other times she recalls: "The nonstop taping we have always continued, and in only a few instances, after the disaster of the first onion soup show, have we had to break off, erase, and pick up again. I can remember only half a dozen occasions, some of which were due to electrical failures, others due to me. Once, doing the 'Lobster *a' l'Américaine*,' every time I touched the cooktop I got a short-circuit in the microphone against my chest, and kept clutching my breast in a very odd fashion. It felt like a bee sting. We wiped out back to the worst clutch, and were able to continue in midstream. Another time, 'The Flaming Soufflé' collapsed in its dish on the way to the dining room; I had forgotten to put in the cornstarch. We merely waited for the standby soufflé to come out of the oven and used that. Otherwise we let the gaffes lie where they fell, and on the whole it is just as well." Julia Child, "About the Television Series," in *The French Chef Cookbook*, drawings and photographs by Paul Child (New York: Alfred A. Knopf, 1961/1968), xiii. In his series *Good Eats*, Alton Brown employs slapstick comedy to go hand-in-hand with his scientific approach to cooking to make the shows more entertaining. For example, in one episode his kitchen is invaded by the Food Police to interrogate him on his ingredients and their quantities. Another time, in applying butter to a turkey at the sink, it slips out of his hands and flies out the kitchen window.
7. Ann Garry, "Pornography and Respect for Women," in *Morality and Moral Controversies*, edited by John Arthur (Second Edition; Englewood Cliffs, New Jersey: Prentice-Hall, 1986), 67-74. Another good source is Susan Dwyer, *The Problem of Pornography* (Belmont, California: Wadsworth Publishing Company, 1995). Many of the ideas I develop for the notion of food porn—in addition to pornography in general—come from Dwyer's anthology.
8. Dwyer, 22.
9. As a side note, there are ways other than sexual gestures to show disrespect for food. We no longer grow our own food, so the idea of respect and disrespect seems remote or even unintelligible to the modern Western mind, but it is not uncommon in other cultures. For instance, most Native American tribes treated food with reverence or deep respect, so most of the practices that make up cooking shows exhibit disrespect or irreverence. For details, see chapter 9.

10. Carol J. Adams, *The Pornography of Meat* (New York: Continuum, 2003). Her two earlier books are: *Neither Man nor Beast: Feminism and the Defense of Animals* (New York: Continuum, 1990), and *The Sexual Politics of Meat: A Feminist-Vegetarian Critical Theory* (New York: Continuum, 1994).

11. Besides educational shows, there are competitive ones among the TV cooking shows. Examples are plentiful: *Iron Chef America, Chopped, Master Chef, Cupcake Wars, Man versus Food,* and *Guy's Grocery Games,* to name a few. It is here that Chan's statement about making viewers feel "inadequate or unconfident in their own culinary prowess" applies.

12. Chan explains the "money shot" as "the commonly used descriptor in pornographic films for the scene containing the climax/orgasm scene, i.e., when the male actor ejaculates for the camera. As Susan Faludi noted in 'The Money Shot,' her [30th October] 1995 *New Yorker* [pp. 64-85] essay on Los Angeles' pornographic film industry, 'The on command male (erection) orgasm is the central convention of the industry: all porn scenes should end with a visible ejaculation. There are various names for it: the pop shot, the payoff shot, the cum shot; most resonant is 'the money shot.' Hence in porn the (usually male) viewer is aroused by the on-screen ejaculation as a trigger for his own. Whether or not it confirms his own masculinity, there is a reciprocity of some transferential [sic.] kind through his own off-screen ejaculation."

13. For the structure of analogical arguments, see chapter 8; and for an exposition of these fallacies (*ad hominem* and the fallacy of false analogy), see Robert D. Boyd, *Critical Reasoning and Logic* (Upper Saddle River, New Jersey: Prentice-Hall, 2003), 57 & 111.

14. Jane Canova (Managing Editor), "Erotic Nightmares," *Gastronomica—The Journal of Food and Culture* III # 4 (Fall 2003): 46.

12

Chocolate and Its World

* * *

This chapter focuses primarily on the chemical properties of chocolate and the reactions or effects of these properties on the human body. What are the health benefits, if any, of chocolate? Are there side effects from drinking or eating it? These two issues as well as the nature of the cocoa plant are addressed in this essay. Some ethical considerations concerning consumption are brought to light. The rich history of chocolate in Mesoamerica and Europe covers nearly four millennia. This history will be discussed in some detail in this chapter.

The Substance. Chocolate consists of over five hundred compounds, with little over half known or identified. This is why it has never been synthesized or artificially reproduced. Those compounds that are well known are caffeine, theobromine, serotonin, and phenylethylamine. The first two, caffeine and theobromine, are alkaloids. Both are plant products found in coffee and tea as well as in chocolate. Their bitterness gives pleasurable sensations to human beings. The amount of caffeine found in chocolate is minimal; for example, a bar of fine chocolate (about 3.5 ounces, or 100 grams) contains less caffeine than a cup of regular coffee. However, the presence of caffeine means that chocolate is a stimulant to the central nervous system and is a diuretic agent. Serotonin and phenylethylamine are mood-changing chemicals that affect the brain. These contribute to the pleasure that eating or drinking chocolate yields. Of the above four compounds, theobromine may be the most interesting. The theobromine alkaloid is unique in this Mesoamerican plant, and modern chemical analysis has been able to identify traces in ceramic vessels that contained chocolate with radiocarbon dates between 1800 and 1400 BCE in Mesoamerica. The presence of this compound in the pots of Mesoamerican cultures established that the drink made from chocolate was consumed much earlier than believed—even before the Olmec period. Theobromine is closely related to caffeine and has the same side effects; it is also found in small amounts in Kola nuts and tea.

Tools and Processing. What is (was) necessary for making chocolate? The first specific tools we know of are from the Mayan period (ca. 500 CE): cylindrical vases or jars were used for a chocolate drink—some of which had a stand and a lid with a handle. Women poured the chocolate preparation from one vessel to another in order to produce a foam or froth. The Aztecs (ca. 1500 CE) considered the foam to be the most desirable part of the drink. The cacao beans were first dried, then fermented, then ground on a heated curved grinding stone called a *metate*. Next the ground beans were soaked, steeped, aerated, filtered, and dried again into wafers or tablets (to which Aztec warriors added water to make "instant chocolate" during military campaigns). Another method for creating the foam or froth was later achieved by beating hot chocolate with a large wooden swizzle-stick called a *molinillo*. The molinillos had different decorative heads with geometrical designs that are aesthetically attractive. These molinillos or rotary whisks with their grooved heads were spun back and forth between the hands with speed to produce the foam. The drink was then served in a gourd or clay cup (*jicara*) by the Aztecs. The drink was accepted by the colonial Spaniards, and it eventually made its way to Spain. By the seventeenth century, the Spanish were making chocolate but adding new ingredients, such as anise seed, black pepper, cinnamon, sugar, and nuts in addition to the ingredients that the Mesoamericans added to the ground cacao beans, which included chiles, vanilla, and various leaves and flowers. The method for making chocolate remained the same in Europe as it was in the New World until the nineteenth century, when the process became mechanized. Until then the Europeans rolled the chocolate by hand into sheets and rolls, and then made them into cakes or bricks that could be further processed into a drink or a wafer bar to eat.

The cacao tree, which grows between three and ten meters high as an understory tree in the rain forest, is pollinated by insects called midges. The tree usually grows within about 20° latitude of the equator; notably in West Africa, Central America, parts of South America, and the Caribbean Islands. But the tree was introduced into Asia and the Pacific Rim in addition to the Hawaiian Islands in the nineteenth century. How it was introduced—by seeds (unlikely) or seedlings or trees—remains a mystery. Three subspecies of trees produce cacao pods: the Forastero, the Criollo, and the Trinitario. Forastero trees account for over 90 percent of world production and are cultivated mainly in Africa and Brazil. The Forastero bean is good but has no special qualities. Criollo trees, native to Venezuela, produce the most delicate, complex, and flavorful chocolates. Unfortunately, the trees are very fragile and expensive to harvest, so chocolate made from their beans is quite rare and expensive. The Trinitario is a cross between the first two and has traits of both parent trees—sturdier and more prolific than the Criollo, but approaching it in subtlety and flavor. It can be harvested twice a year under decent circumstances. Some chocolates are a blend of these different beans to bring about the flavor profile the manufacturer wants. The beans, incidentally, were used as currency by the ancient Mesoamericans—and some Mesoamericans continued the practice until the early part of the last century.

The cacao beans were first dried in the sun for five to seven days. But they had to be selected from fully ripe fruit in order to have maximum flavor or taste. They had to be fermented to develop flavor because the seeds themselves have an intense bitterness, so the cacao fruit had to be cut or stripped of some of the pulp so it could ferment when exposed to the air. After fermentation, the beans were removed from the fruit or remaining pulp and dried, then cleaned, and after that roasted. Roasting insures that the shells can be easily removed to produce the center of the beans, called "nibs." Today a machine that removes the hulls from the nibs is called a winnower. Each nib contains an average of 54 percent cocoa butter, which is a natural fat. The Europeans cooked with it, and after their arrival, the Mesoamericans began to do so, too. The diets of both changed drastically during and immediately after the Columbian exchange. In 1828, Conrad J. van Houten, a Dutch chocolate maker, invented a hydraulic press that reduced the cocoa butter content by nearly half, which allowed the remaining substance to be ground into a powder known as "cocoa." He treated the cocoa with potassium and sodium carbonates—alkaline salts—so it would mix more easily with water. This process is called "Dutching," and produces what we refer to as Dutch chocolate, which has a mild dark taste. Twenty-one years later, Joseph Storrs Fry (and sons) combined chocolate with sugar and remixed it with cocoa butter to make a solid. This became the world's first eating chocolate—what we associate with chocolate bars. During this time, however, actual bars were created by John Cadbury, a Briton who developed an emulsification process that led to making solid chocolate. These inventions led to more production and lower prices, so soon average Americans and Europeans, not just the wealthy, were eating chocolate. The dark side of this mass production was slave labor by imported Africans and forced labor by Native Americans. The practice of using slave labor to produce the cacao for one's morning chocolate dates back to eighteenth century Europe, and was common among the ancient Mayans and Aztecs. Hence, chocolate was not free from this grave immorality until the late nineteenth century. Child labor is still a common practice in West Africa, however, and 75 percent of the world's cacao bean production comes from there. Consequently, most of our chocolate has a moral shadow cast over it. One way for the consumer to avoid abetting child slavery would be for manufacturers to put the place of origin on their labels, just as it is done with most wines.

Health Issues. Is chocolate good for you? Dark chocolate is, but only in moderation because of the fat, calories, and carbohydrates it contains; for instance, one bar of Hershey's Special Dark Chocolate has 12 grams of fat, 25 grams of carbohydrates, and 180 calories. Protein is minimal: two grams. The numbers are more impressive when we look at larger quantities: a pound of dark chocolate contains 2,300 calories, 140 grams of fat, 100 milligrams of cholesterol, 270 milligrams of sodium, 2,070 grams of carbohydrates, and 31 grams of protein. Europeans and Americans consume most of the world's chocolate; the Swiss lead all nations with 22.36 pounds per year per person. Americans are in eleventh place with 11.64 pounds per year. Furthermore, chocolate is not good for other animals; it can kill dogs and cats and possibly horses. The reason for this is theobromine, which they cannot metabolize, so it poisons them rather quickly. It should not be given to infants because their digestive system has not developed enough to process it. It can make them sick. (In fact, children were not given chocolate of any kind until the nineteenth century—it was thought of as an adult beverage and food.) White chocolate does not contain theobromine, and milk chocolate contains only small quantities, so these will not affect infants or other animals. An important question for those who have celiac disease and other similar conditions is: Is chocolate gluten free? The simple answer is yes, it is naturally so, but the problem is that chocolate is almost always mixed with other ingredients and those may not be gluten free, so one needs to read the ingredient declaration on the package. Chocolate maker Lindt is mindful of this dietary restriction and labels their products accordingly. Other manufacturers have followed suit. Speaking of other manufacturers, the American Milton Hershey (1857-1945) built a chocolate empire that matched the Swiss and English giants. A town in Pennsylvania, where his factory turns out the famous Hershey's Kisses and candy bars, bears his name. With the assistance of nutritionists who helped enhance the healthful qualities of his products, he soon took over the American market, and his products made their way to the European market—challenging Europe's supremacy. Some of these healthful qualities of chocolate are the flavonoids *phenolic* and *quercetin*. Phenolic is an antioxidant that helps prevent oxidation of LDL ("bad") cholesterol and helps prevent heart disease. The saturated fat in cocoa butter, which are mainly stearic triglycerides, arguably has no effect on blood cholesterol levels, although this conclusion is somewhat controversial among medical scientists. Phenolics furthermore prevent chocolate from going rancid, which partially explains its long shelf life. Quercetin is another antioxidant that is also an anti-inflammatory agent. So the two flavonoids contribute to the health profile of chocolate. At the beginning of the last century, chocolate was thought to have caused or aggravated acne and cavities or tooth decay; medical studies proved both of these claims to be false. Acne is not linked to diet but rather to one's physiology. Sugar in chocolate could contribute to tooth decay, but cocoa butter would counteract the sugar because it coats the teeth and may help protect them from plaque formation. So sugar and cocoa butter cancel one another out. Dental hygiene (or the lack thereof) is the culprit in cavities or tooth decay, not chocolate. Of some concern is the fact that during production chocolate absorbs lead, even though the level of lead is one of the lowest found in natural foods. The amount of lead varies in chocolates, so there is some concern that it may cause mild lead poisoning. This is another reason to purchase only high-quality chocolate and to consume it only in moderation. Inferior chocolates may have a greater concentration of lead than chocolates of good quality. In eighteenth- and nineteenth-century cookbooks, there are warnings about chocolate adulterated with brick dust and red lead to replace cacao solids and to provide the proper color—all in the name of reducing cost. One hopes these adulterations no longer appear in our chocolate.

Can chocolate be as addictive as a drug? For some people, just thinking about it can stimulate the release of the neurotransmitter dopamine, which can cause the brain to relax control over indulgence and overeating. But more than that, neuroscientists have found that eating chocolate triggers the production of natural opioids. (Opioids are chemicals, such as those found in opium, that increase a feeling of well-being or euphoria and decrease or dull pain.) However, the greatest discovery yet is the presence in chocolate of cannabinoids, which act like cannabis to stimulate certain cannabinoid receptors in cells. What makes a person "high" from ingesting marijuana is a chemical called tetrahydrocannabinol (THC). This chemical resembles anandamide (a kind of neurotransmitter) found naturally in the brain (in traces or very small amounts) and in chocolate (also in small amounts); it acts like a neurotransmitter when ingested. This analysis helps explain why some people crave chocolate—it may extend feelings of well-being. One big difference between THC and the cannabinoids found in chocolate is that the former affects the whole brain, while the latter is limited to just some areas of the brain, and the effect lasts for only a very short period of time. So to get any marijuana-like effects, a person would have to eat one-fifth of his or her body weight in dark chocolate—and given that it is eaten, it would be difficult to determine how much enters the bloodstream and actually reaches the brain. And speaking of the brain, recent studies have modestly shown that a compound (flavanols) in cocoa aids brain health and can reverse age-related memory loss. Accordingly, conservative politicians need not rush to pass laws to forbid or regulate the consumption of chocolate. Presently, regulation of chocolate primarily addresses purity, additives, and known health claims.

Is chocolate an aphrodisiac? At one time or another, almost everything edible was considered an aphrodisiac, and chocolate is no exception. Of course there is the placebo effect: if one thinks that chocolate will have that effect, it probably will. Advocates' arguments (ancient and modern) about this attribute are not convincing and not worth repeating here. At this point there are only social and cultural connections between chocolate and amorous feelings or love—the giving of chocolates, for example, on February 14—Saint Valentine's Day. There is no physiological basis for these associations, however, and the practices are concentrated in the Americas and Europe—although the chocolate trail is making its way through Asia and the Middle East.

Cooking and Baking. In cooking and baking, one must distinguish the different types of chocolate. First, true chocolate consists of cocoa butter and cocoa solids, which together are known as "chocolate liquor." The percentages of these two components determine the type. *Unsweetened chocolate*, also known as bitter chocolate, is unadulterated chocolate liquor that has been tempered (see below) so it can be molded. This is used primarily in baking. The US Food and Drug Administration requires that it contain at least 50 percent cocoa butter. *Bittersweet chocolate*, with a chocolate liquor content of at least 35 percent, also contains flavoring (like vanilla), lecithin (an emulsifier usually made from soy beans), about 27 percent cocoa butter, and sugar (typically about 33 percent). *Sweet chocolate* and *semisweet chocolate* consist of dark chocolate with additional fat and sugar in the cocoa mixture. *Sweet* requires a 15 percent concentration of chocolate liquor. *Semisweet* has a lower sugar content; it is interchangeable with bittersweet in baking. Dark chocolates are the ones that are the healthiest for you. Along with cocoa butter, sweeteners, and flavorings, *milk chocolate* has added dried milk powder to produce this popular eating chocolate. Dried milk powder is added because milk's high water content would render the chocolate too liquid. To be labeled as milk chocolate, the product must have a minimum of 10 percent chocolate liquor and 12 percent milk solids.

White chocolate is not really a chocolate because it has no chocolate liquor in any percentage; it is just a mixture of sugar, cocoa butter, milk powder, and vanilla or vanillin. To select the best white chocolate, make sure that it contains cocoa butter and no other fats. Avoid products labeled "white coating"; it is waxy and bland. The last two chocolates— milk chocolate and white chocolate—have a short shelf life, usually eight to twelve months, because of their milk content. Dark chocolate has a long shelf life and will last indefinitely if it is stored away from light, high humidity, and heat. Ideally, 65 degrees Fahrenheit with 50 percent humidity without variation would be best. Does chocolate ever go bad? Only if it is not kept properly. It should not be put into the freezer due to the fact it will develop condensation and will "bloom" white patches or *oysters* because the cocoa butter crystals will make the chocolate gray when there are temperature and humidity changes. This will also change the texture and it will become crumbly, but the chocolate will still be edible. The only time to avoid eating it is if you see mold on it; then discard. Besides, who would be able to keep chocolate long enough for it to go bad? So this is surely an academic question.

In the seventeenth and eighteenth centuries, the Italians tried cooking with it in their *pasticcie* (meat pasties or dishes) and in pastas—in lasagna, for example, with a chocolate sauce that included nuts and anchovies. Along with the Germans, they experimented with soups that had chocolate as an ingredient. But they soon gave up on the savory dishes in favor of desserts. In Europe during the eighteenth century, chocolate began to appear in pastries, cakes, and sorbets.

What remains today as a savory dish is the Mexican *pavo in mole poblano*. The word "mole" comes from the Aztec word *molli*, which means a saucy dish. *Mole* easily became the National Dish of Mexico, probably in the early nineteenth century. Moles are called sauces, but they were (and are) so rustic and heavy that they could be called stews. Their ingredients usually include a mixture of dried chile peppers, nuts, spices (cloves and cinnamon), tomatoes, raisins, garlic, onion, unsweetened chocolate, dried corn tortillas, and chicken stock.

Recently, new uses of chocolate have emerged on the culinary scene: dishes such as chocolate spaghetti and pasta—both sweet and savory. (You can Google these recipes.) About a decade ago, a competitor in a Texas barbeque cook-off used cocoa powder, cracked black pepper, assorted herbs and spices in a rub for a brisket. (It wasn't my recipe, but I was disappointed that he didn't place—probably too creative for the judges.)

Chocolate candies were perfected through "tempering," a delicate, final process of melting and cooling for mixing ingredients that stabilizes the fat and sugar crystals so that the chocolate will have good texture and snap or crisp bite. It also ensures that no bloom or oysters of cocoa fat will streak the surface of the finished chocolate. A related process, called *conching* (named for the original shell-shaped machine), was invented by Charles Lindt, a Swiss chocolate maker, which involves heating and grinding chocolate solids so that everything is evenly blended to ensure a uniform product that is luxuriously glossy and smooth. This can take up to several days for the best chocolate to develop its full potential of nuances, accents, and aromas. Today Lindt and other manufacturers' candies and chocolates are abundantly present on retail shelves and enjoyed by millions.

Further Reading

Bau, F. 2011. *Cooking with Chocolate: Essential Recipes and Techniques*. Flammarion, Paris.

Bernstein, Lenny, in the *Washington Post*, February 12, 2015. "Chocolates loaded with heavy metals? Watchdog: Levels of lead, cadmium in some brands warrants warning labels." *Santa Fe New Mexican*, A-1 and A-4.

Coe, S. & Coe, M. 2007. *The True History of Chocolate*. Second edition. Thames & Hudson, London.

Daley, R. 2001. *In the Sweet Kitchen: The Definitive Baker's Companion*. Artisan, New York.

Engoron, E. with Goodbody, M. 2011. *Coclatique: 150 Simply Elegant Desserts*. Running Press, Philadelphia.

Herbst, S. T. 1990. *Food Lover's Companion*. Barron's Educational Series, Hauppauge, New York. Chocolate entry, pp. 95-96.

Knukle, Frederick, in the *Washington Post*, October 27, 2014. "Compound in cocoa aids brain health—study"; "Chocolate can reverse age-related memory loss." *Santa Fe New Mexican*, Life & Science section, A-7.

Lebovitz, D. 2004. *The Great Book of Chocolate*. Ten Speed Press, Berkeley, California.

Olney, J. with Klingel, R. 1982. *The Joy of Chocolate*. Barron's Educational Series, Woodbury, New York.

Spadaccini, J. 2011. "Chocolate: Facts, History, and Factory Tour." *Exploratorium Magazine*. http://www.exploratorium.edu/exploring/exploring--chocolate/. Retrieved 10/26/2011.

Thomas, A. 25 December 2011. "Brussels: The Chocolate Trail." *The New York Times*, Travel, 1, 6, 7.

Tomaso, E. d., Beltramo, M. & Piomelli, D. 22 August 1996. "Brain Cannabinoids in Chocolate." *Nature*, 382, 677-678.

US State Dept. 2011. "Estimates 100,000 children in forced (enslaved) labor in chocolate production in West Africa." CNN News Report, January 21, 2012, 11:15a.m. MST.

Williams, G. Winter [Nov. 20th] 2011. "Baliwood: Two Modern-Day Willy Wonkas are building the world's first bamboo chocolate factory." *The New York Times Style Magazine*, 75, 78, 80.

Young, A. M. 2007. *The Chocolate Tree: A Natural History of Cacao*. Revised & Expanded Edn. Univ. Press of Florida, Gainesville.

N. A. [no author cited] 2011. Chocolate from *Wikipedia, the free encyclopedia*. http://en.wikipedia.org/wiki/Chocolate. Retrieved 10/26/2011.

N. A. 2012. Theobroma Cacao from *Wikipedia, the free encyclopedia*. http://en.wikipedia.org/w/index.php?title=Theobroma_cacao. Retrieved 1/25/2012.

13

Eating and Dining: Collingwood's Anthropology

* * *

In *The Principles of History*, R. G. Collingwood (1889-1943) makes an important distinction: "The history of dining is not the history of eating; it is in virtue of his rationality that he not only eats but dines"[1] (PH, 46). Reason has given rise to institutions like dining. He elaborates: "On a foundation of animal life his rationality builds a structure of free activities, free in the sense that although they are based on his animal nature they do not proceed from it but are invented by his reason on its own initiative, and serve not the purposes of animal life but the purposes of reason itself" (PH, 46). It is because of institutions, including dining, that people write histories. I am using "eating" and "dining" as metaphors for the distinction between physical actions and culturally, socially laden actions, respectively. So the right questions to ask are about institutions that humans have made by their reason or rationality. Besides history, Collingwood was interested in physical and cultural or social anthropology, which I will concentrate on in this chapter.

Collingwood describes eating as follows: "The organism perpetually converts its environment into itself; a process whose other aspect consists in a perpetual conversion of itself into its environment by the waste of its tissues" (PH, 256). And "When it [an organism] eats, the organism absorbs food into itself and destroys the food" (PH, 258). It is not eating that interests the historian or anthropologist, however, "but man's thought about it, as expressed in his" dining customs (PH, 93). So eating really doesn't have a history in the strict sense of the term, as he said earlier (PH, 46); there is just eating—the physical actions of masticating and swallowing food. Although there may be some biological interest in this, there is nothing interesting here either historically or anthropologically.

First, let us look at the conception of physical anthropology. Today's anthropologists conceive of it as the study of man as an organism in his environment, and the influences environmental forces have on the social and cultural aspects of human beings. For example, Claude Levi-Strauss declares, "It [the chronological and spatial continuity between the natural order and the cultural order] explains why anthropology, even social anthropology, affirms its solidarity with physical anthropology, whose discoveries it awaits somewhat avidly."[2] From Collingwood's quote above (PH, 46), we see that he seems to deny this intimate interaction between physical and cultural anthropology. He perceived our animal life as separate (free is his term) from the rational structure that our reason develops. So he draws a sharp distinction between them and pretty much collapses the former into the latter. He does not completely dismiss physical anthropology, however. In *Roman Britain*, especially the early chapters, which cover the physical and human geography and the physical characteristics of the ancient Britons, Collingwood utilizes the concepts of physical anthropology[3] (RBES, 1-18, 183-185). In these few pages he treats physical anthropology the way it should be treated. For instance, after a discussion of skulls, bones, and traces of Italian and Germanic blood, he concludes with these remarks:

> The inference from this anthropological material is definite. In some places, notably Richborough and London, there may have been populations whose debt to an Italian ancestry was visible in their bodily appearance; in the north, a Germanic physical type may have had its influence on the army; but elsewhere, in town and country alike, the later part of the Roman period saw Britain inhabited by a race highly uniform in physique, and in that respect definitely and characteristically British, owing nothing physically to the Italian influence to which, culturally, they owed so much. (RBES, 185)

Elsewhere he let it be known that "anthropology—I refer to cultural, not physical anthropology—is a historical science, where by calling it historical as opposed to naturalistic I mean that its true method is thus to get inside its object or recreate its object inside itself"[4] (cited in Boucher's "In Defence of Collingwood," Editors' Introduction, PE, cxiii). What motivated him to make this reductionistic move to collapse the distinction between physical and cultural anthropology? One possible answer is the conversation about race that took place at the time. (It cropped up again during Levi-Strauss's time.) Collingwood mentions *Rassentheorie,* or the "races" of man, and Herder's historical naturalism, which attempts to reduce history to biology (PH, 43, 92, 237). Here is Collingwood's response: "What are nowadays called racial types in the psychological sense are in fact certain cultural traditions built up, not unlike the character of an individual, through a history of many centuries; what are called in the stricter sense psychological types are the product of that historical process which biologists call the evolution of man" (PH, 193). He was also averse to writers like Spengler and Toynbee attempting to find patterns of historical cycles (PH, 19). Historians, for Collingwood, are to look for evidence, to find answers to questions of what happened and why it happened, and this is to be found in the thoughts and actions of historical agents. Similarly, this methodological procedure is to be followed in social or cultural anthropology, which Levi-Strauss denies. Hence, a point of difference between them. There is a major difference between history and anthropology, however, on Collingwood's point:

> The fundamental difficulty of anthropological study lies here. It is not an intellectual difficulty but an emotional one. If we could contemplate the life and mind of the savage without horror, we should not find them hard to understand. This is why the anthropological ideas of people with experience of field-work are so much better than those of the merely book-learned. It is not that through personal acquaintance with the facts they are better informed on points of detail; it is rather that, in human contact with human beings, they have learned that there is no such thing as the abstract savage, there are only men and women, living their own lives in their own way and (surprisingly, perhaps, at first) living them as decently and rationally as ourselves. (PE, 183)

Earlier anthropologists may have created an abstract savage (which we will briefly examine later), but for later anthropologists (like Levi-Strauss) the abstraction is in myths or other phenomena produced by the use of transformation rules. Emotions, however, play a dominant role in his analysis of magic, which is where most of his anthropological conceptions appear[5] (PE, 195-234; PA, 57-77). "We shall do better," Collingwood suggests, "if we seek the source of the idea [magical destruction or construction] not in the savage's intellect, but in his emotions" (PE, 196). Magic is the art of influencing events by occult control of nature or spirits usually conceived of through witchcraft or a mysterious agency or power. Collingwood adheres to this first part of the definition, but he thinks that this influence is achieved through social customs and subconscious communication or control, what he calls emotional sanction. (This will become clearer in the discussion to follow.) Now on to some examples of magic.

Since we started out with eating and dining, let us continue with this topic. This is how he fleshes out the European practice of dining. In *The Principles of Art*, he includes the ceremonies of social life, like dinner parties, as art as magic "which decorate in their fashion the private lives of modern civilized men and women" (PA, 74). What is magical about them is brought out in his description of what goes on in this activity:

> The ceremonial of a dinner-party is intended to create or renew a
> bond, not of understanding or interest or policy, but simply of emo-
> tion, among diners, and more particularly between host and each
> several guest. It consolidates and crystallizes a sentiment of friend-
> ship, at best making each feel what a charming person the other is,
> and at worst, that he is not such a bad fellow after all. It would be a
> poor dinner-party in which these feelings were not to some extent
> evoked, and did not to some extent survive the party itself. (PA, 75)

He speaks of the ritual instruments of dining: a "complicated outfit of
knives and forks and glasses, each with its prescribed function" (PA, 74).
Because we have more ritual instruments, there is as much, if not more,
magic in modern civilization as in primitive cultures. Collingwood remarks: "The actual people who we call savages are as sensitive to good or
bad manners as ourselves; . . . the idea of good [or bad] manners . . . [has]
its emotional sanction" (PE, 224). There is no need of legal or religious
reinforcement; the emotional sanction produces the kind of effects that
the society wants—approval or disapproval of others.[6] He makes this pro-
cedural statement about anthropology: "If our analysis of magic is correct,
this [magical] sanction must be describable in terms of emotion; and if
our method of approach is correct, the emotions concerned must be discoverable in ourselves and may perhaps be found at the basis of certain
customs existing in our own society" (PE, 222). To sum up, *an emotional
sanction* is a conscious or unconscious influence that causes a rule or custom to be observed or followed by an agent. What about someone other
than the agent? How about someone (like a social anthropologist) observing an agent? The concerned emotions of another being discoverable in
ourselves can be an unreliable procedure for understanding others: we
can attribute certain emotional states to persons who may not have them
at all. At best, reasoning from similarities observed in emotional behavior
is an argument from analogy—and this is never certain and can even lead
to the fallacy of false analogy.

   An anthropologist who has followed the above procedure with success
is Howard Morphy. In his *Ancestral Connections: Art and an Aboriginal
System of Knowledge*,[7] he is aware of the pitfalls of this method and employs it in a way in which Collingwood would have approved. Here is one
of his discussions of emotions:

> Emotions of fear and anger generated by death are generalized
> through Yolngu ritual process so that they become a potent force in
> Yolngu society: they are one of the things that contribute to the Yoln-
> gu concept of power. Images and emotions associated with one part

> of a mortuary ritual are taken up and transferred to other aspects of the ritual so that ritual acts become part of a chain of analogues in which the focus of emotion is shifted to the particular referent. We have seen this happen in the case of the smelly and decaying fish, which creates a series of emotionally charged images that can be transferred easily to the dead and decaying human body. Analogous transfers can be effected with the emotions themselves. (262)

These emotions evoked by the rituals and ceremony were not just observed or witnessed but were experienced and felt, because Morphy had felt those emotions in his own experience, especially with the death of his own father, Hugh (xvii), before the book was completed. Put another way, he has a deeper understanding of them since he can empathize with the participants of the ceremony. One analogous transfer of emotion is from the one who died to one's self: the fear of death. Morphy offers some explanation of how this occurs: "Emotions are culturally structured to reinforce the separation between essentially positive and productive powers and angry, unpredictable, and vengeful powers" (106). Through symbolism, however, the negative may become transformed into positive, valued feelings of power (273). And this can be seen in Yolngu art: "The painting of a design on a person's chest . . . becomes *a sign*," and "emotions are generated in ritual which link the person to the design" (131; emphasis added). This is clearly an instance of magic, especially as Collingwood conceived of it.

Now back to dining. In his exposition of magic in *The Philosophy of Enchantment*, Collingwood returns to the dinner party (PE, 222–223). A young man is invited to a dinner party and is told to wear a dinner jacket. He would rather wear flannels, but he complies. Why? If he doesn't comply, there will be "an almost intolerable atmosphere of disapproval," but not of the moral or legal kind. The discomfort he feels is "the emotions attendant on his consciousness of having done it. . . . It is his own feelings that punish him for having broken a ceremonial rule whose essence (for we have seen that such ceremonial clothes are magic) is that it expresses feeling." There is an "increasing importance [that] is attached to those emotional sanctions which, in all societies, attend what we call a breach of good manners" (PE, 224). Collingwood concludes: "Thus the general form of a taboo-system [that is, a system of prohibitions with purely emotional sanctions] for regulating human conduct, which even in our own law-ridden civilization retains its validity over several large parts of life, applies over larger and larger areas according as the society in question is in a legal sense more and more primitive: a conclusion which follows at once, if we grant the premise that the savage's emotional nature is very much like our own, and that where we differ from him is not in our feelings, but in our institutions" (PE, 225). We share feelings and emotions with primitive man, and the principle behind this commonality he calls the Principle of

Primitive Survival, which states that "unless a man reflecting had in him a primitive survival of mere consciousness, he would have nothing to reflect on, and would not reflect"[8] (NL, 65). Shifting from feeling and emotions of modern man to primitive man then building anthropological accounts of the latter's life can lead to false analogies. Moreover, this is dangerously close to Eurocentrism, that is, the modern European mind has elements of the primitive mind and we need to only reflect on those, but I hope he will not be accused of this. He comes close to this again in *The New Leviathan*, where he uses his own consciousness as a model of the modern European mind (NL, 62).

When discussing the magical significance found in social customs of civilized life, one example he uses is washing one's hands before dining. Here in detail is Collingwood's analysis:

> The essence of the civility in question is a feeling that impels me to remove all traces of my labour before I enter the ceremonial atmo-sphere of a civilized meal. For the meal is not a mere taking of food. It is also a social ceremony for which one prepares oneself by a cer-emonial ablution *symbolizing* the dismissal from one's mind of work and its preoccupations. I might express this feeling in a metaphor-ical way (the only way in which it can be expressed in words; the literal expression of it is by the ceremony of washing) by saying that somehow or other I feel the spirit of work sticking to my hands, and I must not bring it in to lunch with me, because its presence would spoil the social *atmosphere* of the meal.[9] (PE, 209; emphases added)

Put another way, human actions can be symbols or signs, and they have an atmosphere that is produced by their situation. The anthropologist is to tease these out of the situation. These ". . . emotions will be those arising out of a certain type of situation" (PE, 202).

In his critique of Hume on human nature and history[10] (IH, 81-83), Collingwood criticizes him for treating the laws of mental process as "ready-made and unchanging from their beginning." Later in *The Philos-ophy of Enchantment*, he treats emotions much the same way that Hume treated the laws of mental process: "In every case we have found that *the magical practice has its basis in emotions which are universally human* and can be verified as existing, and even sometimes as giving rise to definite customs, in and among ourselves" (PE, 221; emphasis added). It is remark-able that Collingwood would make such a bold statement, but then again, this is the basis of his anthropology, which as a study seeks out such uni-versality in the human species. On this point he agrees with Levi-Strauss on the universality of certain rules in human societies (19), and in what he calls *the problem of invariance*—"social anthropology attempts to resolve . . . the universality of human nature" (24). Seeking something universal in human nature is a major premise of anthropology, especially physical anthropology. As Ellen Dissanayake puts it: "It is our specieshood, not our nationhood or race, that unities us."[11] The key for Collingwood is found in emotions (through symbols or signs), where in Levi-Strauss they are found in transformation rules that identify structure among seemingly diverse phenomena, like myths (58).

What was anthropology like prior to Collingwood? He has harsh words for Freud and his followers (PA, 62-64, 77n, 127n; PE, 181-182, 156-169). He rejects Freud's conceiving of magic as neurosis,[12] and criticizes other anthropologists like Tylor and Frazer for looking upon magic as pseudo-science.[13] These developments of anthropology Collingwood described as "a disaster" (PA, 58). Rather, he conceives of magic as the signs and symbols that carry emotional meaning and the resolution to problems that individuals face. The causal factor in magical situations is in signs and symbols, and these are felt and known through emotions. If they are thought out at all, it would be unconsciously.

The association of emotion with magic was also made at this time (in the late 1930s) by Jean-Paul Sartre.[14] He conceived of human emotion as the magical transformation of a situation. Collingwood obviously sees a similar transformation taking place between emotions and situations. One of the better passages that brings out the connection between emotions and magic comes from *The Philosophy of Enchantment*: "The fundamental idea throughout this type of beliefs and customs [i.e., things such as photographs standing in emotional relation to ourselves] is the idea of certain material objects as what I have called outposts or deposits of one's personality in the external world: an idea which arises spontaneously, without any theoretical or intellectual basis, from our emotional nature. Granted this feeling, various types of situation will arise in which it finds expression" (PE, 198-199). These objects can become a substitute for the person associated with them. So to destroy a photograph of a person hated is as satisfying as an attack on the person (PE, 199). The magic consists in the transformation of the emotion released (believed by the agent) to be "an actual assault upon the victim" (PE, 200). And this, Collingwood firmly believes, is the basis of all magic (PE, 201). The cause for the magical beliefs "should be sought in a certain complex of emotions: these emotions will be those arising out of a certain type of situation" (PE, 202). Throughout this chapter we have seen examples from various social customs—whether they came from primitive societies or what we call our civilized life. These examples and the theory behind them raised anthropology to a new level of sophistication and understanding of human nature.

Notes

1. R. G. Collingwood, *The Principles of History*, edited and with an Introduction by W. H. Dray and W. J. van der Dussen (Oxford: Oxford University Press, 1999).

2. Claude Levi-Strauss, "The Scope of Anthropology," in his *Structural Anthropology*, translated from the French by Monique Layton (Chicago: University of Chicago Press, 1976), II, 14. Elsewhere, in "The Work of the Bureau of American Ethnology," Levi-Strauss claims that "[a]nthropology . . . has the same subject matter as history, but for lack of time perspective it cannot use the same methods. Its own methods . . . aim at discovering invariant properties beneath the apparent particularity and diversity of the observed phenomena." (57) An example of the method is what he calls "transformation rules which make possible to include in the same group myths previously held to be markedly different." (58) I shall return to these concepts later in the chapter.

3. R. G. Collingwood and J. N. L. Myres, *Roman Britain and the English Settlements* (Second Edition; Oxford: Clarendon Press, 1937).

4. R. G. Collingwood, *The Philosophy of Enchantment: Studies in Folktale, Cultural Criticism, and Anthropology*, edited by David Boucher, Wendy James, and Philip Smallwood (Oxford: Clarendon Press, 2005), cited in Boucher's "In Defence of Collingwood," Editors' Introduction, PE, cxiii.

5. R. G. Collingwood, *The Principles of Art* (New York: Oxford University Press, 1938).

6. There is a great deal written on the history of manners. See, for openers, Norbert Elias, *History of Manners* (New York: Pantheon Books, 1982); and his *The Civilizing Process: Sociogentic and Psychogentic Investigations* (New York: Wiley, 2000).

7. Howard Morphy, *Ancestral Connections: Art and an Aboriginal System of Knowledge* (Chicago: University of Chicago Press, 1991).

8. R. G. Collingwood, *The New Leviathan: or Man, Society, Civilization and Barbarism*, edited and introduced by David Boucher (Revised Edition; Oxford: Clarendon Press, 1992). Originally published in 1942.

9. Here we see the use of *atmosphere* as a term to describe what goes on in dining or in a social meal, just as we have observed in chapter 1.

10. G. Collingwood, *The Idea of History*, edited with an Introduction by Jan van der Dussen (Revised Edition; Oxford: Oxford University Press, 1994).

11. Ellen Dissanayake, *What Is Art For?* (Seattle: University of Washington Press, 1988), 198; emphasis removed from this sentence.

12. "Savagery is . . . a mental disease to be cured by psychoanalysis!" (PE, 163n).

13. "[T]hey [Tylor and Frazer] concluded, magic is at bottom simply a special kind of error: it is erroneous natural science. And magical practices are pseudo-scientific practices based on this error," e.g., the crops will grow as high as he jumps in a ritual dance. (PA, 58) "This definition of magic is the result of examining customs, whose true basis is emotional, through the spectacles of the utilitarian obsession" (PE, 208) with science.

14. Jean-Paul Sartre, *The Emotions: Outline of a Theory* (1939), translated by Bernard Frechtman (New York: The Philosophical Library, 1948).

Index

About the Author

SPENCER K. WERTZ is an Emeritus Professor of Philosophy at Texas Christian University, Fort Worth. He is the author of *Talking a Good Game: Inquiries into the Principles of Sport* (SMU Press) and *Between Hume's Philosophy and History: Historical Theory and Practice* (University Press of America), and he coedited *Sport Inside Out: Readings in Literature and Philosophy* (TCU Press). He has also written over a hundred articles during his career—some of which are rewritten and published here. He has served as president of four philosophical societies and associations, and has given over ninety presentations at meetings and conferences.

Wertz lived in rural Parker County just west of Fort Worth. He was the head cook of a barbecue team that competed across the Lone Star State. The BBQ team, "Smokin' Asses," was named after the miniature donkeys he and his wife, Linda, raised on their twelve-acre mini ranch. After retirement, they moved to Santa Fe, New Mexico, where they enjoy high mountain desert terrain and the many fine eating establishments that the town has to offer.